HISTORICAL ESSAYS 1600–1750

Photograph by Ivor Fields, Oxford and Abingdon

HISTORICAL ESSAYS
1600–1750

PRESENTED TO

DAVID OGG

EDITED BY

H. E. BELL & R. L. OLLARD

ADAM & CHARLES BLACK
LONDON

FIRST PUBLISHED 1963

A. AND C. BLACK LIMITED
4, 5 AND 6 SOHO SQUARE LONDON W.I

PRINTED IN GREAT BRITAIN
BY R. AND R. CLARK LTD. EDINBURGH

PREFACE

THOSE who have had the privilege of knowing David Ogg as a tutor or a colleague will not need to be reminded of those qualities of wit and intellectual elegance, of originality of thought and expression, of common sense applied in an uncommon way, that characterise his talk as unmistakably as his writing. The deceptive ease with which his exact scholarship and wide erudition have been put at our disposal is no small part of the pleasant debt we all owe him.

The same holds true, though in the nature of the case less personally, for those who know him only through his books. It would be an imperceptive reader who had failed to notice that in both the fields that Ogg has made his own, the England of Charles II and the Europe of Louis XIV, he has challenged both the accepted historiography of the period and the fashionable portrayal of the two eponymous figures of the age. It would be imperceptive, but it would not be impossible. The modulations of irony, the subtle effects of tone, the humility in which, above all, the style reveals the man, will be lost on such as prefer vulgar colours, familiar platitudes, and the techniques of self-advertisement in which modern scholarship can report such notable advances. But the continued and increasing success of *Europe in the Seventeenth Century* and *England in the Reign of Charles II* gives good ground for believing that the rare qualities of which his pupils at Oxford and in America have been the chief beneficiaries have been recognised and valued by a far wider public. Of the influence exerted by these books on students of the period there can be no doubt: of their example there cannot be too many imitators. To their author the present volume is offered with the admiration and affection of the contributors.

CONTENTS

It was originally planned that each essay in this volume should not exceed six or seven thousand words, but unhappily not all of those who accepted invitations to contribute have been able, in the event, to do so. In particular the lamented death of Professor R. R. Betts, two days after his enthusiastic agreement to become a contributor, robbed the collection of what would certainly have been a distinguished paper on the seventeenth century Bohemian peasantry. The necessary re-adjustment that the editors have made has permitted them to allow more space to one or two contributors, the nature of whose subjects demanded treatment at greater length than was initially envisaged.

HISTORICAL ESSAYS 1600–1750

I

THE NORTHERN BORDERLAND UNDER THE EARLY STUARTS [1]

Penry Williams

WITH a fine eighteenth century confidence the Reverend George Ridpath, historian of the northern counties, asserted that after 1603 'the borders, which for many ages had been almost a constant source of rapine and desolation, enjoyed, from this happy era, a quiet and order which they had never before experienced'.[2] Perhaps for that reason, he did not explore closely the state of the border in the generation after 1603. Nor have later historians been much concerned with the task: some have echoed his verdict,[3] others have maintained that the borders had a wild reputation up to Hanoverian times.[4] The intention of the present paper is a closer look at Ridpath's 'happy era'. Two points had best be made at the start. First, this account is concerned only with the English side of the

---

[1] My warm thanks are due to the Leverhulme Trustees for a grant which enabled me to undertake the research for this article. I am also grateful to the Earl of Crawford and Balcarres for allowing me to use and to quote from his MS., 'The Actes of the Commissioners for the Borders, 1605–6', now deposited in the John Rylands Library; and to the staff of that library for giving me the facilities to work on it. The MS. is referred to below as Crawford MS. A copy of the volume is calendared by the H[istorical] M[anuscripts] C[ommission], *Tenth Report, Appendix iv., MSS. of Lord Muncaster* (1885), hereafter referred to as *Muncaster*. I hope to discuss the Crawford MS. in a forthcoming number of the *Bulletin of the John Rylands Library*.

[2] George Ridpath, *The Border History of England and Scotland* (1808), p. 706.

[3] E.g. A. L. Rowse, *The Expansion of Elizabethan England* (1955), p. 28.

[4] E.g. E. Hughes, *North Country Life in the Eighteenth Century; the North-East, 1700–1750* (1952), pp. 14–15.

frontier; conditions on the Scottish side were very different. Second, it leads to no startling or paradoxical conclusions. What happened was what one would expect to happen: slowly and clumsily, with many set-backs, the creaking apparatus of Stuart government brought to the region a degree of order that was at once new, gratifying, and incomplete. The interest of the story lies in its details rather than its generalities.

Life in this remote, mountainous, and infertile region had long been violent and harsh, for the land could support only a small and scattered population, farming mainly oats, cattle, and sheep. From the plains around Berwick and Carlisle the dales climbed towards the Scottish frontier, where high fells protected thieves and outlaws. Here—on the Esk and the Sark, in Liddesdale, Tynedale, Redesdale, and Teviotdale—lived the border clans, the moss-troopers, heroes of the ballads. While their raids were a constant menace to the 'inland' parishes, among themselves they followed the feud—'deadly foed, the word of enmitye in the borders, implacable without the blood and whole family distroied'.[1] They were not, however, the only threat to law, order, and a quiet life in the sixteenth century. Both sides had to fear official invasions from the opposite kingdom, sometimes small, like John Carey's raid in 1596, sometimes massive, like the incursions of Sussex in 1570. Then, both England and Scotland had their great marcher lords—Nevilles, Percies, Maxwells, Johnstones, and others. Although these dynasties remained powerful on the Scottish side into the seventeenth century, on the English side their strength had been effectively reduced in 1569. Lastly, the lesser families of landed gentry, in this area as elsewhere, were none too scrupulous about the law, if they thought that local influence would protect them from it. Their quarrels gave rich opportunities to the more unruly of their servants and followers.

To defend the frontier and to control the borderers both kingdoms had set up elaborate systems of law and authority. In spite of some superficial likenesses the English and Scottish

[1] *Calendar of Border Papers* (1896), ii, no. 323.

systems were in many ways very different;[1] and what is said here applies only to the English side. The region was divided into three marches, east, middle, and west, each ruled by a warden, whose duty was to hold the border against the Scots, to keep order in his own march, and, with his opposite number on the Scottish side, to settle the claims of one nation against the other. Beneath the wardens there was a complex structure of courts, laws, and officials. The courts were of two main kinds: the warden-courts, where each warden administered domestic law upon his own border; and the 'days of truce', at which he met his opposite number, presented the English claims against the Scottish raiders, and received the Scottish counter-claims. The border laws were compounded partly of regulations agreed with the Scots from time to time for the settlement of 'international' disputes, partly of the 'march treasons', designed to keep the Englishmen in order. Beneath the wardens was a multitude of officials: deputy-wardens of each march, the officers of the Berwick and Carlisle garrisons, the captain of Bewcastle, the keeper of Tynedale, the land-serjeant of Gilsland, and so on.[2]

By the last decade of the sixteenth century this system seemed to be gaining some control over the east and middle marches, but to be rather less successful in the west. Then, at the death of Elizabeth, the situation changed, and much of the structure was dismantled. For there succeeded to the throne a high-minded man, determined to abolish the frontier between his two nations, insistent that his subjects should regard 'both the two realmes as presentlye united and as one realme and kingdome'.[3]

[1] For the Scottish side see T. I. Rae, 'Some Aspects of Border Administration in the 16th Century' in *Transactions of the Hawick Archaeological Society*, 1958. I am most grateful to Mr. Rae for an offprint of this important article.

[2] General accounts of the border in Tudor times will be found in: Rae, *ubi supra*; *Calendar of Border Papers*, i and ii; Rowse, *Expansion*, ch. i; D. L. W. Tough, *The Last Years of a Frontier* (1928); C. M. L. Bouch and G. P. Jones, *The Lake Counties, 1500–1830* (1961), chs. i-vi.

[3] T. Rymer, *Foedera* (1715), xvi, 506-7. D. H. Willson, 'King James I and Anglo-Scottish Unity' in *Conflict in Stuart England*, ed. W. A. Aitken and B. D. Henning (1960), pp. 41-56. *The Register of the Privy Council of Scotland* (1885), vii, pp. xxix-xliii.

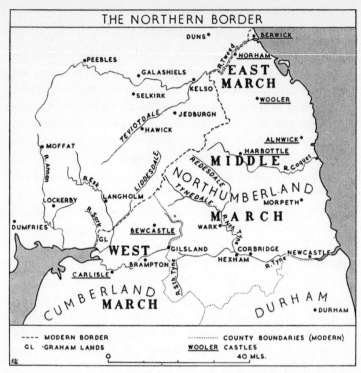

DUNS
BERWICK
PEEBLES
NORHAM
R. Tweed
GALASHIELS
EAST
MARCH
KELSO
SELKIRK
WOOLER
JEDBURGH
TEVIOTDALE
HAWICK
ALNWICK
MOFFAT
HARBOTTLE
LIDDESDALE
MIDDLE
R. Coquet
REDESDALE
R. Ann
R. Esk
NORTHUMBERLAND
LOCKERBY
LANGHOLM
TYNEDALE
MORPETH
DUMFRIES
R. Sark
M'ARCH
GL
BEWCASTLE
WARK
R. Nth. Tyne
WEST
GILSLAND
CORBRIDGE
NEWCASTLE
HEXHAM
CARLISLE
BRAMPTON
R. Sth. Tyne
R. Tyne
C U M B E R L A N D
MARCH
D U R H A M
DURHAM

---- MODERN BORDER .... COUNTY BOUNDARIES (MODERN)
GL ·GRAHAM LANDS <u>WOOLER</u> CASTLES
0 40 MLS.

Map by Miss Anne Lowcock, University of Manchester

On the border itself, however, his accession had accompaniments that were unforeseen, outrageous, and bizarre. Four days after the queen's death, the Bishop of Carlisle saw from the ramparts of Carlisle castle a crowd of armed men riding down from the border. This was the beginning of ten days' vigorous raiding, known as the 'busy week', in which, according to the victims, six men were killed, fourteen men were taken prisoner, sixty-seven horses, 1280 cattle, 3807 sheep and goats were stolen, and damage by burning, spoiling, and robbing was inflicted to the value of £6750. One should not take such statements any more literally than some people's insurance claims today, which indeed they closely resembled; but even scaled ruthlessly down the figures suggest that the border clans—Armstrongs, Elliotts, Grahams, Hendersons, Nixons—had done well for themselves.[1]

[1] P.R.O., State Papers Domestic, Addenda, vi, fos. 179-208. Crawford MS., fo. 141.

Two hundred foot-soldiers and fifty horsemen, sent from Berwick, quickly put an end to the marauding; but the memory of the 'busy week' remained for some years in the 'inland' parishes, perhaps because it was the last raid upon the old scale. Then, the fun over, the excuses began. One of the clans, the Grahams, explained their conduct on the curious ground that[1]

> some among us, of evill and corrupt judgment, did perswade us that untill yor Majestie was a crowned kinge within the realme of England that the lawe of the same kingdome did cease and was of no force, and that all actes and offences whatsoever done and committed in the meane tyme were not by the common justice of this realme punishable.

How far this extraordinary naivety was genuine one cannot be certain; but, since the persons 'of evill and corrupt judgment' were never named, it looks a trifle disingenuous. The Grahams urgently needed excuses, since the crown had decided to cast them as scapegoats. The motives for this decision are, to say the least, suspicious. Certainly the Grahams had plundered enthusiastically during the 'busy week'; equally certainly they were not alone in this. The Armstrongs and the Elliotts had been quite as energetic; other clans had not been idle.[2] Yet in the course of 1603 the crown's pronouncements, speaking at first vaguely of the 'partakers of the fowle incursions made uppon our first cominge to our crowne . . . of England',[3] came gradually to put the whole blame upon the Grahams. No one reading about the 'busy week' in the government correspondence of 1604 and 1605 could know that any other clan had been involved. One must try, therefore, to trace the steps by which this curious turn of policy was reached.

The government was certainly faced with an awkward situation in April 1603. Its troops had stopped the raiding but its gaols were totally inadequate to hold the raiders. The king therefore proclaimed that all who submitted before 20 June 1603 would be shown mercy; at about the same time—a small

---

[1] Crawford MS., fo. 63.
[2] P.R.O., State Papers Dom., Add., vi, fos. 179-208.
[3] Rymer, xvi, 504.

straw in the wind—Robert Cecil ordered an inquiry into the lands occupied by the Grahams.[1] How many submitted by the final date, or what happened in the next four months, one cannot tell. However, in October, George, Earl of Cumberland, who had been appointed warden of the west and middle marches, held sessions of *oyer et terminer* at Carlisle. He had already been ordered by James to show mercy to the raiders of the 'busy week', and, when the Grahams came to ask his help, he promised that in return for submission they would be pardoned and then banished to some place where they could maintain their families.[2] This unenticing prospect they accepted; and in December a royal proclamation announced that they would be transported when means could be found.[3] Two months later a survey of their lands was ordered, in preparation for a grant of those lands to the Earl of Cumberland, who received them shortly after.[4] Thus far the facts will take us. Inference, hypothesis, or guess-work must provide the explanation. The circumstantial case against Cumberland is undoubtedly strong, for he controlled the crown's negotiations with the Grahams, he benefited from their banishment, and the only clan to be banished *en bloc* was the one which occupied his new estates.[5]

The marauders of the 'busy week' were of course only one of the problems of border administration. With the queen's death, 'days of truce' and much of the border law lapsed; the borders were borders no more, but 'the verie hart of the cuntrey'.[6] Even so, since the region could obviously not be governed by the methods that prevailed elsewhere, temporary structures were needed. As we have seen, Cumberland was made warden of the west and middle marches, with powers in

[1] Rymer, xvi, 504. H.M.C., *Calendar of Salisbury MSS.*, xv, 120.
[2] P.R.O., State Papers Dom., James I, x, no. 43. Crawford MS., fo. 19.
[3] Rymer, xvi, 560.
[4] P.R.O., State Papers Dom., Docquets, vii, 7 February 1604.
[5] A similar indictment of Cumberland is given in J. Graham, *The Condition of the Border at the Union* (1907), ch. xiv. This is a prejudiced work whose arguments did not at first seem to me convincing; a closer look at the evidence has shown that they may nevertheless be correct.
[6] *Register of the Privy Council of Scotland*, vi, 560.

many respects as wide as those of Elizabethan wardens. By no means all the old system was preserved, but it is difficult to find out how much was kept, how much was jettisoned.[1] Whatever the arrangements, they were not wholly successful. Cumberland held a gaol delivery at Carlisle on 27 July 1603, six weeks after his appointment, and executed two men from each of the main clans, together with seven others, as a deterrent.[2] The effect did not last long: by the autumn of 1604 the gentry of Northumberland were complaining that the Union of the Crowns and the abrogation of border laws had encouraged, rather than prevented, crime—'the dayly and contynuall theft, wherewith wee are nightly opprest, contrary to all expectacion, being nowe greater then hath bene dyvers yeares heretofore'. Too few sessions had been held; the old defences of nightly watches and 'slew-dogs' had been abandoned; and the customary procedures for recovering stolen goods had been abolished.[3] To their voices the Earl of Cumberland added his own. Criminals could not be brought in, and, even when they were, juries were reluctant to find a verdict of guilty, 'their kinridd and alliance [being] soe greate . . . and their consciences so smalle, that hardlie anie proofe can be gott'. Like Rowland Lee, Lord President of the Council in the Marches of Wales seventy years before, Cumberland believed that the people under his rule were congenitally wicked—'beinge even from their cradells bredd and brought up in thefte, spoyle, and bloode'—and that only severity would keep them down.[4]

Clearly a tighter system of government had to be devised; and in February 1605 a new commission was issued for five gentlemen of the English border and five of the Scottish to form a united administration for the 'middle shires', with Cumberland remaining lord-lieutenant, but no longer warden, on the English side. The commissioners were to meet regularly, put down feuds, and return to his native country any thief who

[1] Rymer, xvi, 507-12. See the Statutes 4 Jac. I c. 1 and 7 Jac. I c. 1.
[2] P.R.O., State Papers Dom., James I, x, no. 43.
[3] *Ibid.*, ix, no. 88. See also vi, no. 42.
[4] *Ibid.*, v, nos. 58, 59; vi, no. 43; x, no. 43.

crossed the border. To help them on the English side, Sir Henry
Leigh was appointed provost-marshal in command of twenty-
five horsemen.[1] With a few alterations of membership and one
major change this commission stayed in force until 1611. The
major change was the appointment, in December 1606, of
James's favourite, the Earl of Dunbar, to a general supervision
of both sides of the border; and in August of the following
year he was reinforced, in a joint lieutenancy, by Francis,
fourth Earl of Cumberland, who had succeeded his brother in
1605.[2]

The most awkward single problem before the commissioners
was the Graham clan, whose banishment had been ordered
more than twelve months earlier, but whose destination was
still unknown. In March 1605 James decided not to transplant
the entire clan at once, but to impress 150 of their men into the
garrisons of Flushing and Brill. The commissioners had to
decide who should go and to get them away. Proceedings
started slowly, for by 28 June, the day appointed for embarka-
tion, only eighty-five of the 150 had appeared. However,
during July, about 130 were laboriously assembled and dis-
patched to the Netherlands.[3] By November most of them had
returned home again, some with passports, some without; only
fourteen remained at Flushing, only thirty at Brill.[4] After a long
and arduous search throughout the winter, some of the fugitives had, by April 1606, been recaptured; but most were still
at large.[5] The king now decided that those who had deserted
the Netherlands service should be sent back there, while the
rest of the clan should be deported to Ireland.[6] An Englishman,
Sir Ralph Sidley, undertook to settle them upon vacant land
in Connaught, on condition that the inhabitants of the border

---

[1] P.R.O., State Papers Dom., Docquets, viii, 21 February 1605. State
Papers Dom., James I, xii, nos. 57, 58; xiii, no. 4. Crawford MS., fos. 1–3.
[2] P.R.O., State Papers Dom., James I, xxiv, nos. 18, 19; xxviii, no. 28;
Addenda, xxxviii, no. 90; Docquets, viii, 21 October 1607.
[3] H.M.C., *Salisbury*, xvii, 87, 289, 309. Crawford MS., fos. 6–12, 16–17,
24–7, 61. *Muncaster*, pp. 230–5, 244.
[4] Crawford MS., fos. 46–7, 56. *Muncaster*, pp. 240–2.
[5] Crawford MS., fos. 97–99.   [6] *Ibid.*, fos. 122–4.

would contribute to the cost of setting them up when they got there.[1] The condition turned out to be an awkward obstacle. One Cumberland gentleman, Sir John Dalston, refused utterly to contribute anything, and many of the others dragged their feet.[2] Tactfully the commissioners suggested that perhaps the king might care to advance the money on a promise of repayment when the contributions came in. Finally, with the help of such loans the Grahams were mostly sent from Workington in mid-September, the rest to follow in the spring.[3] By November they were starting to come back, complaining, perhaps with justice, that Sidley had refused to hand over to them the money due for settling them in their new homes. Promptly the government ordered their return, and, although some of them seem in the next ten years to have infiltrated back, the borders were thereafter relatively free of Graham outlaws.[4] The whole business illustrates both the unsavoury suspicions that lurk behind Jacobean administration, and the extraordinary difficulty of carrying out the crown's decisions.

Looking at the commissioners' work as a whole, one can see that tensions and conflicts made the advance of law and order frustratingly slow. After generations of enmity English and Scots gentlemen could not perhaps have been expected to co-operate very closely, and there were certainly several rubs between them. More than once the commissioners of Scotland failed to send to the English assizes Scots criminals who were accused of crimes committed in England.[5] In return, the Scots provost-marshal, Sir William Cranston, told the English commissioners tartly that he had enough to do on his own side of the border without being ordered everywhere by them:[6]

Sirs, if ye will nedes be comaunders I will desire that your discretion may appeare amid your authoritie; and think not my bodie can be everie where to do all your service on such an instant as yow require.

[1] H.M.C., *Salisbury*, xviii, 191-2, 214-15.
[2] *Ibid.*, 214-15, 224-5.   [3] *Ibid.*, 284-6, 289-90.
[4] *Ibid.*, 342, 350. Crawford MS., fo. 180. *Muncaster*, p. 266. Rymer, xvi, 771.
[5] Crawford MS., fos. 139, 142. *Muncaster*, pp. 258-9. P.R.O., State Papers Dom., James I, xxi, no. 8.   [6] Crawford MS., fo. 94. *Muncaster*, p. 250.

Yet, in general, contacts between the two groups were surprisingly friendly. Sir William Lawson wrote to Cecil that he could not but 'commend the honest care and forwardness we find in the Scottish commissioners to the furtherance of the service'.[1] Although co-operation could perhaps at times have been rather closer, relations might very easily have been far more acrimonious. In any event, all was not entirely harmonious on the southern side of the border. The Privy Council sometimes rebuked the English commissioners for undue severity, drawing from them the angry reply that all the gentlemen of the border counties felt lenity to be disastrous, and that the only instrument for pacifying the region was 'a well tempered sword'.[2] Interference from Whitehall was generally met by a united northern front; but in part this unity was deceptive. The commissioners from Cumberland, Sir Wilfrid Lawson and Mr. Joseph Pennington, faced with the more arduous tasks, complained that they got little help from their Northumberland colleagues, of whom Sir William Selby spent most of his time in the south, Sir Robert Delaval was seriously ill, and Mr. Edward Gray preferred to concentrate upon his private affairs.[3] Even so, one's general impression of the commissioners' work is favourable. Gaol deliveries were regularly held,[4] and, in consequence, most reports upon the state of the borders were optimistic. For example, as early as August 1605, Sir William Selby announced that 'masterful theft and murder are well banished out of the shires within our commission'; and in 1609 Sir Edward Philipps observed that the border shires were as free from crime as any others in England. True enough, there was plenty of petty thieving, and the border country still contained more than its share of outlaws; but the rule of violence was, to all appearances, at an end.[5]

---

[1] H.M.C., *Salisbury*, xvii, 151.
[2] Crawford MS., fos. 100, 114, 116-17. *Muncaster*, pp. 249, 252.
[3] Crawford MS., fo. 198. H.M.C., *Salisbury*, xviii, 368-71.
[4] Crawford MS., fos. 213-14. H.M.C., *Salisbury*, xviii, 212-13.
[5] H.M.C., *Salisbury*, xvii, 382. Also xviii, 78-81, 179, 191-2, 214-5. P.R.O., State Papers Dom., James I, xlviii, no. 25. See also Crawford MS., fos 46-7, 54, 56, 153, 176.

Unfortunately appearances were not reliable, for with Dunbar's death, early in 1611, there began a slow relaxation of control. Dunbar had been particularly well-suited to supervise the government, since he had lands on both sides of the border and lived not far from it. His colleague, the Earl of Cumberland, lived further away, had property only in England, and was, in any case, not the man to inspire much confidence. James decided to end the system by which one or two noblemen supervised the border, and reverted to government by a small commission.[1] It was much less successful than before. A few weeks after Dunbar's death a raiding-party of seventy Elliotts and Armstrongs crossed the border into Northumberland, shooting and plundering. This was the first such raid for many years, and, although it was not repeated, it marked the beginning of a period of crime.[2] A Northumberland man, writing a little later, reported that 'theft and stealth [are] as ordinarye nowe in the most partes of this countie as it was in Quene Elizabethe hir reigne'.[3] By 1616 this concern had spread to the Privy Council, which inquired why 'after so manie yeares of peace . . . there are committed . . . more robberies and spoyles, then in times precedent? And that there dayly growe and multiply more outlawes . . .?'[4]

One reason for the decay of government at this time was, almost certainly, the growing tension between the leading families. During the earlier years of James's reign, factional rivalry had been, to all appearances, subdued. By 1616 it had reached its height. At the centre of all disputes and controversies was Lord William Howard of Naworth castle. Inheriting through his wife a large part of the Dacre lands in Cumberland, he wielded also the strong court influence belonging to any member of the Howard tribe. As a Roman Catholic he soon became the head of the recusant party on the border,

[1] P.R.O., State Papers Dom., James I, lxiii, nos. 9, 12, 13, 15, 43; lxv, nos. 17, 18; cxli, fo. 97.   [2] Ibid., lxiii, no. 99; lxiv, no. 2.
[3] Ibid., lxvii, no. 162. Cf. lxxi, no. 21.
[4] G. Ornsby (ed.), Selections from the Household Books of Lord William Howard (Surtees Soc. 1878), pp. 416-7. Cf. Register of the Privy Council of Scotland, x, 847.

whose leaders until Howard's arrival had been Sir Henry Widdrington of Swinburne castle, near Hexham, and his brother Roger Widdrington of Harbottle. Allied to them were Sir Francis Radcliffe, of Dilston, near Corbridge, whose daughter was married to Roger Widdrington, and John Preston of Furness Abbey, whose daughter was married to Lord William's son Francis. After 1614 this faction gained strong aristocratic support when the lordships of Redesdale, Wark, and Coquetdale were granted to Lord Howard of Walden, son of the Earl of Suffolk. On the other side were ranged Sir Henry Anderson of Newcastle, Sir James Bellingham of Levens, Sir William Hutton of Penrith, and, providing the essential court backing, Henry, Lord Clifford, son of the Earl of Cumberland.

Although the charges flung by both sides were more colourful than accurate, they indicate at least the nature of the conflict. Howard and Roger Widdrington were accused of dominating the whole border country, of promoting recusancy, and of maintaining thieves. Howard's tenants were said to have set up a lord of misrule in the parish of Bampton, 'shotte gunnes in the church, and brought in flagges and banners; others sported themselfes with pies and puddings in the church, using them as bowles in the church-allies'. Roger Widdrington was, according to the Archdeacon of Durham, 'a notorious *bangester*, a patron of al theeves and murderers'. Between them, Lord William Howard, Lord Howard of Walden, and the Widdringtons were reported to rule all Tynedale and Redesdale, where most of the people had become 'papists, theeves, or athists'.[1] On his side Howard sharply criticised the ability of the commissioners for the middle shires:[2]

> Sir William Selby that dwelleth in Kent; Sir John Fenwick, a gentillman that more aimes at a private life then publick imploiement; Sir Wilfride Lawson, dwelling in the inmost parte of Cumberland, and aged neere 80 yeares, Sir William Hutton, of great debilitie of body, both of them learned and sufficient men on a bench, but alltogether unable to serve in the feild.

[1] Ornsby, pp. 423–5, 428, 433. P.R.O., State Papers Dom., James I, clxxxv, no. 43; Charles I, xxii, no. 52.   [2] Ornsby, pp. 418–19.

A few years later he spoke in harsher terms of Hutton: 'the rancor of Sir William Hutton's envious and splenatike humor . . . with the multitude of his yeares, the debilitie of his body, and the totall decaye and defect of his sences'; but that was written after Hutton had accused Howard's wife of abetting the escape of a thief.[1] From this thunder of charge and counter-charge two clear impressions seem to emerge. A recusant faction which had been for long denied public employment was challenging the capacity for government of the respectable, protestant, but now rather aged men who had run the border for a decade; and in the ensuing conflict government suffered.

To repair the damage, the crown gave commissions to Howard and others 'to surveigh and finde oute and infourme us of the moste notorious and lewde persons, and of their faultes, within the said counties of Northumberland, Cumberland, and Westmerland, Riddesdale and Bewcastle within the same'. Larger commissions, to the Lord President of the North and others, were issued for the general government of the borders.[2] Detailed regulations were then set out for the control of the area: any man leasing lands in Hexham, Redesdale, or Bewcastle lordships must find two persons who would stand surety for him in the sum of £20; notorious criminals were to be given bail only in open court; 'the multitude and un-necessarie nomber of hosteller houses and maulsters' were to be suppressed; all cattle and sheep must be sold in open market with their skins; no one—except noblemen, gentlemen, and their servants—might carry pistols and armour or possess horses worth more than 40s.; all landlords were to take recognisances of their tenants, and to be responsible for seeing that their tenants obeyed the warrants of J.P.s.[3] The plan to make landlords responsible for tenants was not entirely successful. Lord Howard of Walden complained that he had great diffi-culty in controlling Tynedale and Redesdale, because he had not the authority possessed by former lords, because he could

---

[1] *Ibid.*, p. 456. Cf. R. S. Ferguson, *Carlisle* (1889), pp. 131-3.
[2] Rymer, xvii, 50, 53, 58, 83, 141.
[3] *Ibid.*, 47-51. *Acts of the Privy Council of England, 1616–17* (1927), pp. 380-3. *Register of the Privy Council of Scotland*, xi, pp. lxxvi-lxxxix.

not persuade any officer to settle there 'from a more civill place', and because of the 'pretended inhumane customs' of his tenants.¹ Within a few years the government's special measures seem to have lapsed. Early in the reign of Charles I, Lord Henry Clifford wrote in alarm to Secretary Conway that 'you had neede bestirr your selfe else the disorders will swell to that height as they will run over'.² During the 1630s, Sir Richard Graham of Netherby warned the king that the 'humor of theivinge' was by no means extinct: the attempt to drop the special border administration and to leave matters to the J.P.s had, in his view, failed.³

Failed in a sense it had; yet even so the border of the 1630s was a very different place from the border of 1603. Given careful supervision and a firmer structure of government than the normal, the region could now be controlled. Thieves and outlaws certainly remained in large numbers around the frontier, their names preserved for us in the returns made to the Privy Council's inquiries in 1618. Hector Nixon, condemned to death in 1603, had broken gaol and stayed out ever since. William Taylor, pardoned for burglaries, had returned from an Irish exile and 'did eate in his sheild in shilding tyme nine barrells of salted beefe, a large proportion for his familie in so short a tyme'. The wanted men made up a substantial band—about sixty all told for Cumberland alone; but mostly they were criminals on a very small scale, taking two or three beasts at a time by stealth, wholly unlike the raiders of Elizabethan days.⁴ This impression is confirmed by the Privy Council's statement in 1611 that most of the thefts were

¹ P.R.O., State Papers Dom., James I, cix, no. 6.
² *Ibid.*, Charles I, xix, no. 71. Cf. vi, no. 46; xxi, no. 36; lxxv, no. 56. *Register of the Privy Council of Scotland*, xii, pp. xxxvii–xliv, 644-5, 775-9; xiv, 667-714.
³ P.R.O., State Papers Dom., Charles I, cccii, no. 107; ccccviii, no. 55. Dropping the special system of government had apparently the same effects in Scotland. See *Register of the Privy Council of Scotland* 2nd series, ii, pp. xx–xxi; iii, 112, 147; v, 496-9.
⁴ Ornsby, pp. 436-47. P.R.O., State Papers Dom., James I, xcvii, nos. 60-4. Crawford MS., fos. 84-7. *Register of Privy Council of Scotland*, ix, pp. liv–lvi, 394-5, 705-14; xii, 776-9; xiv, 667-714.

'pettie and secret stealinges of a verie fewe cattle or sheep, and not with force of multitudes or strong hand'.[1] Just as Welshmen or Irishmen became exceedingly litigious when the government forbade them to solve their disputes by force, so the borderers began to flock to the law-courts:[2]

> According to the nature of the soile, and qualitie of the air (like that in Norfolk) the vulgar people are subtill, violent, litigious, and pursuers of endless suites by appeales, to their utter impoverishment.

Even so, the borders did not for many years come to be so easily ruled as the rest of the country. In 1662 Parliament established a special official, the country-keeper, whose duty was to make good any losses from theft, either by capturing the thief or by making restitution himself.[3] A few years later, Lord Guilford, on circuit in the north, found that the 'country is yet very sharp upon thieves; and a violent suspicion there is next to conviction'.[4] The tradition of the 'well-tempered sword' was still alive, and that tradition must make one ask, in talking of law and order, What sort of law? No doubt the forms were observed, but determination to abolish theft may well have led to unjust convictions. Whether it did, how often it did, one can hardly, at this distance of time, tell.

What effect had these changes upon border society as a whole?[5] Some bold statements have been made about the economic effects: Lord William Howard's rent-roll grew, it is said, from £1042 in 1595 to £3884 in 1611; the income of the Grey estates rose, according to Roger North, from £1000 before 1603 to £7000 or £8000 after 1660.[6] These intimations

---

[1] P.R.O., State Papers Dom., James I, lxv, no. 18; lxvi, no. 91.

[2] The Bishop of Carlisle, quoted in Ferguson, *Carlisle*, pp. 131-3. Cf. Penry Williams, *The Council in the Marches of Wales under Elizabeth I* (1958), pp. 61-4, 321.

[3] J. L. Kirby, 'Border Service, 1662-1757', in *Transactions of Cumberland and Westmorland Antiquarian Society*, n.s. xlviii (1949), 125-9.

[4] Roger North, *Lives of the Norths*, ed. A. Jessopp (1890), i, 179.

[5] I originally included here a discussion of the struggle over tenant-right, but later decided that the subject could not adequately be dealt with in so short a space. For a good account see Bouch and Jones, ch. iv.

[6] Ornsby, pp. xxxvi, 408-9, 413-16. North, p. 178.

of prosperity have been variously used by historians: sometimes
to illustrate the benefits of union, sometimes to explain why
men were prepared to turn away from lives of crime.[1] They
need, however, to be cautiously approached. To begin with,
the evidence for the Howard estates is not at all satisfactory:
the total given for the Northumberland manors in 1611 inex-
plicably exceeds the sum of the individual receipts by the
startling amount of £690; and manors are included in the
second rental which did not appear in the first. Thus one
cannot attribute all of this increase to a rising level of rents.
Even if one could, rents are not to be taken as a reliable
measure of general prosperity: a rising rent-roll might—and on
the Percy estates certainly did—result from changes in the
techniques of management. The substitution of leasehold for
tenant-right, the letting of parks, reduction in the length of
leases, these were some of the ways in which a landlord could
push up his revenue; they do not necessarily indicate general
prosperity, and they may perhaps have involved a fall in the
living standards of the peasants. Until more estates have been
examined with the care devoted by Mr. M. E. James to the
Percy lands, nothing can really be said about the impact of
administration upon the border economy or about the effect
of economic changes upon the habits of the moss-troopers.[2]

Something less negative can be said about the social effects of
the union, a subject which deserves far more space than it can
be accorded here. The gradual establishment of peace had,
from the middle of the sixteenth century, allowed a shift in
architectural styles. The old peel towers were no longer built,
and in their place came, first, fortified manor houses, and
second, gentlemen's houses of a more orthodox type, but still
wholly innocent of the renaissance features that were to be seen
in the south. Not until the eighteenth century did the style of
the border houses come to match that of the rest of England.
In smaller houses too the border lagged behind: the great re-

[1] Ornsby, p. xxxv. Rowse, *Expansion*, p. 29.
[2] M. E. James, *Estate Accounts of the Earls of Northumberland, 1562-1637*
(Surtees Soc. 1955), pp. xxxviii-xlviii.

building, begun elsewhere about 1570, started here in about 1690. Architectural changes were thus gradual: while the union produced no aesthetic revolution, the coming of peaceful ways began a slow assimilation of southern styles.[1] On the border ballads the union had perhaps a sharper effect. The line of heroes—Jock o' the Side, Hobie Noble, Kinmont Willie—had come to an end. In a sense the last of these heroes was Lord William Howard, who hunted thieves with a sportsman's zest and kept a list, like the notches on a western sheriff's revolver, of the outlaws he had taken. Yet Howard was a very different man from Kinmont Willie; for not only was he on the government side, but he interspersed his man-hunts with archaeological excavations and the building of a library. The educated gentleman had come to the border: while helping to suppress the old life, Howard brought in the ways of the new, southern, metropolitan society of Tudor England.[2]

[1] R. W. Brunskill, 'The Development of the Large House in the Eden Valley, 1350–1840' in *Transactions of Cumberland and Westmorland Antiquarian Society*, n.s. lvii (1958), pp. 72-96. Bouch and Jones, chs. i, iv. W. G. Hoskins, 'The Rebuilding of Rural England', *Past and Present*, no. 4 (1953), pp. 47-8. M. W. Barley, *The English Farmhouse and Cottage* (1961), pp. 113-122, 233-8.

[2] W. J. Entwistle, *European Balladry* (1939), pp. 228-42. Ornsby, pp. 463-4, 469-87. A. L. Rowse, 'Nicholas Roscarrock and his Lives of the Saints' in *Studies in Social History*, ed. J. H. Plumb (1955), pp. 1-31. D. Mathew, 'The Library at Naworth' in *For Hilaire Belloc*, ed. Douglas Woodruff (1942), pp. 117-30.

II

TWO SWEDISH FINANCIERS: LOUIS DE GEER AND JOEL GRIPENSTIERNA

Raymond Carr

IT is clear that, while the quantitative extent of the hold of private capital over Swedish public finance in the seventeenth century may not have changed significantly, the nature of that hold was modified. This modification is epitomised in the careers of Louis de Geer, the great Amsterdam merchant of the twenties and thirties, and of Joel Ekman (ennobled Gripenstierna) who was overwhelmed in the destruction of the Gustavian system brought about by the commissions of Karl XI. By the Gustavian system is meant that preference for liquidity which did much to modify the traditional financial structure inherited from Gustav Vasa, a system which lasted from the payment of the Älvsborg Ransom (1616–19) until the reforms of Karl XI in the eighties. These reforms, known collectively as the Great Reduction and accomplished by the great commissions of the reign, besides being directed at the recovery of land alienated on unfavourable terms by Gustavus and his successors, implied a frank acceptance of the closed economy of the sixteenth century as more fitted to the nature of Swedish resources.[1]

[1] The foundations of this paper are E. W. Dahlgren, *Louis de Geer* (Uppsala, 1923), two vols and A. Munthe, *Joel Gripenstierna* (Uppsala, 1941). Some of de Geer's business letters are printed in *Historisk Handlingar*, xxix (1934). This paper was written before the publication of the second volume of Professor Michael Roberts' *Gustavus Adolphus* (1958). This work contains an excellent description of the Gustavian system, pp. 67-88.

(i)

How was it that private capitalists entered the field of public finance in Sweden? Everywhere, under the *ancien régime*, periodic poverty and faulty financial techniques forced governments into reliance on private capital for short-term loans; Gustav Adolf could not pay his baker and was forced to cancel an order for tapestries illustrating his Russian victories.[1] This general cause apart, the place of private capitalists was different in Sweden because of special factors involved in the peculiar nature of the Swedish fiscal system and in the nature of the payments that system was called upon to make.[2]

The Swedish fiscal system reflected the predominant natural economy of the country in that it was based to an unusual extent on payments in kind. It was a constant source of complaint that the king's revenues came in the form of hens, oxen, leather, fish, wheat, eggs, etc. This cumbrous system survived, in part, into the nineteenth century and there is a constant danger of inferring from the more developed areas of the Swedish economy (for example, the metallurgical industries) that the economy in general was nearer to the 'normal' seventeenth century western European pattern than it in fact was.

The demands made by the war on this fiscal system were of a nature that it was particularly ill-fitted to meet: the demand was for *cash* payments *abroad*, for munitions, German cavalry, ambassadors' expenses, etc. Hence two operations were involved to make domestic revenue available for demands of this nature. Firstly, the *transformation* of kind rent-taxes into money, secondly, a pure *transfer* problem, the creation of foreign exchange when Swedish currency (the dollar silver mint) was unacceptable for foreign payments which could only be made

[1] A. Cronholm, *Sveriges historia under Gustav II Adolfs regering* (Stockholm, 1857–72), iii, 233; iv, 84.

[2] For a general description see E. Hecksher, *Sveriges Ekonomiska Historia* (Stockholm, 1935–36), i, pt ii. 209-98 and F. Lagerroth. *Statsreglering och finansförvaltning* (Lund, 1928), pp. 23–74 (mainly budgetary).

in riksdollars. It was the transfer problem that proved the more intractable.

Transformation of kind revenues into cash resources was first accomplished by the typical financial device of the *ancien régime*—tax-farming; revenues in kind were transferred to tax farmers for money payments and the system was applied to the crown revenues as a whole in the years 1620–29. It was through these farms that the private capitalists made their entry into crown finance:[1] the classic example is the farm of the iron works of Finspång in 1618 to William de Besche and it was through a network of such farms that de Geer came to dominate the industrial economy of Sweden, since the taxes farmed included, besides iron works, the labour services (transportation, charcoal burning) that were necessary for iron production.[2] Farming was considered by the government, not merely as a device for the creation of *immediate* liquid resources, but as part of a system that would enlarge the money area of the Swedish economy. That this was conscious policy is clear from the Treasury instructions of 1621: merchants will be able to do more commercially with the kind revenues of the crown than the crown itself and thus promote the growth of a money economy. Elsewhere in Europe the emphasis lay rather on the raising of loans or administrative convenience than on the creation of liquidity as such. 'It is abundantly clear', writes Almquist, 'that the whole policy of Sweden under Gustav Adolf was moving in a direction which made the traditional natural economy increasingly unsuitable. When the wars . . . began to be fought abroad ready money was urgently needed and a conglomeration of various commodities [became] useless. The government, therefore, utilized the possibilities of the tax farming system to create liquid resources.'[3]

[1] The best, if rather confused, account, of the details of the Gustavian farms is contained in Cronholm, *op. cit.*, iv, 455-502.

[2] The Finspång farm is printed in J. O. Carlberg *Historiskt sammlung om Sveriges bergverkens uppkomm och utveckling* (Stockholm, 1879), pp. 269-71. The farm included police powers over the workers.

[3] J. A. Almquist, *Den civila lokal förvaltning i Sverige* (Stockholm, 1917–1922), p. 145.

Tax-farming would not become a permanent expedient for converting kind into cash; after ten years the system was gradually abandoned.[1] To some extent it was replaced by the alienation of crown and tax peasants' land either by sale or outright donation. Sale (*frälseköp*) represented a sale of landed capital (whose income was realisable only with difficulty) in order to realise immediate cash resources for the wars.[2] Donation was, at least in part, inspired by a desire to replace cash wages for services rendered to the crown by gifts of land.[3] In return for donations, in both Gustav Adolf's and Oxenstierna's view, a noble family was in perpetuity bound to serve the state as soldiers or civil servants. When the nobility demanded *more* donations to justify new services and when the landed capital of the crown had been seriously eroded, the system could no longer work. Hence Karl XI reversed it and by the Liquidation and Reduction Commissions sought to reclaim for the crown the landed capital squandered on (or stolen by) the higher nobility. This involved a budgetary revolution: the old kind resources must be rearranged to fit modern needs.[4] Thus Karl XI's recovery of crown lands implied a re-organisation of the military system in order to use up the kind incomes of the crown, scattered as they were, all over the kingdom. The basic idea of Karl XI's military reform was to turn over local revenues to the army for exploitation on the spot.

[1] Tax farmers' exactions were a constant source of peasant complaints which a government that needed peasant support in the *Riksdag* could not neglect: cf. C. T. Odhner, *Sveriges inre historia under Drottning Christinas förmyndare* (Stockholm, 1865), p. 225. The search for new cash resources is evident in the importance of the Baltic Tolls and in the imposition of new taxation paid in cash.

[2] Sales under Gustav Adolf are examined in E. Brännman, *Frälseköpen under Gustav II Adolfs regering* (Lund, 1950): cf. *ibid.*, p. 224: 'The aim of frälseköp was to get money to finance the war'.

[3] For donations see R. Swedlund, *Grev- och Friherreskapen* (Uppsala, 1936) and the older but excellent work of S. Clason, *Till reduktionens för historia* (Uppsala, 1895).

[4] The report of the Skatteförenklingskommitté (1847) gives a curious picture of the complicated kind payments which still figured in the crown revenues. Taxes were accounted for in 295 categories and on 155 bases: see S. Eberstein, *Finansrätt* (Stockholm, 1942), p. 21.

To solve its *transfer problem* the Swedish government had no alternative but to rely on private capitalists: foreign capitalists supplied the crown with its foreign exchange by means of transactions based on Sweden's most valued export commodity—copper. The process was used for the first time on a large scale to meet Sweden's first substantial overseas payment, the war indemnity to Denmark called the Älvsborg Ransom. Swedish dollars, the product of a special tax, were used to buy copper for the crown: this copper was then sold to Dutch merchants and others in return for riksdollars paid to Denmark.[1] Nearly all subsequent foreign payments of Gustav Adolf are a variant of this method with bills of exchange replacing the crude transfer of specie. Here only the foreign capitalists could act—the condition of their activity being that the native Swedish merchant community was weak and timid, itself deriving its working capital from the Dutch. Here it was that de Geer, with his connections with the Amsterdam house of his kinsman Trip and friends like Arnold Huybertson, was indispensable.

Transformation and transfer operations were necessary economic functions. The third method of entry open to the private capitalist was less creditable, less typical of Sweden in that it was common to seventeenth century financial practice generally: the exploitation by private capitalists of the government's need for short-term credit together with the exploitation of the inadequacies of government accounting. Schemes for funding debt or facilitating long-term loan operations failed and the Swedish crown remained at the mercy of its short-term creditors: its only weapon was to play these creditors off against each other as Gripenstierna was used to break the monopoly of the Cronström group. Imperfections of accounting technique gave endless opportunity for private gain; creditors could not be brought to book because the true nature of their transactions lay in their private accounts. Treasury accounting

---

For a description of this process see E. F. Heckscher, *Ekonomiska-Historiska Studier* (Stockholm, 1936), p. 175 *et seq*. Heckscher emphasises the delays and clumsiness of such a system.

could not keep an adequate check. So slow were its procedures that the opponents of Bonde's drive for economy in the Regency of Karl XI could maintain that the crux of the difficulty lay, not in an actual shortage of money, but in the way the Treasury accounted for and administered what funds there were. Moreover the Treasury must avoid drastic measures which would drive the capitalists from supporting the crown —a statement often made by de la Gardie in his quarrel with Bonde.[1] It was in the interstices of an ill-ordered financial system that the private financier inserted himself for his own gain.[2]

De Geer was mainly concerned with transformation and transfer operations: the gains he made out of loans as such were incidental if considerable. Less of a financier than a merchant and industrial entrepreneur, his financial operations were subordinate to his commercial and industrial activities. He facilitated Swedish loan operations in Holland because he wished to sell armaments to Gustav Adolf; he became, via Monier, a shareholder in the Copper Company because he wished for information about probable payments in Amsterdam; he loaned to the crown as a form of investment to get hold of farms of metallurgical works which he wished to manage on his own account. Thus he came to dominate the industrial economy of Sweden as no man has done before or since. Seeing a great opportunity in Sweden when the supply of the armaments industry of the Low Countries was falling away, at the very time that demand was increasing, he came to Sweden to create an armament industry where iron was plentiful. From the beginnings at Finspång, he squeezed out all competitors, taking over a large number of unprofitable enterprises in

[1] Thus it proved impossible to examine the accounts of Drakenhielm for his administration of the Great Toll in spite of a justified conviction that he had been cheating the crown.

[2] For an account of these difficulties see K. Wittrock. *Karl XI:s förmyndares finanspolitik* (Uppsala, 1915), i, 198, 376; ii, 253, 331, 340. The sins of the Treasury were amplified in other departments so that the Treasury itself could get no accurate statements (see the failure to produce accounts for the Inquest of 1675, O. Varenius, *Räfsten med Karl XI:s förmyndaretyrelse* (Uppsala, 1903), i, 111-12, and for Admiralty, K. Wittrock, *op. cit.*, ii, 159 *et seq.*).

the process. De Geer's farms, later converted into outright purchases, became the foundation of the modern iron industry in Sweden, using the new techniques that the Walloon immigrants, organised by de Geer, brought with them.[1] De Geer played a large, though by no means a preponderant, part in transfer operations based on the copper trade, a central feature of Swedish war finance; Sweden's position as a great power corresponded with the domination of the European market by Swedish copper.[2] Concern with copper prices runs through the correspondence of Gustav Adolf and Oxenstierna because it was a vital interest to maintain buoyant copper prices. It was the sharp fall of prices in 1624-25 that forced Gustav Adolf towards his much criticised copper policy: a combination of a copper coinage in Sweden to create an artificial shortage on the Amsterdam market together with a policy of depositing copper as security for loans until the price rose to make sale on the open market profitable. The policy failed because the coinage demand in Sweden was inelastic once the slack had been taken up: thus the coins were exported and exercised a depressing effect on prices. Deposition had a deadening effect on the market because, as Oxenstierna put it, the merchants saw the obvious limits of restraint in sales, given the vendors' pressing necessity for money, and waited round the deposited copper like wolves round a lamb they were

[1] The purchase of farms (the purchase price was the writing off of old crown debt) was an obvious advantage to de Geer: it eliminated competitive bidding when the contract was renewed and made improvements a safe investment. From the point of view of the crown, alienations (*frälseköp*) of this nature meant a permanent loss of income in return for temporary increase. De Geer's purchases amounted to 20 per cent of the whole sales of the minority (Heckscher, *op. cit.*, i, pt. ii, 315) and resulted in a steady loss of annual income from the farms. 1640: 33,521 d.s.m. 1645: 24,416; 1647: 17,427; 1649: 2,734. Some of this fall can be attributed to a contraction of the scale of de Geer's enterprises. (Dahlgren, *op. cit.*, i, 276.)

Abbreviations—d.s.m. = dollar silver mint; RD = riksdollars.

[2] Heckscher's view (*Scandia*, xi, 1938, 214) that Sweden's semi-monopoly position was never seriously threatened in the seventeenth century must be accepted as against A. Olsen's view (*Scandia*, x, 1937, 38 *et seq.*) that Japanese copper was a serious competitor. Cf. G. Lindeberg, *Svensk Ekonomisk politik under den Görtzka perioden* (Lund, 1941), pp. 264-71 for a final destruction of Olsen's Japanese bogy.

waiting to devour.[1] By the late twenties the copper deposited with the house of Trip was paralysing the sale of copper in the open market and the use of new exports as security for loans: if Trip 'let loose' his deposition copper, prices would collapse completely. It is clear that Trip was using his extraordinary position to force the crown to grant him a virtual monopoly of the Swedish copper trade in Amsterdam.

It is difficult to unravel de Geer's complicated connection with the Amsterdam market. At times he appears as the ally of the crown, co-operating with Swedish agents to break Trip's position. In 1632 he claimed that he had forced a sharp rise in copper prices by selling some of Trip's copper on the open market and buying it at an artificially high price—as he called it 'user de pratique'.[2] On the whole his activities are less creditable from the point of view of the Swedish crown, although a rise in copper prices after 1630 allowed the king, but not his chancellor Oxenstierna, the illusion that these complicated manœuvres had succeeded. In the late twenties and early thirties we have the unedifying picture of de Geer, Eric Larsson, and the Trips, either in cut-throat competition or collusion, jockeying for a position from which to dictate terms to the crown. Eric Larsson, sent out to 'free' copper from Trip, ends up by becoming his partner. De Geer promises to drive Trip out of the market if he can become sole 'factor' for Swedish copper: his connections with the Trips, both by marriage and in business, were so close that his motives are suspect. He, too, enters Trip's *consortium* when he is not strong enough to force through his own monopoly. Yet however shady his operations, however large his profits (the fact that he went out of the copper trade would seem to indicate that he found it unprofitable), his transactions were in the nature of genuine commercial transactions.

[1] J. Wolontis, *Kopparmyntningen i Sverige 1624–1714* (Helsingfors, 1935), p. 33 *et seq.* Cf. *Axel Oxenstiernas skrifter och brefvexling* (1888 and after), i, 345.

[2] De Geer to King, 21 August 1632.

(ii)

Gripenstierna was a pure financier, the first pure financier in Swedish history; with few mercantile or commercial connections, his sole interest was government finance and, as a civil servant in the Treasury, he represents that mixture of public and private finance typical of the seventeenth century. The basis of his loan operations was not his own wealth but his political connections, above all his boyhood friendship with Erik Lindschöld: through these connections and his own position as a government servant, he obtained the administration of certain crown revenues and from these revenues he loaned to the crown itself. Whereas the crown came to de Geer, Gripenstierna, to use one of his enemies' phrases, 'insinuated himself with the crown'. Thus Gripenstierna rises and falls, not in relation to his economic strength, but with the reliability of his political connections.[1] He flourished, therefore, in the atmosphere of intrigue of the early years of Karl XI's reign, the period of de la Gardie's ascendancy and of the peculiar rule of secretaries that succeeded it. Made by Erik Lindschöld, he was ruined when he had no secretary friend in the king's confidence.

The foundation of his loan operations was the administration of the French subsidy and, above all, of the Sea Tolls, the crown's largest cash income; once he controlled these revenues he could 'save' de la Gardie by the loan of 1674, after the Bank and all other sources had failed. The nature of his operations is clear: he could use deductions (*decurtations*) from the Sea Tolls to pay his own debts to the merchants and others from whom

[1] That is, in contrast with those financier-industrialists of the earlier period, e.g. the Momma-Reenstierna brothers. As with de Geer they used their loans to the crown as a means to obtain mining concessions, etc., as a form of capital investment. This capital was the result of earlier activity *outside* Sweden. Such investment was not always sound and the Momma-Reenstiernas were ruined because they invested in ventures like the Lapland mines where there was no profit margin. The final blow to this dynasty was a series of expensive law suits connected with the complicated company farms in which they took over various concessions; but they rose and fell for economic, not political, reasons. P. Sondén, 'Bröderna Momma-Reenstierna' (*Historisk Tidskrift*, xxxi, 1911, 144 *et seq.*).

he had raised the money in the first place and then take from the Tolls the crown's debt to himself—an indirect way of financing the crown out of its own resources. His profits lay in the concession of the right to pay 'transported' debts (old crown debts bought up at a discount) out of the Toll revenues he administered. Hence the constant difficulties in separating Gripenstierna's function as a Treasury official from his functions as a moneylender. Moreover, a large part of the 1674 loan took the form, not of a cash advance, but of the acceptance of crown debt to army contractors: this allowed internal adjustments, the sort of brokerage Gripenstierna excelled in.

There were soon signs of a bitter opposition to Gripenstierna. Led by his personal enemies this opposition represented the interest of the Bank which Gripenstierna had defeated in the negotiations of 1674. The Bank policy was to get the cash revenues of the crown, including the Sea Tolls, paid into a consolidated fund, administered by the Bank on the account of the Treasurer.[1] Such a central account would ruin Gripenstierna not merely by revealing the nature of his operations but by taking away his working capital. After an incredibly bitter struggle the Tolls were taken from him and handed over to the Bank. With no crown revenues to play with Gripenstierna could make no loans. He was finished; in 1678 he made one last attempt, in return for a loan, to handle the crown's copper.[2] He failed. The slow machinery of Karl XI's commissions, manned by his enemies, the enemies of the system that had allowed Gripenstierna to prosper, ground him down to total ruin by a remorseless application of the principle that loans to the crown out of its own resources were invalid and that any concessions made on the basis of such a loan were now to be considered as debts to the crown.

[1] For the Bank see S. Brisman, *Den Palmstruchska banken och Riksens ständers bank under den karolinska tiden* (Stockholm, 1918), p. 168 et seq.

[2] i.e. the regalian dues paid to the crown in copper. The sale of this *avrads koppar* is quite distinct from the sale of the total copper production bought up by the crown from the miners which was the basis of Gustavian finance in the days of the Copper Company.

(iii)

There can be no doubt that de Geer, Gripenstierna and others hoped for profit from their crown loans. The question is the degree of that profit and the nature of the profit. Was it usurious, speculative profit or the due reward of services and risks? The nature of the sources makes it difficult to give a satisfactory answer in quantitative terms. What one might call the literary sources give a dusty answer because they cancel each other out and are full of accusation and counter-accusation. There are the statements about the financiers embodied in the protocols of the Råd and in the Treasury minutes. John Skytte talks of 'de Geer and others who lust after lucrum', and the protocols of the minority are full of bitter complaints by de la Gardie and others on the sins of those who put private gain above the public good.[1] In direct opposition to these are the statements of family tradition embodied in the 'official' biographies of the next generation—especially after the commissions of Karl XI endeavoured to prove that all gains were illegal gains made at the expense of the crown. Both de Geer's and Gripenstierna's heirs insisted that the founders of the family fortunes were patriots who spent their time, in the picturesque phraseology of the time, 'gripping the king under the arms'. If they and their loans had not existed the state would have foundered. The Gripenstierna tradition, embodied in the biography of 1758,[2] is built on the theme of the extent of his unrequited loans to the crown and the 'Albanian persecution' brought on him by his enemies. The patriotic hero becomes the martyr.

The second source, the Treasury accounts of settlement for debts and the mass of work accomplished by the Liquidation Commission, is in appearance more objective. But much

[1] De la Gardie accused the Cronberg group of a fixed design to enslave the kingdom by their loans, to engulf 'vires et substantiam totius regni', cf. Wittrock, op. cit., i, 363-5. Cf. Nils Brahe's statement that to give in to Cronberg's demands was 'to change overlords'.

[2] J. Gripenstierna, Riks-Cammar-Rådet Herr Joel Gripenstiernas Lefwerne (1758).

government accounting, especially in the Caroline commissions, was inspired guesswork; inspired, that is, by a desire to make as much as possible for the crown. What strikes one most is the difference between the crown and its creditors' estimate of the same debt. In 1634 the Treasury claimed a debt to the crown of 142,103 d.s.m. as against de Geer's counter-claim of 84,325 d.s.m. When settlement of account proved impossible, both sides settled on a fictional amount in return for some immediate gain at the moment of settlement. In 1636 de Geer accepted the Treasury estimate of 18,599 d.s.m. because he was in process of negotiating a renewal of the Finspång farm. The Treasury quoted a moderate amount in return for a large loan that exceeded the agreed settlement.[1] Gripenstierna's affairs present even more extreme conflicting estimates. In 1696 the Liquidation Commission claimed 1,540,296 d.s.m., Gripenstierna 3,377,823 d.s.m.

The Treasury mind worked in a peculiar way. Absolutely dependent on financiers for its short-term credits, it was convinced that it was being held to ransom and cheated but it lacked the information to prove its case since such information would lie in the private accounts of the financiers. Like the schoolmaster, unable to detect the boy who is talking in form, it punished indiscriminately with the conviction that sharp practice was in the national interest. When de Geer and the Treasury were moving towards the settlement of the 1636 account the Treasury quite arbitrarily refused to reckon any interest on debt since 1636 and reduced, equally arbitrarily and against all accepted accounting practice, the exchange rate of d.s.m. and RD. Its handling of the Trip debt was scandalous. Although it had been judicially recognised as 115,182 d.s.m., the Treasury refused to recognise the debt after the death of Elias Trip in the hope that the debt would be 'forgotten'. Unfortunately the heir Adrian Trip demanded both debt and interest, and, even more unfortunately, became de Geer's son-in-law. De Geer was not the man to forget a debt. He

---

[1] Such considerations lessen the value of de Geer's reckonings with the crown preserved at Leufsta.

immediately appealed to the queen in a moving letter and the Treasury was forced to acknowledge the debt, though de Geer held that the Treasury cheated over the copper contract by which Adrian Trip was to receive payment. In 1830 the Trip heirs were still claiming two million d.s.m.

Authoritative proof of the amount of profit can only be found in the account books of the financiers concerned. Unfortunately these are not always available. The rough methods of the Liquidation Commission and the Reduction Commission made it advisable to do away with any evidence that might support the crown's claims.[1] This destruction in itself would be strong negative evidence of illicit gain did not the unscrupulous methods of the commissions make such destruction less weighty evidence of an uneasy conscience. The commissions' aims in these matters were to prove that the loans to the crown were not made at a fair rate or that they were made in some way out of the crown's own revenues or that the land sold to creditors to write off these debts was sold at an unfair price; if any of these charges could be proved then the lands in question could be 'reduced', i.e. claimed by Karl XI's commissions for the crown. It is scarcely surprising that the account books (e.g. 'the master's big book' of de Geer) which would give us an overall picture of crown indebtedness or otherwise have been destroyed. Important subsidiary accounts have vanished. There was some doubt if the purchase price of Finspång included all the rents that the de Geers had actually enjoyed. To avoid inquiry the family claimed that the accounts were kept by a certain Lina who could not write. The story becomes even less convincing when it is found that letters from Lina actually exist. The crown could not extract from Gripenstierna an account of his own activities, it therefore relied on its own estimates.

To get any idea of the profits we are therefore forced back to the examination of what accounts survive of individual transactions, or in the case of Gripenstierna to even more

[1] The commission officials were not above bribery, cf. A. Levenhaupt, 'Ett blad ur Reducktionens historia' *Historisk Tidskrift*, 1899, p. 327.

general considerations based on the reports of the Liquidation Commission. Deductions from de Geer's capital account or from his will tell us nothing about the nature of his profits; they only prove he was a rich man.

The sale of arms to the crown was, as we have indicated, the origin of de Geer's Swedish fortune rather than any pure financial operations. From accounts of these transactions it is possible to make a rough estimate of trading profit: in the years round 1630 it would seem to be about 40 per cent whereas the profits from crown factories for arms supplied to the crown would seem to range from a minimum of 25 per cent to as high as 180 per cent. These seemingly high profits must be weighed against the risks of trading with the crown; in 1631 Gustav Adolf suddenly cancelled a contract for the supply of armaments to the whole Swedish army and de Geer was left with the task of disposing his stock elsewhere. The crown in Sweden as in other countries had a bad name for repudiation or late payment of debt. Oxenstierna once imprisoned an English merchant who laughed in his face at an offer of prompt repayment. Stenbock counselled moderation in dealing with the crown's creditors 'A merchant is a merchant. He makes profit at one moment and loses all the next and the risks he takes are great.'[1]

In the case of Gripenstierna's individual transactions the evidence of the Liquidation Commission is obviously prejudiced and cannot be taken as evidence of the exact amount of 'illegal' profit. The commission's treatment of Gripenstierna's Copper Contract of 1670 is a case in point. The commission held that this contract was not rescinded in 1674 (it clearly was and only a dubious legal quibble could support the Treasury contention) and consequently declared Gripenstierna liable to pay in the terms of the contract from 1674 the enormous sum of a quarter of a million d.s.m. *plus* interest. The fact that the commission could, as a result of their interpretation of the contract, argue that Gripenstierna had crown incomes in his hands, allowed them to declare all his *subsequent* loans invalid because

[1] A. Munthe, *op. cit.*, pp. 51-2.

made to the crown out of its own resources. It would be clearly wrong to accuse Gripenstierna of cheating the crown to the tune of 1,540,296 d.s.m. as the commission claimed.

In spite of this sleight of hand the commission's findings cannot be the monstrous fiction that Gripenstierna claimed them to be. What damns Gripenstierna is his inability to prove, by his own accounts, that the greater part of his loans to the crown came from other sources than the internal manipulation of crown revenues and the profits he derived from their administration. If Gripenstierna, as he maintained, loaned his own money, or money that his credit had raised from others, he had to prove one of two things:

(i) That he had the necessary capital to start with,
(ii) By means of evidence, that he had loaned the money from others.

Since (i) was obviously untrue his failure to prove that most of his loans were the result of negotiations with third parties on the basis of his own credit was fatal. His connections with merchant houses for instance were obviously slight. He was involved with the German house of Wolters and some Stockholm merchants, but what is most significant is that when his credit was shaken and his ruin imminent, apart from Wolters, no one seems to have sued him for large outstanding claims which would have undoubtedly existed had the basis of his loan operations been credit raised from third parties. The conclusion seems clear. The 1674 operation apart, he loaned the crown its own money.

De Geer accomplished valuable economic functions in meeting Sweden's need for capital imports and foreign investment in Swedish industry, and in introducing the new Walloon techniques in the iron industry. He made his profits: but it is clear from the nature of the settlement with the Treasury at the end of his career that these profits were not all considered by the crown as illegal gains. Thus, in the Reductions, his family kept much of his landed fortune. Gripenstierna fulfilled no such functions; a born Swede, a career civil servant, who was the son of a poor priest, he had no private capital nor is there any indication that he was an important channel by which foreign capital reached Sweden. Unlike de Geer, he did the state no service: the state knew it and his fortune vanished in the commissions.

The relative parts played by de Geer and Gripenstierna are indicative of an increasing contraction of the Swedish public economy towards a system more suited to the nature and extent of Swedish resources. There is in Bonde's system, in the minority of Karl XI for example, a desire to get away from foreign commitments that would entail heavy foreign payments.[1] Karl XI, in his reversion to the methods of Gustav Vasa, was to cut Sweden off from the international money market; but this process had been going on imperfectly beforehand in spite of the financial excesses of de la Gardie. Such a contraction implied that Sweden had less use for the de Geers, the Larssons, the Mommas with their connections with Amsterdam. Gripenstierna was a Swede and he and Cronberg are the first Swedes to play any significant part in the financing of the crown. They could do so because financing the crown demanded technical agility in domestic finance, not the import of foreign capital.

The distinguishing feature of this uneasy period before the reforms of Karl XI is the deterioration of standards of government finance generally: the contracted system could only work, given the limited resources of the crown and the country, if new standards of financial probity and exactness of account were introduced into public finance. Karl XI, whose heart was in his counting house, imposed such standards. In the early years of the Gustavian system the prestige and temper of Gustav Adolf and the great financial abilities of Oxenstierna kept government finance above the standards of western Europe. By the late seventies these standards had been undermined by the incapacity of Kristina and the faction fights of the

---

[1] This connection was restored in the attempts of Görtz to raise loans for Karl XII.

minority of Karl XI. Budgets became battle-grounds between de la Gardie and his opponents and the whole atmosphere of the Treasury is one of intrigue. It was such a deterioration that gave Gripenstierna his chance and the deterioration is reflected in the corruption of Gripenstierna himself.

III

PROPAGATING THE GOSPEL

Christopher Hill

(i)

In the century before 1640 the existence of the Council in the North and the Council in the Marches of Wales bore witness to official recognition that there were special problems of government in those areas. They were also areas in which Catholicism and paganism survived longest. Puritans like Bernard Gilpin and John Penry, John Preston and Sir Benjamin Rudyerd, called for the evangelisation of these 'dark corners of the land'. The Feoffees for Impropriations devoted much attention to Wales and the Marches; London merchants endowed schools and lectureships, especially in Lancashire, Yorkshire, and on the Welsh border. Behind this activity of Puritans and merchants there was a triple concern: for the glory of God, the salvation of the souls of men, and the political security of protestant England. Wales and the North were long regarded, by Catholics and Puritans alike, as potential allies for a Spanish invasion: and in the civil war Wales and the North were the main source of royalist strength.[1] One western area in which there was spontaneous popular support for Parliament during

---

[1] W. K. Jordan, *Philanthropy in England, 1480-1660* (1959), *passim*; *The Charities of London* (1960), *passim*. Professor Trevor-Roper notes that the zeal of pre-revolutionary London merchants was inherited by the Commissioners for the Propagation of the Gospel (*Econ. Hist. Rev.*, New Series, xiv, 140). Detailed evidence for some of the statements in the above paragraph will be found in my 'Puritans and "the dark corners of the land",' *Trans. R. Hist. Soc.*, 1963. See also D. Ogg, *England in the Reign of Charles II* (1934), pp. 41-50, 78.

the civil war was the Forest of Dean. In 1631 the Rev. Peter Simon had been accused of fomenting revolt there and preaching the equality of all mankind; it transpired that he had been presented to his living by the Haberdashers' Company of London, under the will of one of their company of Welsh origin.[1]

From the earliest days of its existence the Long Parliament showed great interest in the problem of the North and West. In December 1640 a committee was appointed to inquire into the shortage of preaching ministers, and to consider some way of removing those who were scandalous—what later became the Committee for Scandalous Ministers. It included Sir Robert Harley, who had long been a patron of Puritans in Herefordshire, and all the M.P.s of Wales, Northumberland, Cumberland, Lancashire—the only areas so heavily represented.[2] Next year the Committee on Preaching Ministers authorised Walter Cradock and other ministers to preach in Wales.[3] In March 1644 the Westminster Assembly appointed a committee to select a suitable person to translate its Directory into Welsh.[4] Three months later the Commons appointed a Committee to provide ministers able to preach in Welsh, for the parliamentary armies as they advanced into Wales.[5] Sir Thomas Myddelton —son of the ex-Lord Mayor of London who had financed the translation of the Bible into Welsh in 1630—who appropriately commanded the army which conquered North Wales, was empowered to replace scandalous ministers by religious and learned men.[6] An ordinance of 28 March 1646 provided

---

[1] *Calendar of State Papers Dom., 1631-33*, p. 36. The Haberdashers later gave a lectureship to the vicar of Monmouth (T. Richards, *A History of the Puritan Movement in Wales, 1639-53*, 1920, p. 41). The men of the Forest of Dean again supported Parliament in 1651.

[2] *C.J.*, ii, 54.   [3] *Ibid.*, ii, 189.

[4] Ed. A. F. Mitchell and J. Struthers, *Minutes of the Sessions of the Westminster Assembly of Divines* (1874), p. 67.   [5] *C.J.*, iii, 565.

[6] Richards, *op. cit.*, p. 46. Fairfax had in February 1644 similarly been given a free hand to place 'able and learned divines' in the North (Ed. C. H. Firth and C. S. Rait, *Acts and Ordinances of the Interregnum*, 1911, i, 391-2). Cf. *Memorials of the Civil War* (Ed. R. Bell, 1849), i, 337-8—a plea to Fairfax to use his power to make the Gospel flourish 'in this your blind county' of Yorkshire.

for the maintenance of preaching ministers in Herefordshire.[1]

Parliamentarians had always claimed that one of the objects of invading Wales was 'to plant the Gospel among the Welshmen'. After the fighting was over Morgan Llwyd, Ambrose Mostyn, and Vavasor Powell were appointed itinerant ministers for North Wales, an appointment regularised in June 1648. They received £100 a year each.[2] In August 1645 the House of Commons sent Henry Walter, Walter Cradock, and Richard Symonds to South Wales to preach 'itinerantly' in Welsh, also at £100 a year each, to be found from the revenues of the Bishops, Deans, and Chapters of Llandaff and St. David's.[3] Preachers in South Wales and Monmouthshire also received money from the sequestrated estates of the catholic Marquis of Worcester.[4]

In 1644–45 there had been a revulsion of feeling against the royal forces in Wales and its Marches: armies of Welsh clubmen helped the parliamentarian generals to finish off the war.[5] This reinforced feelings among supporters of Parliament that the common people of Wales were 'but a seduced ignorant people': the words are attributed to Oliver Cromwell.[6] 'At length the moles have eyes', wrote *Mercurius Britanicus*. In

[1] Firth and Rait, *op. cit.*, i, 846-7. A similar ordinance of April 1645 had provided for the maintenance of preaching ministers in York, Durham, Carlisle, Newcastle, Berwick (*ibid.*, i, 669-71).

[2] Ed. A. H. Dodd, *History of Wrexham* (1957), pp. 57-8; Richards, *op. cit.*, pp. 40, 65.

[3] *C.J.*, iv, 242, 622, 707. This was not confirmed by ordinance (i.e. with the concurrence of the Lords) for fifteen months (*L.J.*, viii, 463, 569), since the Westminster Assembly complained that the ministers had not received its authorisation (Mitchell and Struthers, *op. cit.*, pp. 267, 301-2). Symonds ultimately got their blessing, but not apparently the others. Thomas Edwards was worried that such men should be sent into Wales (*Gangraena*, Part III, 1646, 163, 241-2). It is the recurrent story of the radicals being prepared to take on the tasks of evangelisation which others shirked. Vavasor Powell managed to obtain a certificate from the Assembly, after some argument (*The Life and Death of Mr. V. Powell*, 1671, pp. 15-16).

[4] A. Clark, *Raglan Castle and the Civil War in Monmouthshire* (1953), p. 63.

[5] J. R. Phillips, *Memoirs of the Civil War in Wales and the Marches* (1874), i, ch. vi, *passim*; ii, 129, 139, 246, 268, 273-4, 279-81; *Portland MSS.* (H.M.C), i, 256, 294.   [6] Phillips, *op. cit.*, ii, 377-8.

August 1645 the House of Commons ordered that Parliament's case should be explained to the people of South Wales. Parliament was also confident that the people of North Wales, although not so active in rejecting the royalists, could be won over by propaganda. It ordered a declaration to be drafted 'to inform them aright of the Parliament'.[1] *The Parliament explained to Wales* was published in 1646 by John Lewis, who claimed to be 'the first of my country that did publish anything in order to the Parliament'. His book was dedicated to Sir Robert Harley, Sir Thomas Myddelton, and John Glynn, all M.P.s. Since Lewis was later one of the Commissioners for the Propagation of the Gospel in Wales, his book neatly links the Propagators with pre-1640 attempts to spread light in the dark corners of Wales.[2]

So by the end of the civil war it was being assumed, as a correspondent with the army besieging Carnarvon put it, that Parliament 'will take care to send a powerful ministry so soon as North Wales is totally reduced', since 'the country towns hereabouts have been quite without all manner of preaching almost'.[3] 'Doubtless we are deep enough in their [the Parliament's] thoughts', John Lewis agreed; 'and ... they do mind our happiness more than we do ourselves. The only compendious way to make us happy is to have the Gospel come amongst us. . . . It will presently purge church and state'.[4] 'Churches . . . will be your strongest castles, if you furnish them well with ministers,' a preacher told the Commons in September 1646.[5] From 1646 onwards petitions flowed in to the London classis asking for ministers to be sent to the former royalist areas of Wales and the North, over which God had now cleared up 'those misty clouds of affliction and oppression'.[6]

[1] Phillips, *op. cit.*, i, 319-21; *C.J.*, iv, 342, 622. There is no evidence that this order was ever carried out (Richards, *op. cit.*, p. 79).

[2] J. Lewis, *The Parliament explained to Wales*, pp. 4, 6. I quote from the 1907 reprint.   [3] Quoted in Richards, *op. cit.*, pp. 9, 79.

[4] Lewis, *op. cit.*, pp. 34-5.

[5] H. Palmer, *The Duty and Honour of Church-Restorers* (1646), p. 44.

[6] Ed. C. E. Surman, *The Register-Booke of the Fourth Classis in the Province of London, 1646-49* (Harleian Soc. Publications, lxxxii-iii, 1952-53), pp. 20-8 and *passim*.

The time seemed ripe; and the political as well as spiritual advantages of evangelising the dark corners were clear. 'The people are desperately ignorant and profane abroad; and from profane priests and ignorant people, you know the other party have fomented this war, and may begin it again, if the Word prevent not the sword.' So Hugh Peter told Parliament, the Lord Mayor and Aldermen of London and the Assembly of Divines in 1646, reminding them that he had formerly been an active associate of the Feoffees for Impropriations.[1] He had found the Marches of Wales 'ripe for the Gospel'.[2] John Owen, himself a Welshman, made the same point to Parliament in the same year: 'Doth not Wales cry, the North cry, yea and the West cry, "Come and help us. We are yet in a worse bondage than any by your means we have been delivered from. If you leave us thus, all your protection will but yield us a more free and jovial passage to the chamber of death".'[3] Cradock hammered the point home in a sermon preached before the Commons in July: 'And what if you should spend one single thought upon poor contemptible Wales? It's little indeed and as little respected, yet time was the enemy made no small use and advantage of it. . . . Is it not a sad case that in thirteen counties there should not be above thirteen conscientious ministers who in that time expressed themselves firmly and consistently faithful to the Parliament, and formerly preached profitably in the Welsh language twice every Lord's Day?'[4] (We note in passing Cradock's simple assumption that regular preachers would of course be constantly faithful to Parliament.) In *The Parliament explained to Wales* John Lewis complained of 'that swarm of blind superstitious ceremonies that are among us, passing under the name of old harmless customs' — worship of saints, pilgrimage to wells, superstitious veneration of chapels. It 'is still to this day undispelled, and hinders us from the primitive light of the

[1] H. Peter, *Gods Doings and Mans Duty* (1646), p. 44.
[2] *Mr. Peters Last Report of the English Wars* (1646), p. 13.
[3] Quoted by J. Moffat, *The Life of John Owen* (n.d.), p. 23.
[4] W. Cradock, *The Saints Fulness of Joy* (1646), quoted by J. Ballinger, *The Bible in Wales* (1906), p. 30.

Gospel'.[1] The task of enlightening Wales was therefore a dual one: darkness had to be dispelled as well as truth preached. For this preaching *in Welsh* was essential. But there were grave obstacles. Livings in Wales were desperately poor. Parliament did much to end pluralism, to divert the revenues of sinecures to preachers, to augment stipends, and to find Welsh preachers. The practice of reducing royalists' composition fines on condition that impropriated tithes were made over to the minister of the parish greatly increased the maintenance available for many ministers, especially in the North and West.[2] But the Army was a competitor for sequestrated impropriations: some time before 1650 three royalists' livings in Pembrokeshire were assigned to Colonel Horton's brigade.[3] Finance was crucial to the provision of preaching: only after Pride's Purge were dean and chapter lands sold and £20,000 a year made available for this purpose.[4] But the nature of the preachers was also at issue: so long as it was assumed that they must be ordained ministers, preferably university men, the supply fell short of the presumed demand.

Hugh Peter had a simple and traditional solution, which he put forward on every occasion: itinerant preachers. These, he thought, should be established by the state in all parts of the kingdom, especially in the dark places. 'What you have gotten by the sword must be maintained by the Word.' The Westminster Assembly, by concentrating on creating presbyteries in London, was tackling the problem from the wrong end, he thought.[5] What Britain most needed was 'justice, charity and

[1] Lewis, *op. cit.*, pp. 30, 33. Ten years later Lewis assumed that 'hardly . . . half the people of Wales would be granted to belong to Christ', though by that time he had moderated his destructive zeal (J[ohn] L[ewis], *Some seasonable and moderate Thoughts in order to the furtherance and promoting the affaires of Religion and the Gospel especially in Wales*, 1656, p. 8). Contrast p. 51 below.) Cf. John Jones's question to Morgan Llwyd in 1651: 'Where more ignorance, where more hatred to the people of God, where the word saint more scorned . . . than in Merionethshire?' (ed. J. Mayer, 'Inedited Letters of Cromwell, Col. Jones, Bradshaw and Other Regicides', *Trans. Hist. Soc. Lancs. and Cheshire*, New Series, i, 185).
[2] For examples in Wales, see Richards, *op. cit.*, pp. 38-42, 47-52, 63-70.
[3] *Ibid.*, p. 2.   [4] See my *Puritanism and Revolution* (1958), pp. 168-83.
[5] Peter, *Gods Doings and Mans Duty*, pp. 43-4.

industry,[1] the only upholders of that flourishing neighbour-nation, the Netherlands'. A preaching ministry was the way to attain all these desirable objectives. 'How long therefore shall I entreat some three or four itinerary ministers in a county? ... How easily might the land be (in some measure) reduced to God and their own civil interests, if provision was laid in of this kind?' A college should be set aside, at Oxford perhaps, to train 'godly youths out of shops' to act as travelling preachers. A committee should be set up to approve preachers who 'cannot answer the narrow examination of an Assembly', even though 'they should fall short of arts and tongues'.[2]

A year later Peter proposed that tithes should be pooled, and was more specific about the central examining committee which he had in mind. No doubt recalling the Feoffees, he said it should consist of 'godly men, ministers, gentlemen and others', and should test would-be itinerants, of whom two or three should be sent to each county.[3] In 1651 he proposed that each university should maintain at the public charge 'able, fit, godly and learned men', who would travel through the country settling all religious disputes and disposing of errors.[4] Peter was to be an enthusiastic supporter of the Propagators of the Gospel in Wales, and actively assisted them in Pembroke-shire.[5] He thus forms another link between the Propagators and the pre-1640 attempts to evangelise the dark corners.

In fact missionary enterprise started in Wales as soon as the war was over: and it rapidly got out of the control of Parliament and the Assembly of Divines. 'In some parts where the Gospel came', said Vavasor Powell, 'they far and near pressed

[1] My italics.
[2] *Mr. Peters Last Report of the English Wars*, pp. 12-13; cf. p. 8.
[3] H. Peter, *A Word for the Army* (1647), in *Harleian Miscellany* (1744-6), v, 573.
[4] Peter, *Good Work for a good Magistrate* (1651), pp. 6-14. Peter also proposed that universities 'to train godly ministers' should be set up in Wales, Yorkshire, and Cornwall, to serve the three darkest corners of the land (*ibid.*, p. 3). When Durham University was established in 1657 it was instructed to maintain two itinerant ministers (*V.C.H., Durham*, ii, 53). John Lewis supported the idea of a college or two in Wales, subordinate to Oxford and Cambridge (*Some seasonable and modest Thoughts*, p. 30).
[5] R. P. Stearns, *The Strenuous Puritan* (1954), pp. 362-3.

to hear it, night and day.'[1] Walter Cradock, in a sermon preached in 1648, said: 'I have observed and seen, in the mountains of Wales, the most glorious work that I ever saw in England, unless it were in London. The Gospel is run over the mountains, between Brecknockshire and Monmouthshire, as the fire in the thatch. And who should do this? They have no ministers; but some of the wisest say that there are about 800 godly people there, and they go from one to another. . . . Shall we rail at such, and say they are tub-preachers, and they were never at the university?'[2]

Peter and Cradock posed the question that Wales and the North were setting. 'Tarrying for the universities' in the decades before 1640 had left the problem of preaching in Wales virtually untouched. Even the generous augmentations of the forties and fifties did not furnish many livings rich enough to attract graduates. In any case there were not enough Welsh-speaking graduates. One of the ministers ejected by the Propagators admitted in 1650 that scarcely one in fifteen of his clerical contemporaries could read and write Welsh.[3] So there was a case for pooling parochial funds in state-controlled livings, and for employing non-graduate Welsh speakers—if anything was to be done to evangelise Wales at all. Preaching the Gospel in the dark corners was a tough job, which called for many enthusiastic participants. But enthusiasm was what the parliamentary Presbyterians and the Westminster Assembly most dreaded, since it was most obviously to be found among the sectaries and in the New Model Army. 'Godly youths out of shops' were not to everybody's liking: yet how else could preaching ministers in sufficient numbers be provided? 'Shall we rail at such, and say they are tub-preachers, and they were never at the university?' The Presbyterians, like the bishops before them, inclined more and more to shelve the problem. It was tackled only after Pride's Purge. Acts for the Propaga-

[1] Quoted in Ballinger, *The Bible in Wales*, p. 30. Cf. J. Lewis, *The Parliament explained to Wales*, p. 31.
[2] Quoted in T. Rees, *History of Protestant Nonconformity in Wales* (2nd ed., 1883), p. 67.
[3] *Ibid.*, p. 77.

tion of the Gospel in Wales and in the four northern counties followed in February and March 1650.

These acts attempted to do for preaching in the dark corners what the generals had done for the Army in the summer of 1647: to take over and canalize a rank-and-file movement which they could not suppress and with whose objects (if not with whose methods) they to some extent sympathised. Even the Petition of the Six Counties of South Wales, a fierce attack on the activities of the Propagators, agreed that the Act for the Propagation of the Gospel 'filled all the inhabitants of Wales with joy and gladness.'[1]

(ii)

On 22 February 1650, the Act for the Propagation of the Gospel in Wales was passed, 'according to the plan laid down by Hugh Peter'.[2] Since the livings at Parliament's disposal—church and crown livings, and sequestrated livings of royalists—could not all be filled with learned and Welsh-speaking ministers, their revenues were to be pooled. In each county a group of itinerant ministers was set up, at £100 a year each, with the further inducement of a pension of £30 a year for widows. In addition the use in their own neighbourhood of gifted lay preachers was authorised; these received £17-24 a year. There were seventy-one commissioners, all laymen, including significantly few representatives of the old ruling

---

1 *The Petition of the Six Counties of South Wales* (1652), p. 3; cf. p. 29—the speech of Col. Edward Freeman when presenting the Petition. A Petition in favour of the Propagators was said to have been signed by 19,000 people, as against the 15,000 claimed for the 1652 Petition (*ibid.*, p. 9; *Mercurius Cambro-Britannicus*, 1652, p. 14). Neither figure is to be taken too seriously; but the Petition of the Six Counties came later, and might be expected to wish to claim more than its rival. The petitioners were certainly not deterred by excessive scrupulosity. Even Anthony Wood said that the Act for the Propagation of the Gospel in Wales was 'so really intended, by the pious care and charity of those members of Parliament' (*Athenae Oxonienses*, 1817, iii, col. 913).

2 J. Walker, *Sufferings of the Clergy* (1714), pp. 147-50. The text of the Act for the Propagation of the Gospel in the Four Northern Counties has not survived, but it was presumably similar. Each act originated in response to petitions in the area in question, whether spontaneous or not.

families but most of the local parliamentary officials. But the commissioners were by no means a revolutionary body. A majority had been royalists and churchmen before 1646, and conformed after 1660. Two were executed as regicides, but Colonel Philip Jones, the leading Welshman on the commission, co-operated in bringing about the restoration, retained the lands he had acquired during the interregnum, and was High Sheriff of Glamorgan in 1671.[1] The commissioners had power to examine and where necessary eject the incumbents of Welsh livings, for delinquency, scandal, malignancy or non-residence: pluralists had to opt for one of their livings. 278 ministers in all were ejected, some of them because they could not preach in Welsh.[2] Twenty-five ministers (six of them itinerants) were named as approvers or triers of ministers and schoolmasters.

Even more significant were the political powers entrusted to the commissioners, which strongly recall those previously wielded by the Councils in Wales and the North. So do the reasons given for granting these powers. 'The remoteness of the said counties from the courts of justice at Westminster occasioneth many acts of high misdemeanours, oppression and injury to be committed there, which often times escape unpunished.' The commissioners were therefore authorised to hear complaints of such offences, to call the parties before them, and 'with the consent of both parties . . . to hear and determine the same'. This was particularly designed for the protection of 'persons well-affected to the Parliament', who could not afford to travel to London to seek redress. The only appeal from the commissioners lay in religious matters to Parliament's Committee for Plundered Ministers, in civil matters to its Committee of Indemnity.

For three years the Committee for the Propagation of the Gospel remained 'the real government of Wales',[3] which

---

[1] Rees, op. cit., p. 74; cf. Richards, Religious Developments in Wales, 1654–1662, pp. 419-20.
[2] The proceedings of the Commission for North Wales are printed in An Act for the Propagation of the Gospel in Wales, 1649 (Cymdeithas Llên Cymru, 1908), pp. 18-32.   [3] Dodd, History of Wrexham, p. 148.

enjoyed complete independence in religious matters. But the independence was relative, since a majority of the commissioners, headed by Major-General Harrison, commanding the army in South Wales, were English.¹ The chief Welsh Propagators 'were men who, through a forced sojourn in England' during the war 'had come into contact with the fertile thought of a new liberty', rather as Penry had done in his day.² Dr. Richards speaks, perhaps a trifle strongly, of 'the peculiarly English atmosphere of the Puritan conquest of Wales, with the hordes of English officials who infested the country'. 'A jury will do no good in that county [Cardiganshire],' said Colonel Philip Jones in June 1651, 'where little of the gospel hath yet been.' So he advocated a court martial.³ The propagation of the Gospel meant also the extension of English law, order, and civilisation.

'Hath any generation since the Apostles' days had such powerful preachers and plenty of preaching as this generation?' asked Vavasor Powell.⁴ Powell himself—the 'metropolitan of the itinerants'—often preached in two or three places a day, especially at 'fairs, markets or any great concourse of peoples'.⁵ Even so some areas were left uncovered. For the Commission lasted only three years. In August 1652 the Declaration of the Army to Lieutenant-General Cromwell had put propagation of the Gospel first in its demands.⁶ Cromwell must have favoured bills for continuing the authority of the Propagators, despite allegations that Harrison was using the Commission to enlist 4000 men for his own purposes. One of these bills was

¹ Harrison, it is worth noting, came from Newcastle-under-Lyme.
² Richards, *History of the Puritan Movement in Wales*, p. x. Dr. Richards sees the Propagators as carrying out Penry's suggestions for reform (*ibid.*, p. 1.)
³ H. Cary, *Memorials of the Great Civil War in England* (1842), ii, 279. Cf. *Calendar of State Papers Dom., 1656–57*, pp. 55-6, for the unreliability of Welsh juries.
⁴ V. Powell, *The Bird in the Cage* (2nd ed., 1662), p. 9. See Richards, *op. cit.*, pp. 171-5, 220, for favourable comments on the activities of the itinerants. There was, after all, gospel precedent for itinerant ministers.
⁵ Alexander Griffith, *Strena Vavasoris*, 1654 (1915), p. 1; *The Life and Death of Mr. V. Powell*, p. 108.
⁶ W. C. Abbott, *Writings and Speeches of Oliver Cromwell*, ii (1939), p. 572.

rejected on 1 April 1653, and an order was made for replacing the twenty-five approvers or triers by more 'moderate' men.[1] This was one of the reasons for the dissolution of the Rump on 20 April. The dissolution was welcomed by some at least of the commissioners; Vavasor Powell and his party, Thurloe said three years later, 'were the occasion of destroying the Rump'.[2] As with the events of Thermidor, the fall of the Rump was brought about by a temporary coalition of right and left. On 25 April, immediately after the dissolution, Cromwell urged the Welsh commissioners to continue their work.[3]

'God did kindle a seed there indeed hardly to be paralleled since the primitive times', Cromwell said of Wales under the Propagators. He was speaking to the Barebones Assembly, and he continued, 'What discountenance that business of the poor people of God had (who had men watching over them like so many wolves ready to catch the lamb as soon as it was brought into the world), how signally they [the Rump] trod that business under foot, to the discountenancing of the honest people and the countenancing of the malignant party. . . . The state of that business of Wales' seemed to Cromwell 'as plain a trial of their [the Rumpers'] spirits as anything.'[4]

When we try to assess the achievements of the Propagators we must take into account not only the ecstasies of Vavasor Powell and Oliver Cromwell but also reports like that accepted by the sober lawyer Whitelocke, that in September 1652 'there were 150 good preachers in the thirteen Welsh counties; most of them preached three or four times a week. In every market town there was placed one schoolmaster, and in most great towns two schoolmasters, able, learned and university men.'[5] Among the successes of the men who ran the Propaga-

---

[1] S. R. Gardiner, *History of the Commonwealth and Protectorate* (1903), ii, 250-1.   [2] *Thurloe State Papers* (1742), iv, 373-4.
[3] Abbott, *Writings and Speeches of Oliver Cromwell*, iii (1945), p. 13.
[4] *Ibid.*, p. 57.
[5] B. Whitelocke, *Memorials of the English Affairs* (1682), p. 518. Whitelocke's experience of the problems of preaching in Wales dates at least from 1628, when he encountered the vicar of Mostyn, who could not preach in English (R. H. Whitelocke, *Memoirs, Biographical and Historical, of Bulstrode Whitelocke*, 1860, p. 51).

tion, we must count the dissemination of the Bible in Welsh. In seven years from 1647 to 1654 three editions of the New Testament (over 3000 copies) and one edition of the Bible in Welsh (up to 6000 copies) were distributed.[1]

The Committees for the Propagation of the Gospel then were the culmination of two or three generations of puritan aspiration and effort. This tends to be forgotten by those who dismiss the Welsh Propagators as 'a knot of Tammany demagogues'.[2] Inevitably, the operation which they had to perform was political as well as religious: the areas concerned were those which had needed to be governed by the special processes of the Council in Wales. The noted preacher Rice Williams of Newport commanded a party of soldiers which searched Walter Powell's house in Monmouthshire for arms in January 1650.[3] The Propagators' task was doubly difficult in view of hostility from London as well as from Wales. Both the Propagators and frightened conservatives looked on the Welsh campaign as a model which could be extended to other regions: from June 1650 to its dissolution the Rump was continually discussing 'the advance of the Gospel in all parts of this Commonwealth'.[4] The Propagators were feared less because of their methods of overcoming tough resistance in a tough area than because it was feared that those methods might be extended to the rest of Britain.[5]

The case against the Propagators has frequently been disproved,[6] yet it goes on being repeated. It is based largely on the evidence of Alexander Griffith, a clergyman who had the misfortune to be deprived of two livings (for immorality) by

[1] Powell, *The Bird in the Cage*, Sig. B.3; Ballinger, *The Bible in Wales*, pp. 10-32. Powell and Cradock were responsible for these editions.

[2] H. R. Trevor-Roper, 'Oliver Cromwell and his Parliaments', in *Essays Presented to Sir Lewis Namier* (ed. R. Pares and A. J. P. Taylor, 1956), p. 21.

[3] Ed. J. A. Bradney, *The Diary of Walter Powell, 1603-54* (1907), p. 40.

[4] The best discussion of the significance of this is in D. Masson, *Life of John Milton* (1877), iv, 387-98.

[5] Dr. T. Ranger made a similar point very well about Strafford's rule in Ireland ('Strafford in Ireland: a Revaluation', *Past and Present*, No. 19, 1961).

[6] E.g. by Rees, *op. cit.*, pp. 74-90, and Richards, *op. cit.*, esp. pp. 184 and 247-61.

the bishops before 1640, and to be ejected by the Propagators on the same grounds, though in 1650 the charge of drunkenness was added.[1] His is not the most reliable of testimony. The Propagators handled large sums of money, and in accordance with seventeenth century custom accusations of corruption were laid against them. But peculation was never proved, despite repeated attempts. In August 1654 Cromwell set up commissioners 'for taking an account of the moneys received' by the Welsh Propagators, and their accounts were allowed and passed a year later. Nevertheless the House of Commons in October 1656 created a commission of its own to examine the disposal of moneys by the Propagators of Wales and the four northern counties. The matter was raised again in the Commons in February 1659.[2] A very strict inquiry held after the Restoration by the commissioners' fiercest enemies could produce no scandals.[3] Even Anthony Wood only says that Vavasor Powell and the agents of the Propagation 'had the disposal of above £40,000 *per annum*', leaving his readers to draw conclusions.[4]

To the accusations of peculation social sneers were added, and there is more truth in them. After 1649 control of local affairs, in Wales as elsewhere, passed to more extreme Puritans, yeomen and tradesmen who held the lower commissioned ranks in the Army.[5] The traditional ruling gentry either withdrew or were removed (in so far as they had not already been

---

[1] Rees, *op. cit.*, p. 75. Walker's accusations against the Propagators in *The Sufferings of the Clergy* are based almost entirely on Griffith.

[2] Firth and Rait, *op. cit.*, ii, 990-3; *C.J.*, vii, 448; ed. J. T. Rutt, *Burton's Parliamentary Diary* (1828), iii, 82-4.

[3] Richards, *op. cit.*, pp. 215-17, 245-69, 272-3; *Calendar of State Papers Dom. 1660–61*, pp. 4, 260; R. S. Bosher, *The Making of the Restoration Settlement* (1951), p. 233. Some of the Commissioners seem to have thriven during their period of office (Richards, *op. cit.*, p. 216; cf. p. 52 below). But at least one—Major John Sadler—was in such abject poverty in October 1659 that he was granted a pension of £8 a year by the J.P.s. It ceased of course at the Restoration (A. N. Palmer, *A History of the Older Nonconformity of Wrexham*, 1889, p. 4). For Vavasor Powell's asseverations about his own incorruptibility, see his *Brief Narrative* prefixed to *The Bird in the Cage*, Sig. B2-2v.

[4] A. Wood, *Athenae Oxonienses*, iii, col. 913.

[5] Dodd, *History of Wrexham*, p. 60.

extruded as royalists). 'Wales during the Propagation régime was governed by a military middle class'.[1] 'The gentry and all the considerable persons of Wales [are] dejected and oppressed', said a pamphlet of 1652.[2] Alexander Griffith was horrified at oppression when it was directed against 'a gentleman of good estate and quality, and some time a Justice of Peace'.[3] 'By means of Harrison', a letter from Glamorgan said in 1653, 'all the honestest, ablest and most understanding gentry are put out of commission'.[4]

But the most serious allegations were those affecting the itinerants. 'These wandering apostles', Clement Walker said in 1649, 'are to preach anti-monarchical seditious doctrine to the people (suitable to that they call the present government) to raise the rascal multitude and schismatical rabble against all men of best quality in the kingdom, to draw them into associations and combinations with one another in every county and with the army, against all lords, gentry, ministers, lawyers, rich and peaceable men, and all that are lovers of the old laws and government, for the better rooting of them out'.[5] That was the authentic note of alarm felt by conservatives, and set the tone for the stories which were repeated so frequently later.

Some of the itinerants could not read or understand English.[6] Their enemies complained of men who were 'continually thundering out in the ancient British tongue'.[7] There were never enough preachers, and some of them were enthusiastic young craftsmen and ex-soldiers who preached in English. Vavasor Powell admitted to one weaver, one smith, two or three officers. In the mouths of opponents this became the

---

[1] Richards, *op. cit.*, p. 94. For the North, see J. Musgrave, *A True and Exact Relation* (1650), p. 47.

[2] *Mercurius Cambro-Britannicus*, p. 8. Cf. the observations of John Jones on the necessity of breaking the great men in Scotland, quoted in note 2 on p. 53 below.

[3] Griffith, *Strena Vavasoris* (1654), p. 10. I quote from the reprint of 1915.   [4] *Thurloe State Papers*, ii, 129.

[5] C. Walker, *History of Independency*, Part II (1649), pp. 156-7.

[6] Griffith, *Strena Vavasoris*, p. 5.

[7] Richards, *op. cit.*, p. 8; cf. pp. 21, 45-6.

unqualified generalisation: 'soldiers and unordained tradesmen'.[1] The grand jury of Montgomeryshire—i.e. the gentry
of the county—in April 1652 dismissed the itinerants *en bloc* as
'a few illiterate poor traders'.[2] George Griffith, post-restoration
Bishop of St. Asaph, indulged in what seem today rather
unpleasant sneers at Powell's weakness in Latin and his ignorance of university rules for disputation. When Griffith and
Powell debated in 1652, 'the better sort' wanted them to speak
in Latin, the majority demanded English. Griffith thought the
object of this was to arraign him 'before an ignorant multitude'.[3]

We can see the other side of this medal in Morgan Llwyd's
denunciation of woe to the 'evil gentry, licking the sweat of
the poor, making your tenants groan'. His attack was extended
to lawyers, priests, beggars and ignorant labourers.[4] William
Erbery defended the poor against the rich;[5] Vavasor Powell
attacked lawyers and spoke up for the people against the
government.[6] The 'richer sort' of his followers were soon to
disavow his Fifth Monarchist views.[7] Another of the approvers
was denounced in 1659 as 'a Leveller', anxious to imitate John
of Leyden.[8] Such accusations of social revolution must be related to the mounting social conservatism of the years after 1653.

We should be especially wary when reading post-restoration
accounts like that by Bishop Lucy of St. David's, who alleged
that churches in Wales 'have had no divine duty' for years
together.[9] In many churches in this diocese, its bishop told
Laud in 1634, the chancels had been pulled down or allowed

---

[1] *A Relation of a Dispute between Dr. Griffith and Mr. V. Powell* (1653),
p. 16; (G. Griffith), *A Welsh Narrative Corrected* (1653), p. 22.
[2] (A. Griffith), *The Petition of the Six Counties of South Wales* (1652), pp.
15-16.
[3] (G. Griffith), *A Bold Challenge of an Itinerant Preacher Modestly Answered*
(1652), *passim*; *A Welsh Narrative Corrected*, *passim*.
[4] Morgan Llwyd, *The Book of the Three Birds* (1653), quoted by Palmer,
A History of the Older Nonconformity of Wrexham, p. 18.
[5] *The Testimony of William Erbery* (1658), p. 75.
[6] Griffith, *Strena Vavasoris*, pp. 20-1, 12.
[7] *Thurloe State Papers*, ii, 124.   [8] Richards, *op. cit.*, p. 253.
[9] Richards, *Wales under the Penal Code, 1662–87* (1925), pp. 167-9.

to fall, 'leaving them so open and cold, as that the people in those mountainous parts must endure a great deal of hardness'.[1] But the itinerants' habit of preaching in the open air sprang not only from the deplorable state into which the churches had fallen. It was also a matter of deliberate policy, to counteract the Welsh superstitious regard for church buildings.[2] Whether it was successful or not is another question. In 1652 John Taylor the Water-Poet observed that 'in many . . . parishes in Wales . . . they have neither service, prayer, sermon, minister or preacher, nor church door opened at all, so that people do exercise and edify in the churchyard at the lawful and laudable games of trap, cat, stool ball, rackets, etc., on Sundays'.[3]

What remains, however, after we have sifted and discounted the accusations against the Propagators, is the disunity which their régime created among the radicals. A moderate man like John Lewis thought in 1656 that too much emphasis had been laid on preaching, to the exclusion of other ordinances; and perhaps the attack (of which he had originally approved) on traditional customs, festivals and set prayers had been too savage.[4] Erbery believed there had been too much discussion, which had led to divisions and confusion among a people unaccustomed to it.[5] Erbery even joined in the social sneers, when he referred to 'such itinerants, who make a trade of teaching: only what formerly he sold in a shop, is now set to sale in a pulpit'.[6] But Erbery's criticisms came from the left, not from the right. What outraged him was the Propagators'

---

[1] W. Laud, *Works* (1847–60), v, 329.

[2] Lewis, *Some seasonable and modest Thoughts*, pp. 14–17. Contrast his *Parliament explained to Wales*, p. 30.

[3] J. Taylor, *A Short Relation of a Long Journey* (1652), p. 23. The royalist Taylor wished to suggest that the Parliamentarians were responsible for this state of affairs, as indeed they no doubt were for closing the churches. But the use made of the churchyard was highly traditional, and had been encouraged by James's and Charles's Books of Sports.

[4] Lewis, *Some seasonable and modest Thoughts*, pp. 10–12. Contrast his *Parliament explained to Wales*, pp. 33–5.

[5] *The Testimony of William Erbery, passim;* cf. Richards, *Puritan Movement in Wales*, pp. 214–15.

[6] *The Testimony of William Erbery*, p. 147; cf. pp. 50–4.

acceptance of payment from tithes, after so many of them had denounced hireling ministers before 1650.

This brings to the surface a dilemma which had long lurked in the background of radical puritan thought—their attitude to the state and their willingness to use Beelzebub for the purpose of casting out devils. Penry in 1587 had appealed to the secular power against the bishops, and in 1593 he made a frank attempt to bribe the Earl of Essex by offering him the plunder of the Church.[1] But those were dark days. In the intoxication of the early fifties, 'those halcyon days of prosperity, liberty and peace',[2] the millennium seemed too near at hand for such compromises to be necessary. As the case of Erbery shows, disestablishmentarianism was already becoming an ideology among the radicals in Wales. Not everybody was as satisfied as Hugh Peter with a situation in which 'the state pays them, and thus they have a dependence upon the state'.[3] Too many of the professors showed spiritual pride and worldly-mindedness, said John Miles in 1656, 'while they associated themselves with the rich and honourable, despising the poor'.[4] Even Vavasor Powell was horrified at the way in which some of his allies enriched themselves. In 1654 he 'told the sword-men that the spirit of God was departed from them; that heretofore they had been precious and excellent men, but that their parks and new houses and gallant wives had choked them up'.[5]

So the enthusiasts who had taken up the task of preaching fell out among themselves. But they could not afford disunity. Beelzebub was still necessary. The commissioners were trying to do too much too quickly, perhaps aware that they might not last long. The attempt to impose English standards aroused hostility, and did not last long enough. As soon as the

---

[1] Ed. A. Peel, *The Notebook of John Penry* (Camden Soc., 1944), pp. 85-93.
[2] Ed. E. B. Underhill, *The Records of the Church of Christ meeting in Broadmead, Bristol, 1640-87* (Hanserd Knollys Soc., 1847), p. 39.
[3] Peter, *Good Work for a good Magistrate*, p. 11.
[4] Ed. T. Shankland, J. Miles's *An Antidote against the Infection of the Times*, 1656 (Welsh Baptist Historical Soc., 1904), pp. 25-35. Cf. Richards, *Wales under the Indulgence (1672-5)*, (1928), p. 232.
[5] Griffith, *Strena Vavasoris*, pp. 18-19.

preachers ceased to itinerate we hear again the familiar complaints: 'Here are very few good ministers and schoolmasters'; for 'want of able preachers . . . these people will some of them become heathens', something which Major-General Berry 'knew not how to remedy'.[1]

The correspondence of John Jones shows with great clarity the dilemma of the godly minority who hoped to Christianise England through army rule—a dilemma which existed in its most extreme form in Wales. No amount of electoral qualifications, Jones thought, would 'persuade a people sensible of their present burdens, and not of the reasons and necessity of them, to choose those persons that laid the burdens on them. . . . What interest in England is like to carry the universal vote?' he asked. 'If the hearts of the people be generally for the present government and governors, what need armies and garrisons to be kept on foot?' This appalling frankness led him to a conclusion similar to Cromwell's 'What's for their good, not what pleases them', though the paths of the two men were soon to diverge. 'I had rather do a people good though against their wills', Jones continued, 'than please them in show only. . . . Let the Commonwealth have some time to take root in the interests of men.'[2] It is the recurring dilemma of all revolutionary minorities, stated by Rousseau in the doctrine that it may be necessary to force men to be free. The dilemma was especially painful for a Welsh Puritan, acutely conscious that his party was a tiny minority. If God's cause was to be forwarded at all, it *must* be against the wishes of the majority of the population.

[1] *Thurloe State Papers*, iv, 334-5, 565.

[2] Mayer, 'Inedited Letters', p. 190. Jones's remarks about Scotland are relevant. 'It is the interest of the Commonwealth of England to break the interest of the great men in Scotland, and to settle the interest of the common people upon a different foot from the interests of their lords and masters. . . . The great men will never be faithful to you so long as you propound freedom to the people and relief against their tyranny.' But, Jones added in this startlingly naked class analysis, Scotland lacked a bourgeoisie which could be given a vested interest in the new régime 'The people will hardly comprehend the excellency of a Commonwealth and a free people, . . . they having no money to buy lands in England' (*ibid.*, p. 192).

5

In the South and East of England the election of delegates
to the Barebones Assembly from the Independent churches
could be defended as no less democratic than the old franchise:
it merely brought a different minority to Westminster. But
this could not be argued for Wales. Even after 1660 Vavasor
Powell himself claimed only a score or so of gathered churches
in Wales.[1] So it is hardly surprising that Harrison in London
and Jones in Ireland should discuss who were suitable nominees
'to serve on behalf of the saints in North Wales'.[2] Saints
were so few that they must have almost selected themselves.
It is difficult to see anything sinister in this correspondence.

Most of all perhaps we should emphasise the educational
activities of the commissioners. Sixty or more new schools
were started in market towns in Wales, free, and some at least
of them open to both sexes: the first provision for education
ever made by the state in Great Britain. When we recall the
virtual exclusion of the lower classes from grammar schools
founded under the Tudors and Stuarts—an exclusion contrary
to the intentions of the founders—we get some idea of the
revolutionary nature of the Commonwealth's educational
innovations. Before 1640 schools had been subject to strict
ideological control by the hierarchy; but there is no evidence
of interference with existing schools by the Propagators, or of
ejection of schoolmasters.[3]

(iii)

In 1660 all but one of the sixty new Welsh schools came to an
end. So did Durham University. So did the augmentations to
ministers' stipends. As with so many of the ideals of the puritan
revolutionaries, the achievement fell far short of completion.
Yet the revolutionary decades saw a great expansion of sec-

---

[1] Powell, *Bird in the Cage*, Sig. B.3-3v.
[2] Mayer, 'Inedited Letters', p. 227.
[3] Phillips, *Civil War in Wales*, i, 24; Richards, *Puritan Movement in Wales*,
pp. 223-4. For education in the North under the Propagators, see W. A. L.
Vincent, *The State and School Education, 1640-60* (1950), pp. 21, 54, 135;
R. Halley, *Lancashire: its Puritanism and Nonconformity* (1869), i, 176; *Yorkshire Archaeological Soc. Miscellanea*, vi, 23-4.

tarian activity. In 1649 emissaries were sent from Glamorgan to the London Baptist Society, in the hope that labourers would be sent 'into those dark corners of the land'.[1] Many of the London gathered churches, Baptists and Independents alike, in fact sent missionaries to Wales and the North.[2] George Fox brought the Quaker light to many dark corners of Yorkshire, Cumberland, and Westmorland which even the Propagators missed; and from 1654 onwards, as conservatism triumphed in the South and East, itinerant Quakers—yeomen, craftsmen, ex-soldiers—organised a series of missionary tours to evangelise Southern England, Cornwall, and Wales. In 1656 Richard Davies was told of 'a sort of people come up in the North, called Quakers'; and two years later a Quaker came to settle in Davies's 'dark corner of North Wales'.[3] Some of the Welsh itinerants joined the new movement.[4] Merionethshire, of which John Jones had asked in 1651, 'Is that county denied the tender of gospel mercies?' later contained the greatest proportion of Quakers to population of any Welsh county.[5] The Quaker Edward Burroughs in 1655 exulted in this demonstration of the victory of the Gospel in the North: 'and thou, O North of England, who art counted as desolate and barren, and reckoned the least of the nations, yet out of thee did the branch spring, and the stem arise, which gives light unto all the regions round about'.[6] Parliamentary debates in 1656 show that

---

[1] Rees, *Protestant Nonconformity in Wales*, pp. 90-3.

[2] Underhill, *Broadmead Records*, p. 37; Edwards, *Gangraena*, Part II (1646), p. 122; Richards, *op. cit.*, pp. 77, 151-2, 206.

[3] *An Account of the Convincement . . . of . . . Richard Davies* (1928), pp. 5, 27.

[4] Underhill, *Broadmead Records*, pp. 515-17; Richards, *op. cit.*, pp. 217-18.

[5] Mayer, 'Inedited Letters', p. 185; G. F. Nuttall, *The Holy Spirit in Puritan Faith and Experience* (1946), p. 111.

[6] 'To the Camp of the Lord in England' (1655) in *The Memorable Works of Edward Burroughs* (1672), p. 66. There is a similar apocalyptic attitude to the North and West in Erbery's *A Whirlewind from the South* and *The Children of the West*, in *The Testimony of William Erbery*. 'The whirlwind comes from the North.' 'In South Wales and in all the west parts of England and Ireland, the baptized churches do most multiply'. 'To me the present form of churches this day . . . are . . . the children of the West' (pp. 126, 137).

the respectable classes reacted very differently to a movement which seemed to reproduce some of the least desirable ideas of the Levellers and the Welsh itinerants. 'Those that come out of the North are the greatest pests of the nation', said Samuel Highland; 'the Diggers came thence'.[1]

The national sectarian organisations established during the revolutionary decades survived the dark generation of persecution which followed the Restoration; through these links ideas and mutual influences passed backwards and forwards between the capital and the former dark corners of Wales and the North. On the other hand, the movement to form voluntary associations of ministers (of which Baxter's Worcestershire Association is the best known) found its main strength in the outlying regions.[2] This 'Presbyterianism from below' helped to prepare for the restoration of a less tolerant state Church. So both in producing the Quakers, and in producing the most organised reaction against them, the dark corners were now a beacon for the rest of England.

The sword which the Propagators brought into Wales left deep and lasting divisions. The gentry, even the parliamentarian gentry, hated the methods and social doctrine of the itinerants no less than did the university-trained clergy. Yet the Gospel could not have been propagated in Wales by traditional means. In so far as it was propagated, the work was done by 'tradesmen', by men less formally educated perhaps than the incumbents of the established Church, but better able to speak to their compatriots and less concerned about a living in the financial sense. The sectarian churches took over where the Propagators left off. By 1660 the Gospel had penetrated into most corners of England and Wales, inadequate though the achievement would have seemed to John Penry or Hugh Peter

---

[1] Ed. Rutt, *Burton's Parliamentary Diary*, i, 155-6.

[2] There were voluntary associations in Cumberland, Cheshire, Shropshire, Worcestershire, Somerset, Dorset, Wiltshire, Devon, Cornwall, North Wales, Ireland; and in London, Essex, Cambridgeshire, Norfolk, Hampshire, and Nottinghamshire. The Cumberland Association (of Presbyterians and Independents) seems to have been formed as a direct result of the spread of Quakerism (*V.C.H., Cumberland*, ii, 94-5).

or Vavasor Powell. Puritan preaching had extended laterally, into the North and West; it had also, thanks to the sects, extended in depth, to social strata previously left untouched. In Wales nonconformity lost its alien quality, but it became a lower-class religion. Before the civil war there had been no protestant nonconformity in Pembrokeshire. After it, the working and middle class were largely dissenters: but the squires, whether Tory or Whig, were churchmen almost to a man.[1] Dissent after 1660 was not a political conspiracy, as some bishops and M.P.s believed, or pretended to believe: the dissenters themselves had abandoned policies of violence. But dissent still remained a social phenomenon, and its social overtones still disturbed the respectable.

After the Restoration Thomas Gouge—son of the Feoffee for Impropriations—resumed the work of the Propagators. He was described for his pains by the Bishop of Bangor in 1666 as 'an itinerant emissary of the leading sectaries', and in 1672 was excommunicated by the Bishop of Llandaff for preaching without a licence. But Gouge—an occasional conformist himself—went very prudently to work, made his peace with the bishops and secured the co-operation of some Anglicans. ('How shall we Welsh bishops look if we refuse to take part?' one of them asked, with reference to Gouge's scheme for reprinting the Bible in Welsh: so much at least had been gained by the ending of the Anglican Church's monopoly.) Gouge organised a trust, which included Stillingfleet and Tillotson; he distributed the Book of Common Prayer in Welsh, and *The Whole Duty of Man*. 8000 copies of the Welsh Bible were printed, of which 1000 were given to the poor, and the others sold at 4s. apiece, 'much cheaper than any English Bible . . . of so fair a print and paper'. Gouge collected money for education in Wales, especially from 'that perpetual fountain of charity, the City of London, led on and encouraged by the most bountiful example of . . . the Lord Mayor and

---

[1] J. Phillips, *History of Pembrokeshire* (1909), pp. 549-50; Richards, *Wales under the Penal Code*, p. 46; cf. Dodd, *Studies in Stuart Wales* (1952), p. 63 for Wales as a whole.

Court of Aldermen'. More important perhaps, Gouge received 'large and bountiful contributions' from 'the nobility and gentry of Wales and the neighbouring counties': many Welsh towns were stirred up to emulate this activity, until some 1500-2000 children were being taught to read each year.[1]

But despite Gouge's caution, hostility remained, and his 3-400 reading schools seem to have come to an end after his death in 1681.[2] The distribution of Welsh books continued; but the main result of their circulation was an increase in dissent in Wales, said an Anglican sourly in 1697. ('If the growth of dissenters in Wales be an effect of the increase of knowledge there, we can't help that', Calamy commented. The desirability of keeping the lower classes in a state of ignorance was a popish, not a protestant, doctrine, he hoped.[3]) The propagation of the Gospel was still a sword to divide. When Gouge's edition of the Bible ran out, it was Oliver Cromwell's friend, the Whig Lord Wharton, together with 'ministers and citizens of London', who financed the printing and distribution of a new edition.[4] Once the Toleration Act had given freedom of action to dissenters, it was only a matter of time before the majority of the Welsh people was won for dissent.

So the illumination of the dark corners came ultimately by private enterprise. Yet state action between 1640 and 1653 was as important in the extension of London civilisation over the whole of England as it was in transforming agrarian relations

[1] E. Calamy, *An Account of the Ministers . . . Ejected or Silenced after the Restoration in 1660* (1713), pp. 8-13; J. Tillotson, 'A Sermon Preached at the Funeral of the Reverend Mr. Thomas Gouge', 1681, in *Sermons on Several Subjects and Occasions* (1748), ii, 104; A. G. Mathews, *Calamy Revised* (1934), pp. 229-30.

[2] For the deplorable state of education in the diocese of St. David's in the early eighteenth century, see Erasmus Sanders, *A View of the State of Religion in the Diocese of St. David's* (1721), p. 32. For Wales generally, see Richards, *Wales under the Penal Code*, pp. 62-70.

[3] Calamy, *op. cit.*, p. 10, referring to W. Wynne's edition of Powell's *History of Wales* (1697).

[4] Calamy, *op. cit.*, p. 720. Wharton in 1662 had settled lands sufficient to pay for 1050 Bibles and catechisms to be distributed, mainly in the North of England (Ballinger, *op. cit.*, p. 37).

(abolition of feudal tenures, land confiscations) and foreign policy (Navigation Act) and finance (excise, assessment). Private enterprise could consolidate once the obstacles had been removed which had baffled generations of effort: bishops, prerogative courts. The Commissioners for Propagation acted as a sort of Council of the North, a Council in Wales, in reverse: even after they were abolished the field was left open to voluntary effort, thanks to the failure to restore prerogative courts and High Commission, and above all to the change in the climate of opinion which made even bishops reluctant to proceed to extremes against Thomas Gouge. Wales, the North and Cornwall went straight from Anglicanism (or indeed popery) to the sects, with little Presbyterianism except in the old frontier county of Lancashire.[1] In this evangelising effort, merchants co-operated with Puritans; the ideals of the latter were curiously blended with the interests of the former.

By the end of the seventeenth century the 'civilising' process, in England and Wales, was for all practical purposes complete. In 1688–89, 1715, and 1745 there was no significant support for the Jacobites from the former royalist areas of the North and West. In Wales nonconformity established itself as an indigenous religion, like popery in Ireland and Presbyterianism in the Scottish Lowlands; but at the price of perpetuating a split in Welsh society. The extension of English influences among the common people of Wales was not primarily the work of the Anglican Church, to which the mass of the gentry adhered. For this outcome the credit, or the blame, must go chiefly to the Propagators. For in their brief years of rule they carried out in a way that could never be reversed some at least of the tasks which Penry and the Feoffees for Impropriations had set themselves and which the bishops had before 1640 always been able to frustrate.

---

[1] 'Having marched up and down the kingdom, to do the work of God and the state, we have met with many Christians who have much Gospel-light . . . in such places where there hath been no Gospel-ministry', William Dell observed ('The Building, Beauty, Teaching and Establishment of the truly Christian and Spiritual Church', 1651, in W. Dell, *Several Sermons and Discourses*, 1709, p. 79).

IV

'A DRAUGHT OF SIR PHILLIP SIDNEY'S ARCADIA'

John Buxton

THE manuscript of this unpublished poem is written in a neat and legible hand on seventeen pages of an unbound octavo booklet, of which all but one of the other fifteen pages are blank. On that page, facing the first page of text, are written the notes to line 15 of the poem, here printed as a footnote. There are no indications in the MS. of authorship or of ownership. It was acquired by Bertram Dobell early in this century when he was discovering the history of the composition of the *Arcadia*,[1] and by me about a dozen years ago. In the Sidney Exhibition in the Bodleian Library in 1954, held to commemorate the fourth centenary of Sir Philip Sidney's birth, this MS. was included as item 23. Fifty copies were printed in 1961 on the hand press in the New Bodleian Library by members of the bibliography class under the supervision of Professor H. J. Davis and were privately distributed. Here, apart from a very few amendments of the punctuation, which is generally excellent, I print the text as it stands in the manuscript.

There are various clues to the date of composition of the poem, but none (so far as I am aware) to its authorship. The paper is watermarked with a mid-seventeenth century English mark (Heawood 3534), and the handwriting is obviously of about this period. The manuscript is almost entirely uncorrected and must therefore be a fair copy, whether made by the author himself or by a friend or scribe. Probably it was one of several copies that were circulated at the time among members of the faction whose opinions it presented or encouraged.

In the poem the author adapts Sidney's famous book to the

---

[1] 'New Light on Sidney's *Arcadia*', *Quarterly Review*, ccxi, 1909.

circumstances which led to the outbreak of the civil war, and though many of the points he makes are such as any royalist might have made—attacks on the Puritans' contempt for the Altar and Communion Service, on the cant of Parliament's professed wish to rescue the king from his evil counsellors, on the pious humbug and general hypocrisy of the rebels, on the atheism of those who regard religion as a 'knack of State'— there are also references to events of the 1640s by which the date of composition may be determined.

The king is still alive and at liberty, so that the poem must antedate his surrender to the Scots in May 1646. A reference to attempts

To settle the Militia

suggests a date later than the winter of 1641–42 when the king and Parliament were in conflict over the Militia Bill. Immediately after this passage the line,

An armies raised to guard their Leige,

seems likely to refer to the raising of the royal standard at Nottingham in August 1642; but mention in the next line of besieging the enemy could equally well refer to the siege of Manchester that autumn, or to the siege of Gloucester a year later. Next we learn that the rebels come to treat, but on

termes so extreme high

that if Charles accepts them he will be unkinged: these might be the terms of the treaty proposed by Parliament after the king had been repulsed from London at Turnham Green, and which he rejected in November 1642, or they might be those of the Treaty of Uxbridge proposed in the autumn of 1644.

The 'forreigne Agents' whose double-dealing with both parties is designed so that

the Crowne at last
May on the forreigner be plac'd.

ought to be identifiable, and so ought the foreign candidate for the English throne. For various reasons the members of the House of Palatines seem to be the foreigners whom the poet is attacking. Prince Rupert and Prince Maurice had been with the king at Nottingham at the outset of the civil war; Prince Rupert had 'changed his name' when he was created Duke of Cumberland; he might with some reason and more malice be accused of 'leading the King up and down' the country. The claimant for the crown would then be the Elector Palatine, Prince Charles Louis, who landed in England, to the deep embarrassment of his younger brother, on 18 August 1644. There was talk at the time of putting forward Prince Charles Louis as a successor to King Charles, and though this was perhaps never anything more than rumour there can be few occasions when rumour seems more serious than in the midst of civil war.

If these interpretations are correct (and they seem to fit better than any possible alternatives) then the poem must have been written during those unhappy months when the arrival of the Elector Palatine in England had given plausibility to Lord Digby's envious distrust of Prince Rupert, and which were to culminate in the revocation of the prince's commission and his arrest in September 1645. Further, the poem (which is scarcely a model of perspicuity) seems to derive from some supporter of Digby against the House of Palatines who, in the eyes of his party, as a correspondent of Edward Walsingham observed, 'do think themselves assured of the Crown'.[1]

It is tempting, but unprofitable, to seek identifications for those characters in the *Arcadia* whom the poet names in *A Draught*. An elaborate manuscript index to the *Arcadia*, written in similar booklets and probably in the same hand as *A Draught* (and which came into my possession from the same source), gives some clues here, though there is no reason to think that it has any direct reference to the poem. The index is in two parts: the first is a subject-index which 'may readily lead to the most remarkable passages in the Booke', and the second is 'A Clavis opening the names and referring to the Characters'. This *Clavis*, which is arranged alphabetically, may help to elucidate the poem. Thus Kalander is described as 'a noble man, in him is represented nobilitie', which suggests that it

---

[1] *Calendar of State Papers Dom.*, *1645-47*, p. 134.

may be useless to attempt precise identification of Kalander in the poem. Dametas is 'the plebeian, or yeoman, tribunus plebis, poplicola': the 'Kings clownish minion' of the poem may therefore, like Kalander, represent a class rather than an individual. Dametas's daughter Mopsa, described as 'complaint, or an over curious meddler', must not lead us to seek out some unsuitable bride for Prince Charles; and the ludicrous low-life character of Sidney's invention could hardly be identified with the daughter of the Prince of Orange. Mopsa is simply Complaint, as her mother Miso is 'hatred, from μῖσος, odium'; and the line

> Thus odium breeds complaint,

suggests this relationship: indeed here if anywhere may be some connection between poem and index. Clinias is described in *A Clavis* as 'an instrument or prompter of a faction, one that wilbee of any side'; but again the reference is not particular, though it is easy to see how the passage in the *Arcadia*[1] where Clinias attempts to persuade the rebels to return to their allegiance to Basilius, and then recounts the origin of their rebellion, might seem very apposite in the 1640s.

The use of the word *odium* as an English word is one of several examples of the unknown poet's liking for words that were only just becoming current. The *New English Dictionary* gives only one instance of the use of *odium* before the date of *A Draught*, where in Warner's *Epitome of the whole Historie of England* Richard II was observed 'to be in Odium with his subjects', a phrase which might well have come back into the poet's mind when he was writing of the rebellion against King Charles. One or two other passages suggest similar reminiscence.

> This *Heterogeneous* body made
> Of allmost some of every trade,

is not far from Prynne's 'The members of a heterogeneous body are discrepant and various in themselves', which might then

---

[1] Page references in the margins of the poem, and in the index, fit any edition from 1621 to 1638, of which there were about ten. In these the passage here referred to is on pp. 199-203.

have provoked a royalist by its pretentious pomposity. Prynne's *Anti-Arminianisme*, where this passage occurs, was published in 1630. In the following year, in a sermon preached before the Court, Bishop Sanderson had been the first to use the phrase 'to play an aftergame': 'He had need be a good gamester to play an aftergame'. Both expressions, the one from the pen of a puritan propagandist, the other on the lips of a loyal bishop, may have stuck in the mind of a courtier of King Charles. Other words and phrases in *A Draught* were of recent introduction: *previal* had been used as early as 1613, but *to comply with* is not quoted in N.E.D. earlier than 1642, and more surprisingly *trustee* is not known before 1647, a year or two after the composition of *A Draught*. These are small points, but taken with other evidence that the poem provides they suggest that the author was more probably a courtier than a journalist, that he wrote his poem because he had something to say, not because someone was paying him to say it. It is not the work of an unprincipled hack, like Marchamont Nedham, but of a highly educated gentleman who believed in the justice of his cause.

Many a Cavalier could and did write better poetry than the author of *A Draught of Sir Phillip Sidney's Arcadia*, but this man, whoever he was, had a certain vigour of expression, and could manage the octosyllabic couplet so that it does not rush the reader out of breath. He has neither the fantastic wit of Cleveland nor the felicitous pace of Cleveland's friend and disciple Samuel Butler, but his poem has some literary merit, and is more than a perplexed, and perplexing, 'historical document'. His knowledge of Sidney's *Arcadia* means nothing: everyone knew the *Arcadia*, which was the most widely read work of fiction in England, and not only in England, from the time of the Armada to the '45, between, say, Lyly's *Euphues* and Richardson's *Pamela*. But use the here made of the *Arcadia* requires some brief comment.

From the first the readers of the *Arcadia* had been divided into what I may call Lady Pembroke's party, and Fulke Greville's party. The book, whose full title is *The Countess of*

Pembroke's Arcadia, had been written by Philip Sidney for his sister's amusement, and in his charming dedication of it to her he invites her to read it at her idle times. For her, and for the ladies (with whom especially it was a favourite book for a century and a half), it remained a romance. But when Sidney left England for the last time in 1585 he gave his most intimate friend, Fulke Greville, the manuscript of his unfinished revision of the book, from which, in 1590, the first edition, in quarto, was published. And in this revision Sidney had converted a simple romance into a heroic poem: for to Sidney the *Cyropaedia* of Xenophon and the *Aethiopica* of Heliodorus were each of them 'an absolute heroicall poeme',[1] no less than the *Iliad* or the *Aeneid*. (The note to line 15 of *A Draught* suggests that its author was familiar with *An Apology for Poetry* as with the *Arcadia*; as we should expect, for it was constantly reprinted with the folio *Arcadias*.) To Greville and those who thought like him therefore Sidney's *Arcadia* was a heroic poem, and it is clear that the author of *A Draught* was of Greville's party, and may even have known Greville's comments on the book, though these were still unpublished when he wrote. In his *Life of the Renowned Sir Philip Sidney*, which was published in 1652, Greville asserted that in the *Arcadia* Sidney's end 'was not vanishing pleasure alone, but moral images and examples (as directing threads) to guide every man through the confused labyrinth of his own desires and life'. Greville would have agreed that the *Arcadia* contained warnings

> By which this nation might have learned
> And at distance something discerned
> Threatning a change in church and state.

He had said as much in the *Life*, written long before, in King James's time:

'In all these creatures of his making, his intent, and scope was, to turn the barren Philosophy precepts into pregnant Images of

---

[1] *An Apology for Poetry.*

life; and in them, first on the Monarch's part, lively to represent
the growth, state, and declination of Princes, change of Government, and laws: vicissitudes of sedition, faction, succession, con-
federacies, plantations, with all other errors, or alterations in
publique affaires.'

There is a similarity of phrasing in the poem,

> The rise, growth, fall of *Monarchie*,

which may be coincidental; but it cannot be denied that the
author of *A Draught* regarded the *Arcadia* very much in the
same way as did the austere Calvinist statesman and poet whose
epitaph proclaims his belief that friendship to Sir Philip Sidney
was of equal merit with service to his sovereign.

He, too, this unnamed poet, recognised the influence of
Sidney the ideal Courtier :

> Hee was the first that did excell,
> And our young gallants are content
> From him to learne their complement.

Among the more articulate of these gallants were Edmund
Waller, Richard Lovelace, Thomas Bancroft, and Charles
Cotton. But the Puritans, no longer of Fulke Greville's liberal
temper, refused to be charmed by Sidney's reputation into
thinking well of his book. For them it was a frivolous work
which took women's minds off their serious tasks: 'Instead of
reading Sir Philip Sidney's Arcadia, let them read the grounds
of good huswifery.'¹ Indeed yes, for to these people the femi-
nine ideal was the *hausfrau*. Milton, though at one moment
willing to admit that the *Arcadia* was 'a work of worth and
wit', the next moment was belabouring King Charles for
using, in *Eikon Basilike*, Pamela's prayer from this 'vain,
amatorious poem'.² The king's admiration for the *Arcadia* was
no more necessary to its popularity than was his enjoyment of
the *Faerie Queene* to Spenser's reputation, and not even Milton
could allow political prejudice so far to cloud literary judgment

---

¹ T. Powell, *Tom of All Trades* (1631).
² *Eikonoklastes* (1649).

as to find fault with our sage and serious Spenser for delighting Charles Stuart. Paradoxically, after fifty years the elegant courtiers were regarding the *Arcadia* as a serious heroic poem, and the puritan successors of Greville were condemning it as empty romance.

It continued to be read and to be drawn upon by many writers—poets, novelists, opera librettists, dramatists—but this use of it for a satirical purpose is probably unique. There were precedents enough for taking a well-known story as a framework for satire: to go no further back than the greatest of the poets who had enjoyed Sidney's patronage, Spenser in *Mother Hubberd's Tale* had relied on his audience's familiarity with the medieval romance of *Renard the Fox* to give point to his attack on Burghley. Spenser's method was to suggest to the reader certain identifications, and so to stimulate him to construct others: innuendoes would crowd into a mind predisposed to contempt. Dryden, in the most famous of all such satires, was to follow out the story of Absalom and Achitophel in such detail that his very virtuosity almost persuades the reader that history has been repeated. Dryden astonishes us by perfectly fitting together two unrelated patterns; Spenser proposes means by which the two patterns may be related and, by leaving the reader more to do, excites his imagination where Dryden satisfies it. The method of *A Draught* is the less precise, but not necessarily less effective, method of Spenser: the method which the author himself recognises in the modern treatment of Aesop's *Fables* and Ovid's *Metamorphoses* and Virgil's pastorals. He can safely assume in his readers a familiarity with Sidney's *Arcadia*, and can therefore use it to provoke in them a distrust and dislike of those whom he satirises. The satire becomes confusing because he distrusts some of his own, royalist, side as much as he dislikes the rebel enemy. This is a defect in literary tact no less than in political judgment. The author, doubtless, had many other things to do besides writing verses in that disastrous year. Yet he wrote a poem which is of some significance in the development of English political satire, and of which a minor Samuel Butler need not have been ashamed.

A DRAUGHT OF SIR PHILLIP SIDNEY'S ARCADIA

Hee that would read and understand
What this best Author tooke in hand,
Must I ſuppoſe have ſuch a witt
That's knowne to his, who framed it.
A worke as 'tis ſurpaſſing good,
So better if well vnderstood.
T'is like ſome building, where the nice
Eie dwells vpon the frontiſpice
Wherein ſuch art hath vſed bin,
Men ne're examine what's within.
Or like a Curtaine vnder which
A picture drawne exceeding rich
Meerely to tell the standers by
The author studied ſecrecie.
A feign'd diſcourſe framed to shew[1]
Things that are reall; thus wee knowe
The fables Æſop did deviſe
Fictions, left us to moralize.
And Ovid that best Roman witt,
A Metamorphoſis once writt
Wherein hee shadowed forth in h's mind
Things incident to humane kind.
And Virgill when hee would relate
What did concerne perſons of State,
Least truth too plaine should danger call,
Did sport it in a Pastoral.
And here our Author is ſoe wiſe
Hee walks the world in a diſguiſe.
Unmaske him, and you'l clerely ſee
The riſe, growth, fall of Monarchie.
What 'tis that doth uphold a state,
And what the ſame doth ruinate.

[1] Soe did Xenophon give vs the portrature of a iust empire in his Cyres.
Soe did Helidore give vs the picture of love in Theagenes and Chariclea.
Soe did Virgill give vs a vertuous man in all fortunes in Æneas.
Soe did Sir Thomas Moore give vs the pletforme of a whole Commonwealth
in his Eutopia.
Soe did Sophocles give vs the deſcription of anger in his Aaiax.
Soe the feigned storie of Vliſses and Diomedes; ſetts before vs wiſdome and
Temporance.

Hee shewed what danger in a *Court*

lib. 1.　　When wholly given up to fport.
pag. 14.　　When nurfed up in vanitie
15.
It doth prefage a chang draw nigh.

lib. 1.　　Hee shews when Kings themfelves forfake
pag. 12.　　And others trust they pitt-falls make
13. 14.
To their owne ruine: innocence

lib. 1.　　In them disarm'd is noe defence.
pag. 10.　　Hee shewes the peasant and the Clowne
11. 12. 13.
But poore guardians of a Crowne.

lib. 2.　　And Princes doe but tottering stand
pag. 203.　　Who pull the power out of their hand.
204.

When Kings their favours doe bestowe
On fome, because their humors foe,
And raife up thofe about their Throne
In whom defert was never knowne.
Like to earth-gendred vapours they
Darken the Sunn they're raifed by.

lib. 1.　　Befides theife fauorites thus drest
pag. 10.　　With honours, foe orelooke the rest,
49. 50.
And Lord it in their new Commaund
lib. 1.
pag. 10. 11.　Thus they beget odium i'th Land.

lib. 1.　　Thus odium breeds complaint, thence fprings
pag. 14.　　Warr arming subiects against Kings.
lib. 1.
pag. 56.　　Warr once denounc'd, then pollicie
12. 31.　　Fills all men's heads with iealousie,
lib. 2.
pag. 200.　　And fends her agents in all parts
lib. 3.　　For to distill in people's hearts
pag. 235.
236. 237.　Defire of Change. Thus faction bred
238.　　Growes to a body, getts a head.
lib. 2.
pag.　　This *Heterogeneous* body made
195.　　Of allmost some of every trade,
196.
197.　　But Cheifly those whom discontent
198.　　Under the former government,
199.
200.　　Hath foe fpurr'd up, that they will range
201.　　Through worst of hazards for a change.
202.
203.　　With others, whom their well-knowne want
lib. 3.　　In hopes of prey, make valiant.
pag. 141.　　With the Ambitious who difdaine
Any befides themfelves should raigne.
Theife and the like bodied in one
For what amongst themfelves fcarce known

6

Scarce two agreeing in one mind
Only to mifchiefe all inclinde,
Waighting upon their generall
in whom they were united all,
March up and downe, hee in the head
The burden of the Land them bred,
To tell I will not undertake,
What dolefull Scratches thei will make
Upon the face of Government,
Being all as one to mifcheife bent,
Nor long in Citing will I stand
Who fall under their fatall hand,

lib. 1.   Religion, Hofpitality,
pag. 37.   Are first that fuffer Maffacre,
38. 39.
40.   Here one, and there the other lies,
      Though ufed a while for a disguife

lib. 1.   Patience stands out to the last Cast
pag. 16.
17. 18. 19. That alfoe overthrowne at last,
27. 28. 30. Vertue not brookeing bafe deniall
      Made better by its often triall

lib. 3.   At length ith dust doth huddled lye,
pag. 273. And trophies of impietie
274. 275.
276. 277. Erected over it, nay more
288.   The Temples are with Mofse growne ore
The Alter and the Sacrifice
Most doe neglect, and some defpife
Whil'st Machivilian policie
Cries there's noe God but destinie,
Perfwading vulgar ignorance
All things are carried on by Chance,
Soothing men up there is noe god
Hath either eies to see, or rod
To punish; nay shee doth not sticke
To fay Religion's but a tricke
Devif'd for to deceive the blind,
And in obedience men to bind
A knack of State, and humane fence
To keepe men in obedience.
This is the doctrine she writes
To all that are her profelites
But yet her Sonne, her only hee
That shee hath dandled on her knee

And nurſed up her only one
For whom shee doth intend the Throne,
To mock the world hee must appeare
Under a better Character.
Nothing in him but Courteſie,
Nothing but affabilitie,
Nothing but holy and preciſe,
Arm'd only faults for to Chastiſe,
His worth must bee blaz'd up and downe
And noe man fitter for a Crowne.
And then she prates what good he'l bring
Unto the Land if hee were King.
And if his mother chance to flie
Alofte and vaunt in terms too high
Good man hee must ſeeme wrath for this
For hee intends nothing amiſſe,
Hee meanes noe harme unto his King,
But would him from his thraldome bring,
Reſcue him from thoſe minions hands
That doe abaſe both him and lands,
Hee would him to his rights restore
And antient dignities, nay more
Make him most glorious and unshrowd
His glorie though't bee underclowd
For preſent, and the Civill iarrs
And ſad Comotions breathing warrs
Raiſe ſuch a dust i'th kingdomes ſkie
As dusks the face of Maiestie,
Goodman though wrested in wrong ſenſe
Hee takes arms for his Kings defence,
And peoples good; to ſettle things
For good of people, and of Kings.
This the pretence that doth beguile
The eaſie Commons for a while,
How are they taken with their paint,
And who in their esteeme more Saint
Then the most Rebell? thus they goe
Decoyde to their owne overthrowe.
The King thus ſuddenly surpricd
First by his owne faults, next by the diſguiſ'd
Sonns of Rebellion, whom the flie
and workeing braine of pollicie

Hath taught a trick for to Commaund
All Royall rights into their hand,
Juggled out of the hands of thofe
in whom the King did most repofe,
With theife weake trustees fometimes held
A thing too great for them to weild
And mannage long, for now the stronge
And full growne Babe of faction
Hath gott start of the minion Clowne
And become guardian of the crowne,
Pamela's under their commaunds
And *Philoclea* in their hands
Castles they build and fortifie,
Ufing both force and pollicie
To bring to iffue their laid plott,
And keepe what is already gott;
The King by this time is alarm'd
Whom fecure pleafure had long charm'd
Lulled in the downie bedd of peace
And never dreaming a difeafe,
Suppofeing hee had trusted thofe
were able dangers to oppofe,
And to beate any faction downe
That should bee catching at the crowne,
Seeing himfelfe deceived at last
Bethinks himfelfe, about doth cast,
Being with danger hemm'd about
How for to worke himfelfe cleare out
Hee calls his statesmen choyce and best
who are more faithfull then the rest
(whofe councell had hee not difdain'd
Att first to followe, hee had reign'd
Still undifturbed in happie blifse,
And never brought himfelfe to this)
Takes their advice when tis too late.
To strengthen his declining state,
Unhappilie they now affay,
To fettle the Militia,
They levie forces, and applie
All strengths to fight the enemie.
Little good can come of the fame,
For the King doth play an after game,

It had beene eaſier at the first
Thus to prevent, then now to worst;
The people they are wavering
Whether to fight or ayd the King,
The faction's great they must ſubmitt
And yeeld themſelves as ſlaues to it;
Yet the Kings partie now doth grow,
And gathers like a ball of ſnow,
An armies raiſed to guard their Leige
The enemie they cloſe beſeige
Yet of his strength growne confident
Hee will not yeeld, cannot relent
The[y] come to treat, treaties wee knowe
Doe but forerunn Kings overthrowe,
When Kings are forced for to treate,
It is a ſigne they wilbee beate.
This may bee for a Maxime held
The Kings the partie that must yeeld
To all demaunds; the rebells fly
To termes at last ſoe extreme high,
Which will unking him if hee doe
Orecome by words ſubmitt thereto.
First they would make him glorious
Ridd him from counſaile dangerous
Next they'l reforme but whats amiſſe
In government; a third to this,
Except to them hee condiſcend
To murder him they doe intend
This was the plott hidd from the rude
And nought diſcerning multitude.
Things at this paſſe yow then shall heare
The King traduced every where.
All mouths are open to let flie
Their malice against Maiestie,
Some raile against his heavie hand
Imposing tribute on the Land,
Others amids't their cupps doe prate
against the officers of state
Some to have things reformed content
Others for chang of government
Thus doe they vote confuſedly
In one thing ſcarcly two agree.

But (becaufe god will have it foe
To bring fuch men to overthrowe),
A difcontent amid'ft them's begott
And that doth bring to light the plott
A Clineas falls oft and hee
of them makes full difcoverie.
Now whilest fuch things are in debate
Within the bowells of one state
In peices torne by inbred iarrs
Subiects and King at Civill warrs,
There lurke unknowne within the Court
Which daylie to the King refort,
Some forreigne Agents, who have bin
By travaile much experienc'd in
Matters of state, theife doe complie
With either partie cunninglie
Cherish the difcords, and confpire
To kindle, not to quench the fire
Theife wind themfelves like Serpent flie
I'th bofomes of all companie,
They carry it faire on either hand
To gaine refpect ore all the Land
That by their meanes the Crowne at last
May on the forreigner bee plac'd
And then a forreigne state shall fitt
In the King's feat as heire of it,
And bring't about againe to bee
An independing Monarchie
A King of abfolute Commaunds
Settled by wife *Evarchus* hands
Theife forreigners a Compass goe
before they can complete it though
They change their habit and their name
And *Proteus* like themselves they frame
To bee whatever is the best
To forward their owne interest;
Their first acquaintance they begin
With men of worth the Realme within,
Such as *Kalender* act it foe
That they erect where ere they goe
Trophies of vertue leave a name
Behind them for to fpeake their fame

Next they doe covett for to bee
Neare to the King to heare and fee
In what state hee is, there unknowne
State Ielousies by them are sowne
Like *Dauus* in the comedie
They trouble all, but cunningly
The King they doe lead up and downe
As if of them hee held his crowne
Ravish the Queene that shee can fee
Noe good but in their companie,
And the Kings clownish minion
Dametus doth foe dote upon
Their parts for paffing excellent,
That hee is verie well content
To match his *Mofpa* to the rare
Dorus, which his, her fervant were
Theife forreigners that thus betray
The people steale their harts away
Haveing prepared all men's hearts
Till a fitt time to act their parts
offers it felfe; fitt close within
Expecting till the warr begin
(Like spiders in their nett) the flame
Breakes out they add vnto the fame
Supplie of fuch, till at last
There is on either fide a wast,
Sufficient, that a partie fmall
Of forreigne force may Conquer all.
To beate the Rebels thei maintaine
The Kings caufe; and the Rebels slaine
They act about againe, beguile
The Royall party with a wile
They cheate Dametas of small know,
His *Mifo* and his *Mopsa* too,
Beefoole *Guinecia*, and they bring,
Such a strange slumber on the King,
That hee doth sleepe untill hee see
A forreigner where hee should bee;
This if men serioufly but looke
Is the thinge hinted in this booke,
By which this nation might have learned
And at diftance fomething difcerned

Threatning a change in church and state,
Not forfeene, but feene when too late,
The phrafe foe high that all can tell
Hee was the first that did excell,
And our young gallants are content
from him to learne their complement:
His fimilies foe proper are
That they alone would fpeake him rare.
His fentences foe pithie too
They may for *Apothegms* goe,
He's excellent throughout the booke
In whatfoever hee undertooke.
Within this booke defcribed youle find
Everie paffion in its kind,
Places, perfons in ech degree
According to their qualitie;
Their vertues, vices proper graces
Fitted, and anfwereing their places.
Ruins, and change of States, withall
The previall caufes of their fall,
The travailour hee will yow shew,
The statesman, and the souldier too,
The sheepheard yeoman and the clowne,
The coward, and man of Renowne
For fenceing duell; here yow shall
Meete with the complete generall
The Artist, Atheist, every thing
Even from the peafant to the king:
The complete Judge; the fingle life,
blest couples, and the married strife,
The rebel, Traitour, Couetous,
Conceited, and Ambitious,
The Iealoufe; and thofe men that goe
About fedition for to fow,
The Martir and the patient,
The man refolued, the Malecontent,
The inconstant, whom nothing can pleafe
Still tumbling in uncertainties,
The hidebound mifer, and the free
Patron of Hofpitality.
All kinds of fports that doe belonge
To gentry, or to vulgar throng.

In this *Arcadia* men may find
Whatever they fancie in mind,
And weomen too even to the dreffe
That shadowes ore their nakednes,
Court follies hee difcovers, and
What makes comotions in a Land.
To head a faction who are
The likest men hee doth declare,
How great ones are to faction bent
Meerely ftirred on by difcontent,
How Iealoufies 'mongeft them are fure
Vnhappie mifcheifes to procure,
Thofe Mistriffes which hee in fport
Brings in for worthy Knights to Court,
Are vertues, honours, and those things
Which either marr, or elfe make kings.
It is a worke, which if men knowe
T'wil learne them wit, and wifdome too.
Clofetts of Ladys entertaine it,
The Statemen too may not difdaine it.
Of England Sidney was the glorie
And his the best of feigned storie.

V

SCOTLAND AND THE PURITAN REVOLUTION

H. R. Trevor-Roper

BETWEEN the Union of the Crowns in 1603 and the Union of the Parliaments in 1707, the relations of England and Scotland were thoroughly unhappy. Unequal in strength, different in history, the two countries had enough similarity to force them together and yet enough diversity to make their contact always explosive. Moreover, each feared the other. To some Scots—to the 'beggarly blue-caps' who streamed down to the golden court of James I and set up dynasties in the north on the unearned profits of England—the Union of Crowns was a great gain; but to Scotland in general it was a great loss: the King of Scotland became an absentee captured by a foreign establishment, and able, if he wished, to use foreign resources against the liberties of his native country. For the same reason, England too had its apprehensions. The resources of Scotland might be slight, but they were not negligible. In internal English affairs they might give a narrow but decisive margin of superiority to the crown over its opponents—as they afterwards did to its opponents over the crown. From the earliest days of the Union of Crowns, the profoundest of English statesmen, Francis Bacon, foresaw that a revolution in England might well begin in Scotland. A generation later, it did.

The English Puritan Revolution, at every stage, was affected by Scottish affairs. Without Scotland it could not have begun; having begun, without Scotland it might have been over in a year. But again and again—in 1641, in 1643, in 1648, in 1651— Scotland reanimated the flames in which England was being consumed. Thereafter, when the revolution had triumphed in

England, Scotland paid the price: the revolution was carried to it. The uneasy half-union of 1603 was completed, as even James I had not wished to complete it then, but as the statesmen of Queen Anne would be obliged to complete it afterwards, by a full union of Parliaments. Indeed, the Union of 1652 was far closer than that of 1707: for it was a union of Church and Law as well. Moreover, I shall suggest, it entailed a social revolution in Scotland such as would not occur in fact till after 1745. Only it did not last. Within a few years all crumbled; yet another army set out from Scotland and ended by restoring, with the monarchy, the old half-union of 1603. With that restoration the last age of Scottish independence, the darkest age in its history, began.

The character and effect of Scottish intervention in the English Revolution is well known. Everyone knows how the Scots were driven into revolt by Charles I's Act of Revocation and Archbishop Laud's Liturgy; how the leaders of the 'puritan' opposition in England enlisted them as allies; how, thanks to that alliance, they were able to force Charles I to call a parliament and to prevent him from dissolving it; how Charles I, in the summer of 1641, by a personal visit to Scotland, sought and failed to reverse that alliance; how the English Parliament, in 1643, renewed it, and brought a Scottish army, for the second time, into England; how Charles I, in reply, sought once again to raise up a rival party and a rival army in Scotland, and this time nearly succeeded; how the Marquis of Montrose, in his career of triumph, offered to lay all England as well as all Scotland at the feet of the king; but how, in fact, after his disaster at Philiphaugh and the surrender of the king not to his English but to his Scottish subjects, the Scottish Covenanters, in 1646, sought to impose their terms both on the King and Parliament of England; how they were disillusioned and returned to Scotland, selling their king (as the royalists maintained) for £400,000 to the revolutionary English party which was to cut off his head; how the Scottish parties then sought, in vain, by yet other invasions of England, to stay or reverse the revolution: to snatch Charles I from the scaffold

or to impose Charles II as a 'covenanted king' on the throne;
how Oliver Cromwell destroyed the first attempt at Preston, the
second at Dunbar and Worcester; how all Scottish parties were
thereafter pulverised by the victors, the Hamiltons executed,
Argyll driven back to obscurity in Inveraray, the Committee
of Estates rounded up, the General Assembly dissolved, and
the whole country reduced to obedience, and blessed with order
and tranquillity, for the remaining lifetime of the Protector.

All this is well known. Every English historian admits it.
And yet, how many problems are left out of this summary!
Even as we recite the facts, the questions force themselves upon
us. For why did the Scots intervene so constantly, and at such
cost, in English affairs? What springs of action prompted them,
again and again, in the 1640s, to impose a new pattern on a
reluctant English society? And what was the nature of the
revolution which, in the 1650s, was imposed on Scottish
society by England? English historians, who have worked so
intensively on the Puritan Revolution in the last half century,
have seldom asked these questions. To them, as to the English
Independents of the time, the Scottish forces were 'a mere
mercenary army', which King and Parliament in turn summoned to their aid in their purely English struggle. They do
not see them as the expression of social forces in Scotland.
Indeed, they hardly look at the social forces of Scotland. Scotland, to them, is not an intelligible society responding to intelligible social forces. Like seventeenth century visitors to Scotland, they tend to dismiss it as a barbarous country populated
only by doltish peasants manipulated, for their own factious
ends, by ambitious noblemen and fanatical ministers. And
equally, they see the English occupation of Scotland merely
as imposed, for the sake of order, on an exhausted land. Even
Scottish historians have hardly sought to fill this gap. As far as
published work is concerned, the sociology of seventeenth
century Scotland remains a blank.

Into such a blank it is rash for a foreigner to intrude, and in
this essay I shall only offer, with prudent caution, some general
suggestions. They concern the two problems which I have out-

lined above: the attempt of the Scots to impose 'Presbyterian-ism' on England in the 1640s and the attempt of the English Puritans to carry through a social revolution in Scotland in the 1650s. But fundamental to both these problems, and to the failure of both attempts, is the pre-existing difference between the two societies: a difference which was masked, even at the time, by superficial similarities, but which was in reality pro-found: so profound that it made the attempt of the Scots to impose their own form of Presbyterianism on England futile, even absurd, and the attempt of the English to reform Scottish society in the 1650s premature and hopeless except under con-tinuing force.

For in fact, behind all similarities, England and Scotland were poles apart. Consider the century before 1640, the century (some would say) whose new strains, in England, gradually built up the pressures leading to revolution. In that century both England and Scotland had rejected the Roman supremacy. To that extent they were similar. But after that similarity, what a difference! In England population, trade, wealth had con-stantly increased. New industries had grown up and found new markets in a richer, more sophisticated lay society at home. The economic growth of England had been extraordinary and had created, however unequally, a new comfort and a new culture. But in Scotland there had been no such growth. There was little trade, little industry, no increase of population. Always poor and backward, it now seemed, by contrast, poorer and more backward still. That contrast is vividly illustrated by the comments of those who crossed the Tweed, in either direction. We read the accounts of English travellers in Scotland. Their inns, cries Sir William Brereton, are worse than a jakes; and he breaks into a sustained cry of incredulous disgust at that dismal, dirty, waste, and treeless land. Then we turn to the Scottish travellers in England. 'Their inns', exclaims Robert Baillie, 'are like palaces'; and Sir Alexander Brodie of Brodie, goggling at all the wicked fancies and earthly delights of London, reminds us of a bedouin of the desert blinking in the bazaar of Cairo or Damascus.

Nor was the contrast merely one of material progress. Material progress brings its strains. In England there had been a remarkable centralisation, both of population and of wealth, in the twin cities of London and Westminster. There the new industrial wealth was centred, there the swollen bureaucracy of government, the 'court' so resented by the 'country', was rooted. The population of London, in that century, had been quadrupled. Behind the political errors of the statesmen and churchmen in the 1630s, these inescapable social facts provided the solid substance of discontent. 'The country', starved and drained (as it felt) by a monopolist City and an anachronistic, parasitic 'court', was determined to assert its rights; and it felt able to do so because the same century had bred up an educated lay estate, independent of Church and government, and organised in a powerful institution: Parliament.

From all these new forces, and new strains, Scotland was exempt. In Scotland, as there was no inflation, so there was no pressure; nor was there any such concentration either of commerce or of government. Edinburgh was, as it would long remain, destitute of mercantile spirit. There was no court. While the other princes of Western Europe had built up bureaucracies round the throne, the kings of Scotland had been the playthings of great, incorrigible feudatories from whom they had finally fled to England. Without merchants, without 'officers', Scotland lacked altogether the new class of educated laymen on which the greatness of Tudor England had been built. For practical purposes its educated middle class consisted of lawyers and clergy, the two pillars of conservatism which the laity of England sought to reform. Consequently it lacked also their institutions. The Scottish Parliament was as feeble as the Castilian *cortes*. It was because it represented so little that the country acquiesced, in 1707, in its ultimate migration to London.

Finally, there was a third difference. Scotland had already had a religious revolution. By an irony which seems also a law of history, the new religion of Calvinism, like Marxism today, had triumphed not in the mature society which had bred it but in undeveloped countries where the organs of resistance to it were also undeveloped. And because it had triumphed in backward countries, it had adapted itself to the circumstances of such countries. It had become dictatorial, priestly, theocratic. In England, in the reign of Edward VI, the Calvinist clergy (John Knox among them) had sought to determine the nature of the Reformation. They had failed and, in the reign of Mary, had been forced to flee abroad. On the accession of Elizabeth, they had returned eager for the power which seemed to await them. But the self-confident laity of England had soon reduced them to order. Only in moments of crisis—as in 1588—did the organised Calvinist clergy seem temporarily to represent the English people. But in Scotland, where there was no such laity, the Calvinist clergy had established their hold on society. They saw themselves as the educated *élite* which would impose a new doctrine, a new church, a new morality on an indifferent people, and drag them upwards. And the laity of Scotland, recognising its own weakness, accepted them, largely, as such. Kings and courtiers might dislike these insufferable dominies. Individual Scotsmen of culture might prefer the more tolerant, more civilised clergy of the Anglican Church. But those who wished to mobilise the people in Scotland had to use the tribunes of the people; and by 1640 those tribunes were the most highly organised force in Scottish life. If the Scottish Parliament, the organ of the Scottish laity, was a poor thing, the General Assembly, the organisation of its clergy, was not. In times of crisis it could be, like the lay Parliament of England, the voice of the nation.

Thus between England and Scotland there was, by 1640, an immense social gulf which the preceding century had widened. Beneath their common Protestantism and common language, concealed by their common opposition to the same threat, their whole structure differed. Because it had not shared the expansion of England, Scotland was exempt from the strains of growth. Because it had experienced a more radical religious reformation, it no longer felt certain ancient pressures. And because there was little or no independent, educated laity, the

Calvinist clericalism, which in England or France might have been a transitory stage, in Scotland (as in New England) became a conservative tyranny. These different social facts entailed a radical difference of ideas. English Puritanism, though articulated by its clergy, was essentially a lay movement. It was also radical, looking forward to complete the half-reformation of the Tudors by a full emancipation of the laity. Scottish Presbyterianism, though sustained by its laity, was essentially clerical. It was also conservative, seeking not to go forward, to a lay society, but to secure, against the new, creeping episcopalianism of the Stuarts, the clerical reformation which had already been won. In 1640 this was a very real problem: it imposed on the Scots the need of a new, forward policy.

The policy of the Scottish Kirk in the 1640s was the natural result of its conservatism and its weakness. In this it did not differ from the other Calvinist societies of Europe. Everywhere, in 1640, established Calvinism was on the defensive. Having triumphed in weak and backward countries it had automatically exposed their weakness. For Calvinism, by then, had been rejected by all the military monarchies of Europe. Catholic, Lutheran, and Anglican alike regarded it as a revolutionary doctrine and hoped, openly or secretly, to see it ultimately stamped out in the few, obscure corners where it still throve. The King of Spain longed to crush it in Holland; the Duke of Savoy dreamed of the destruction of Geneva; the French monarchy would not long tolerate the 'republic' of La Rochelle; the King of England planned to undermine the Kirk of Scotland. Everywhere Calvinist rulers knew that their society was in danger from powerful neighbours, and to protect it they had, perforce, to adopt one of two policies. Either they must attenuate their Calvinism in order to secure the patronage of non-Calvinist princes, the enemies of their enemies, or, if such patronage were unattainable, they must fall back on themselves, call up their most radical preachers, appeal to the Calvinist international, and, in self-defence, carry the revolution abroad. The former policy was adopted by the Dutch in the sixteenth century, who needed the support of England and France; it was also adopted by the Scots, who sheltered under the wing of that useful, though Anglican neighbour, Queen Elizabeth. The latter was adopted by the Calvinists of the Palatinate and Bohemia in 1618–20; it was also, increasingly, adopted by the Scots when the successors of Queen Elizabeth, who were also their own kings, turned against them and left them isolated in the world.

At first, it was not necessary to adopt it in all its rigour. The Scottish Kirk, in 1638, might be threatened by the crown of England and Scotland, but the errors of Charles I had given it powerful allies in both countries. The king might think that he had divided the classes in Scotland. He might suppose that by his 'innocent Act of Revocation' he had freed the gentry from their '*clientele* and dependence' on the great lords. Many of the Scottish lairds, he claimed, had thanked him for their emancipation from that 'intolerable bondage'.[1] But in fact, as so often, he was wrong. Noble patronage was not broken; the gentry were not rendered independent; and by 1638 the former, as patrons, and the latter, as ruling elders, formed the strength of the National Covenant. Moreover, looking abroad, the architects of that Covenant could see, or thought they could see, a similar alliance of classes in England, all equally determined, with them, to bring the crown to reason. Thanks to this internal solidarity and to these external allies, the Scottish Covenanters were able to overthrow the new episcopacy which had been planted among them and 'restore' the Kirk to its purest form.

Undoubtedly it was a great victory. But how long would it last? When the Scottish leaders looked about them, they had to admit that it had been a very close thing, the result of a remarkably favourable conjuncture such as could never be predicted, could hardly be expected to last, and might never recur. And of course, in changed circumstances, it might easily be reversed. Obviously, while the favourable conjuncture

---

[1] The king's view is expressed for him in [W. Balcanquhall] *A Large Declaration concerning the Late Tumults in Scotland . . .* (1639).

7

lasted, they must do whatever was necessary to make their victory permanent. And after the experience of the last generation they knew what was necessary. They must export their revolution. Theoretically the Scotch Kirk might co-exist with 'moderate episcopacy' in England. It had done so in the previous century. But that was when Queen Elizabeth had reigned in England, and the two kingdoms had been separate. King Charles and the Union of Crowns had changed all that. And anyway, how long would 'moderate episcopacy' remain moderate? Episcopacy had been 'moderate' in Elizabethan England and in Jacobean Scotland; but insensibly it had been transformed, as it could be transformed again. So the Scots leaders were clear. In England, as in Scotland, episcopacy must be rooted out. There must be no compromise, no return to the Elizabethan system. Only one form of church-government in England was compatible with the permanence of Presbyterianism in Scotland: England must become presbyterian too. The full-blown, bishopless, clerical Calvinism of 1639 must be accepted, *in toto*, by the stronger kingdom.

Moreover, thought the Scots, it could easily be done. There was no need of compulsion, hardly even of pressure. As they looked at England they saw only the resemblances, never the differences. Admittedly England was much richer and more powerful than Scotland, but the social and political structure, to their eyes, seemed exactly the same. Was not the parliamentary opposition, which had triumphed, there too bound together by noble patronage, inspired by 'Calvinian' clergy, made solid by the gentry? Was there not a general outcry against the bishops? And did not the English, in that triumphant winter of 1640–41, looking back on the immediate causes of their triumph, 'all everywhere profess' that, under God, they owed 'their religion, liberties, parliaments and all they have' to the victorious army of their brethren the Scots? What wonder if, in the exaltation of the moment, with Charles I's policy in ruins, Strafford and Laud in the Tower, and the citizens of London submitting monster petitions for the abolition of episcopacy, the ever-complacent Scottish clergy overlooked the great social gulf which really separated the two countries, and supposed that 'the Scots discipline' could be established in England by a mere hint from them, the experts, the teachers, and the saviours of England?

So, that winter, four Scottish clergymen set out from Edinburgh to guide the grateful English towards the true doctrine and perfect system of Presbytery. It was a planned operation: each had his set task: one was to bring down 'his little Grace' the Archbishop of Canterbury and the whole episcopal system; one was to destroy the Anglican ceremonies which accompanied it; the third was to define the presbyterian system; the fourth to dish the sectaries who might have other ideas, of 'the New England way'; and all four were to preach by turns to the Scots commissioners and all else who would come to hear the saving gospel from the North. The main advocate of Presbytery among these four evangelists was Alexander Henderson, the framer of the National Covenant; the confident grave-digger of Anglicanism was the voluble, invaluable letter-writer, that incomparable Scotch dominie, so learned, so acute, so factual, so complacent, so unshakably omniscient, so infallibly wrong, Robert Baillie D.D. (Glasweg), regent of Glasgow University and minister of Kilwinning, Lanarkshire.

The four clergymen set to work. They preached, they wrote, they lobbied; and always they saw the end of their labours just round the corner. Baillie's letters home are a continual purr of complacency. Of course, he admitted, the poor benighted English could not leap all at once up to the Scotch level; but he found them eminently teachable; and though his arms, as he said, were 'full of my old friend, his little Grace', he was always ready to open his mouth too, to teach them. (Indeed, Baillie admitted that he opened his mouth 'somewhat to his own contentment' and that it 'weighted his mind' to keep it shut.) So on one occasion, he preached for an hour on God's singular mercies to the Scots, whereupon (he said) 'many tears of compassion and joy did fall from the eyes of the English'. Everywhere, he observed, there was not only a crying need, but also a general desire for Presbytery. There might be a few separatists, pursuing 'the New England way', but 'the far greatest part are for our discipline'; and anyway, it would be easy to use the separatists in the work of demolition and then discard them: once the 'rubbish' of Anglicanism was swept away, it would be easy to 'build a new house': the house of the Lord according to John Calvin, John Knox, and Andrew Melville. In May 1641, when the English Parliament signed the 'Protestation' of solidarity against Strafford, it was, Baillie confidently declared, 'in substance, our Scottish Covenant'.

So Scot to Scot smugly blew his tribal trumpet; but the walls of the episcopal Jericho were strangely slow in falling. First there were excuses: the matter, it was said, must be deferred 'till first we have gotten Canterbury down'. The Scots took up the challenge. Baillie threw himself at 'his little Grace', prepared to give him 'the last stroke', and looked eagerly forward to his 'funeral'; but somehow nothing happened. To hasten the matter, all four ministers wrote pamphlets, which, they felt, were 'much called for': in particular, Alexander Henderson himself wrote 'a little quick paper' against English bishops, giving 'very good reasons for their removal out of the Church'. The result was most unfortunate. The king, who had just publicly declared his faith in episcopacy was 'so inflamed as he was never before in his time for any other business'. He told the Scots that, by such interference, they had forfeited their privileges; the English reformers maintained a prudent silence; and even 'divers of our true friends' (lamented Baillie) 'did think us too rash'. Internal English affairs, the Scots were told, were an English matter: they should mind their own business. Thereupon, to Baillie's dismay, the House of Lords set up a committee to reform episcopacy: an infamous 'trick', to 'caulk the rotten hulk of episcopacy' and set it afloat again. The Scotch lay commissioners interposed discretion and, according to their instructions, submitted papers requesting a conformity of church government as a special means of preserving peace between the two kingdoms; but it made no difference. It was with difficulty that the English

Parliament was prevented from telling them, too, to mind their own business. In the end they were simply told that the two Houses had already considered the reform of church government in England, and would proceed along their own lines 'in due time, as shall best conduce to the glory of God and peace of the Church'.[1]

So that was that. In the summer of 1641 the Scots were finally paid off and sent home. Pym had used them and dismissed them, just as he had used and then dismissed the Irish Catholic enemies of Strafford. Both had secured their immediate aims: Strafford was dead, and the king, that summer, ratified the Scottish revolution. But neither had obtained the long-term guarantees which they sought: there was to be no recognition of Catholicism in Ireland, and the Scottish revolution was not to be exported to England. And indeed, Pym could reply, why should it be? The English Church was the affair of Englishmen. The Scots had indeed been very useful, but they had been serving their own interest; they had been well paid; and they should be satisfied with what they had got: they had helped to restore, in England, that Elizabethan system which had protected the rear of the young Kirk of Scotland, and would do so still. So, in England, on 7 September, all the church bells were rung, to give thanks to God for a peace with Scotland, the departure of the Scots, and the basis laid for a purely English church-reformation.

Unfortunately history did not stop there. Those who call in foreign aid cannot complain if their enemies do so too. Charles I had not accepted the English reformation of 1641; and if the Scots and the Irish thought themselves double-crossed, why should he not exploit their resentment? In a year much had happened in Scotland; the unity of the Covenant was dissolving as the ambitions of Argyll showed through it. Much had happened in Ireland too since the great unifier of discontent, Strafford, had fallen. So in both Scotland and Ireland the king

[1] R. Baillie, *Letters and Journals* (Edin., 1841), i, *passim*; W. A. Shaw, *A History of the English Church . . . 1640–1660* (1900), pp. 127-33.

sought new allies to continue the struggle. In Scotland he failed: his personal presence there only served, in Clarendon's words, to make 'a perfect deed of gift of that kingdom' to the Covenanting Party. But in Ireland the troubled waters yielded better fishing, and before long a train of events had begun which led insensibly to civil war in England, and thereby once again brought the English Parliament and the Scotch General Assembly together.

As soon as civil war appeared imminent, the English Parliament approached the General Assembly: would their brethren the Scots stand by the English Houses in their just struggle? But this time the Scots were not going to be double-crossed, as in 1641. Once bitten is twice shy, and they were resolved to have legal guarantees before they gave any help. The essential condition of help, they replied, was 'uniformity of Kirk government'. Prelacy must be 'plucked up root and branch' in England, and presbyterian government 'by assemblies, higher and lower, in their strong and beautiful subordination' must be substituted for it. The English Parliament was prepared to renounce episcopacy, at least on paper; it was prepared to utter pious general formulae; but it absolutely refused to give any guarantee of Presbyterianism. It preferred to fight the king alone. At that time it thought it could win quickly. A little later, it had doubts, and applied again to the Scots. But still it said nothing about Presbyterianism. Baillie waxed sardonic about the strange 'oversight'. 'It was a wonder', he wrote, 'if they desired any help, that they denied to use better means for its obtaining'. It was not till the summer of 1643, when the Parliamentary cause seemed hopeless—when the king was preparing for the final onslaught, and the radicals in Parliament were in revolt—that Pym decided to seek a Scotch alliance even, if necessary, on Scotch terms. And those terms had not changed. They never would change. The Scots themselves, by 1643, were thoroughly apprehensive. They were almost as eager for an alliance as the English. But even so, they would stand out for the old price. As Baillie wrote, 'the English were for a civil league'—mutual assistance without reference to religion—'we for a religious Covenant': a binding covenant of exact religious conformity.

Such was the origin of the Solemn League and Covenant. How hard the English fought against it we know. Every phrase which alluded to it was contested in both Houses. All the verbal subtlety of Vane was needed to find a formula which could both mean and not mean it: mean it for the Scots, not mean it for the English. All the mental reservations of Cromwell were needed to slip out of that formula when it had been accepted. Pym himself, in his last recorded speech, pleaded sheer necessity as its only justification. Nevertheless, it was accepted; and because the name was accepted, the Scots, those incorrigible nominalists, supposed that the thing was accepted too. In December 1643 Robert Baillie, now a professor and more self-assured than ever, set out once again with his colleagues to London, confident, in spite of all past experience, that this time the cat was in the bag. All that was needed was to keep it there. And this now seemed easy. If only a 'well-chosen committee', packed with Scots, were established in London, 'they would soon get the guiding of all the affairs both of this state and church'.

So the Scots set to work again. Their aim was constant and clear: 'to abolish the great idol of England, the Service Book, and to erect in all the parts of worship a full conformity to Scotland'. From the start there was to be no compromise. They refused to hear even Pym's funeral sermon, delivered by the pope of English 'Presbyterianism', Stephen Marshall, 'for funeral sermons we must have away, with the rest'. In the Assembly of Divines as in Parliament 'we doubt not to carry all clearly according to our mind'. By adjuration from Scotland, reinforced by the Calvinists of France and Switzerland, all deviation from the true doctrine was to be forbidden; schismatics 'and the mother and foster of all, the Independency of congregations' were to be suppressed; all suggestions of toleration were to be crushed. The English Parliament had double-crossed the Scotch General Assembly once. It must not do so again. Nor (thought the Scots) could it do so again. It was committed now by a greater need and chained in redoubt-able syllables of assent.

Alas, even the most pedantic, professorial syllables cannot alter historic, social facts. In spite of the Covenant, in spite of Marston Moor, in spite of much ink and much breath, facts remained facts, and before many months had passed Baillie's letters become, once again, a series of anguished ejaculations. It was not only that Vane and St. John, 'our former friends', the framers of the alliance, who owed all (said Baillie) to the Scots, had turned against them. Vane and St. John, it soon transpired, were acknowledged 'Independents'. Even the pro-fessed English 'Presbyterians', even Denzil Holles, their lay leader, even Stephen Marshall, their religious oracle, were no better. England, exclaimed Baillie, in a moment of truth, even parliamentary England, was either 'fully episcopal' or 'much episcopal'; Presbytery, to the English, was 'a monster'; and the only hope of establishing 'the Scots discipline' south of the Tweed was by means not of sermons or pamphlets, com-mittees or advice, but of 'our army at Newcastle'. 'If by any means we would get these our regiments, which are called near thirty, to 16,000 marching men', then 'by the blessing of God, in a short time, we might ruin both the malignant party and the sectaries'. Already, before the king was defeated, the Scots were thinking of a military conquest of England.

Vain hope! It was not the Scottish army that was to decide the English civil war. It is true, when the first war was over, an English party called the 'Presbyterians' was in power. It is true, this party confirmed the abolition of episcopacy, putting the bishops' lands up for sale. It is true, the name and form of Presbyterianism was accepted to fill the void. But why were the bishops' lands sold? To raise money to get rid of the Scots who, once again, as in 1641, had served their turn and were to be sent home. And what was the Presbyterianism which was set up in the place of episcopacy? Was it 'full conformity with the Kirk of Scotland'? Certainly not. It was, as Baillie himself lamented, 'a lame erastian Presbytery' in which all the essentials of the Scottish system—the divine right of ruling elders, the judicial independence of the Church, its 'strong and beautiful' internal structure, its formidable power of excommunication—had been sacrificed not only to the 'sectaries' in Parliament and 'the sottish negligence of the ministers and gentry in the shires', but also to the stubborn refusal of the so-called 'Presbyterians' themselves.

For in fact—whatever compliance they made for the sake of Scottish help—the English 'Presbyterians' were not Presbyterians. Perhaps no label has caused such political and historical confusion as the label 'presbyterian' attached to an English political party. Because of that label, seventeenth century Scottish clergymen built up impossible hopes and modern historians have tied themselves in unnecessary knots. Why, asked the former, did the English Presbyterians not carry out the terms of the Solemn League and Covenant? Why, ask the latter, did the English Presbyterians, whose Scottish brethren clung to their church through thick and thin, become 'Independents' in the 1650s and Anglicans in the 1660s? The answer to these questions is simple. Except for a few clergymen, tempted by clerical power, there were no English Presbyterians. Whatever history may call them, whatever events sometimes forced them to appear, the Englishmen who attempted to stabilise the revolution in 1646 were, as they had been in 1641, as they would be in 1660, 'moderate Anglicans', believers, under whatever name, in a temperate, lay-controlled, 'Elizabethan' episcopacy.

If we look at the men, if we look at their policy, always making allowances for circumstances, this is clear enough. Clarendon, going through the list of the 'great contrivers', all of whom he had known, marvels to think of the damage done by these men, nearly all of whom, on examination, turned out to be so 'well-affected' to the Anglican Church. John Pym himself, to his dying day, extolled 'moderate episcopacy' as the ideal church-system, and the words in which he nevertheless urged his fellow 'rebels' to swallow the Solemn League and Covenant, show that he was addressing men who shared those ideals. Whatever words they might utter in the heat of the moment, whatever measures might be forced upon them by the necessity of war-finance or the mounting passions of civil war, those men would always have gladly settled for the system which divided them least. They might abolish episcopacy on paper, but all through the first civil war they took care not to abolish it irreversibly in fact. Even when, at long last, under Scottish pressure, the fatal step was taken and the bishops' lands put up for sale, the consequences were not accepted. The 'Presbyterians', having got rid of the Scots and their absurd demands, were prepared to settle for a three-year probationary period which, as everyone knew, would be a half-way house to the restoration of episcopacy. Even the 'presbyterian' Lord Mayor of London of the time could afterwards be praised by a 'presbyterian' minister of the time, for his constant fidelity to the episcopal Church of England.[1] And as a matter of fact, those who became 'Independents' were not very different in this. In 1647 when it was their turn to offer terms to the king, they offered to restore 'moderate episcopacy'. Oliver Cromwell himself, once the violent years were over, sought to reunite the Anglican clergy in his 'puritan' Church[2] and gave a state funeral, with the Anglican liturgy, in Westminster Abbey, to the great figurehead of moderate episcopacy, Archbishop Ussher. For 'moderate episcopacy' meant laicised episcopacy. Whatever form of church-structure (that is, of social structure) the English 'Puritans' were prepared to accept, the one essential ingredient was laicisation. If they could not have 'moderate episcopacy', the next best thing might be called Presbyterianism. It might borrow presbyterian features. But essentially it would be Independency: a decentralised, laicised, protestant church.

To the Scots ministers this fact was never clear. Provincial, complacent men, accustomed to pontificate from their pulpits, tenacious of the dogma and discipline which had served them

---

[1] See *The Royal Commonwealthsman* (1668), being the funeral sermon preached at the death of Thomas Adams, the 'presbyterian' Lord Mayor of London in 1646, by Nathaniel Hardy, whose own sermons in 1646–47 show him to have been a 'Presbyterian'.

[2] See R. S. Bosher, *The Making of the Restoration Settlement* (1951), pp. 45–6.

at home, inured to the nominalism of the Schools and accustomed to the docility of their flocks, they never dreamed that similarity of words could conceal such divergence of meaning. So they alternated between absurd confidence and righteous indignation. At one time—in 1646, when Montrose had been defeated in Scotland and the king in England, and the English 'Presbyterians' had won control in the English Parliament—they would be triumphant. Total victory, it seemed, was theirs. In that year the General Assembly ordained that all Scotsmen who had been in arms with Montrose, or had dealt with him, or drunk his health, should be excluded from communion till they had made public confession of their sins, and the Commissioners of the Church insisted that, in all future treaties, they should be consulted as to the lawfulness of the terms. Meanwhile, at Newcastle, the Scots were demanding that the king accept the Covenant himself and enforce it in all England, and Baillie was confidently distributing the church-patronage of England among his friends. There was Mr. Lee, for instance, 'a very able and deserving man', and very hot against Independency. Now was the time, Baillie instructed the English Parliament, to reward his merits: 'the deanery of Christ Church is his due'. But England, unlike Scotland, refused to accept these peremptory clerical commands; Mr. Lee was not made Dean of Christ Church; and before long Baillie would be expressing bitter, petulant disappointment. The 'Presbyterians' in Parliament, he found, would not do his bidding; the 'presbyterian' aldermen were really 'malignants' at heart; even the 'presbyterian' ministers turned out to be either royalists or Independents. When Cromwell, with his 'army of sectaries' overthrew the English 'Presbyterians', who would have thought that half the 'Presbyterians'—including Stephen Marshall himself—would have supported him? It was all most bewildering. It only showed, to Baillie, that almost everyone in England was extremely wicked, and that 'no people had so much need of a Presbytery'.[1]

[1] W. L. Mathieson, *Politics and Religion, a Study in Scottish History* . . . (Glasgow, 1902), ii, 82-3. Baillie, *op. cit.*, ii, 177, 393.

So the Scottish intervention of 1643 proved, in the end, as vain as that of 1640. Each time the Scots had done their work; each time they had insisted on the same terms; each time they had been paid off in cash only. They had not exported their revolution. They had not done so because, between England and Scotland, there was a social difference which made Presbyterianism, in their sense, impossible; and by insisting on the impossible, by dragging the heirs of Pym further towards 'the Scots model' than they would willingly go, they had ended by provoking a revolution and placing in power a party which was determined to have no more to do with them, but would settle England on an English model only: a model which, in the Church, might be laicised episcopacy—that is 'moderate Anglicanism'—or might be laicised non-episcopacy—that is Independency—but would not be Presbyterianism.

From the moment of the Cromwellian revolution of 1647, the unity of the Scottish classes, forged in 1638, collapsed. It collapsed because the English policy of the Kirk had proved impossible. After 1647 the Scots politicians, 'the Engagers', recognised that the Presbyterianism of the Kirk could not be imposed on England. As far as religion was concerned, they would gladly have taken Scotland out of English politics. They would have settled for Presbyterianism at home and an allied, though not identical, Protestantism in England, as in the days of Queen Elizabeth. If they did in fact invade England in 1648, that was no longer to impose the Covenant: it was because the King of Scotland needed to be rescued from his English subjects. It was yet another fatal consequence of the Union of Crowns. On the other hand the Kirk still clung to its old policy. It opposed the invasion of 1648 not because it had given up a policy of coercion, but simply because this particular invasion was not consecrated by the old purpose. As Baillie wrote, 'that Scotland at this time has a just cause of war against the sectarian army in England and their adherents, none of us do question': the English, by failing to erect a full Presbyterianism, had broken the Solemn League and Covenant and the Scots had every right to enforce its terms. For these reasons, he and his friends were 'most cordial for a war'. But this war of the 'Engagers' was the wrong kind of war. At best it could only lead to 'ane Erastian weak Presbytery with a toleration of Popery and episcopacy at court, and of divers sects elsewhere'. That was no reason for the Kirk to go to war.[1]

So the forward policy of the Scottish Calvinists, like that of the Palatine Calvinists, ended only in catastrophe. They did not export their revolution: they only created a counter-revolution against their interference, and, as a result, brought division and disaster to themselves. One by one the Scottish parties were defeated: the politicians at Preston, the zealots at Dunbar, the nationalists at Worcester. By the autumn of 1651 Scotland lay prostrate before the arms of revolutionary England. All its national organs were destroyed. The king had fled abroad; the Committee of Estates had been seized; the General Assembly, 'the glory and strength of our church upon earth', would soon be dissolved. Instead of the old Scottish revolution being forced upon England, the new English revolution was about to be forced upon Scotland, now a part of the united, kingless Commonwealth of England, Scotland, and Ireland. 'Full conformity', with a vengeance, had come.

The rule of the Commonwealth and Protectorate in Scotland is often regarded as a mere military operation. Certainly Scotland was governed, like England, by the sword. Certainly the nation and the Church had been defeated and were not reconciled to their defeat. Certainly the Scottish, like the Irish, members of Cromwell's Parliaments were largely nominees of the English government. But it would be wrong to stop there, or suppose that the English government did nothing more positive in respect of Scotland than grant it freedom of trade, which it was too disorganised to use, and impose a welcome peace upon its Highland clans and Lowland factions. Within the English Revolution there was a positive social content,

---

[1] Baillie, op. cit., iii, 25, 42, 52.

implied in the word 'Commonwealth'; and this positive content it retained even when it was exported. Originally, of course, the English exported their revolution for the same reason which had impelled the Scots to export theirs: because it was insecure at home. As long as Charles II was accepted as King of Scots, as long as Catholic Ireland did not acknowledge the revolutionary government of England, that government did not feel safe against counter-revolution. Therefore Scotland and Ireland must accept the revolution too. But acceptance was not to be mere submission: it was to entail the same social content: Scotland and Ireland were to become 'free commonwealths' too. In the midst of the fire and slaughter which they carried over Ireland, Cromwell's soldiers believed that they were engaged on a great constructive work, 'the forming and framing of a commonwealth out of a corrupt, rude mass'.[1] In Scotland there was less need of fire and slaughter; the mass was less corrupt, less rude; but the object was the same. A social revolution in Scotland comparable with that of England would be the basis of a stable union between the two countries, a natural defence not, this time, of the Scottish Kirk but of the English Commonwealth.

What was the nature of the social revolution which Cromwell sought to export to Scotland? In England that revolution was not essentially radical, though it had needed radical methods for its achievement. Essentially it was a seizure of power in the state by the classes who had been accustomed to power in the country but who, under the Stuarts, had been, or had felt themselves, more and more excluded by a parasitic 'court' and its church: in other words, by the laity, the gentry. In opposition these men had demanded, and now in power they sought to realise, a general policy of decentralisation and laicisation. The feudal taxes, the antique patronage which had sustained the court and its peerage were to be abolished, together with the court and the house of peers: the parliament was to be reduced to a parliament of gentry, and country gentry

[1] The phrase is that of a Cromwellian soldier in Ireland, Colonel John Jones. (Nat. Library of Wales MSS, 11440-D).

at that—the reduction of borough seats and the multiplication of county seats would achieve that purpose. Education was to be decentralised by the foundation of new local schools and colleges, and laicised by the reform of teaching and the adoption of new 'Baconian' subjects. Religion was to be decentralised by the break-up of episcopal and capitular property, the redistribution of patronage, and the use of both for the 'propagation of the Gospel' in remote, neglected areas; at the same time it was to be laicised by practical lay control and systematic toleration. Law was to be decentralised by breaking the monopoly of the London law-courts and setting up 'county registers' and 'county judicatories' and laicised by the simplification of procedure and language. The whole policy was summarised as 'reformation of law and clergy'.

Of course there were differences of interpretation. Some men interpreted the policy in a conservative, some in a radical, even a revolutionary, spirit. Oliver Cromwell himself interpreted it in a conservative spirit. He believed that the policy should and must be carried out by the gentry. But equally he insisted that its benefits must be enjoyed by those humbler allies whose voices, in the counties and more democratic boroughs, had carried the 'puritan' gentry into Parliament in 1640 and whose arms, in the New Model Army, had since carried them through radicalism into power. All his life Cromwell would never betray 'the godly party'—that is, the country party in depth, the alliance of gentle and simple which alone could preserve the gains of revolution—and many of his apparent inconsistencies, from his surrender to the Agitators in 1647 to his rejection of the crown in 1657, are to be explained by this genuine resolve never to betray his followers or split the 'godly party'.

But if Cromwell was always determined to earn the support of his radical followers, equally he would never adopt their radical policy. To him, the radicalism to which he had sometimes surrendered had always been a tactical necessity. It had been an inconvenient necessity because it had split the united front of 1640, driving some men into royalism, some into 'Presbyterianism', some into 'Independency'. Ultimately,

Cromwell sought to restore that united front and, on the new basis of an England without Stuart kings, to continue the old reforming policy of 1640. The bigots of radicalism or republicanism might protest at his 'reconciling' of royalists, 'malignants', 'cavaliers'; but he did not care. To him radicalism, republicanism, had been stages only; and, anyway, the original aims of the English Parliament were often better represented by men who, since 1640, had become royalists, like Antony Ashley Cooper or Lord Broghil or Sir Charles Wolseley, than by the doctrinaires of a now obsolete radicalism, like the Levellers or the Fifth Monarchy men, or of a fossil republicanism, like John Bradshaw or Sir Arthur Hesilrige or Thomas Scot. So, from his basis in the Army and in the 'godly party', whose vertical unity was his strength, Cromwell reached out horizontally to re-unite the gentry whom war and revolution had divided, to find supporters among old 'Presbyterians', even among old royalists, and so to realise at last, in new circumstances, the old policy of decentralisation and laicisation, 'reformation of law and clergy'.

Such was Cromwell's policy for England. If we wish to see the application of it we must not look at his Parliaments, those sterile assemblies which (he complained) always cavilled at the admittedly questionable basis of his rule instead of making 'good laws'. We must look at his direct administration. This we can do particularly in two periods: in the nine months between the setting up of the Protectorate in December 1653 and the meeting of his first protectoral Parliament in September 1654, the great period of rule by ordinance of the Protector and Council; and in the period between his two protectoral Parliaments, from the summer of 1655 to the end of 1656, the period of rule by major-generals. And the same is true for Scotland. For in Scotland too he could legislate by ordinance; there too he had military commanders. And so, if we look, we can see the same policy applied in Scotland too: not systematically of course (even in England it could not be applied systematically), but in the intervals of financial and military distractions, and yet with sufficient constancy to show the same positive aims as in England.

The parallel between Cromwell's policy in Scotland and in England can be seen, first of all, in the character of his advisers. If we wish to see the continuity and consistency of his English policy, we can look at the group of civilians whom he kept around him. These men who were his ablest supporters in his nominated Parliament, the Barebones Parliament, and who continued with him in the Council of State of the Protectorate, are first found as a group, significantly enough, in that committee for the reform of the law which Cromwell personally forced the Rump Parliament to set up. Similarly, in Scotland, the nucleus of Cromwell's closest advisers was formed by the three Scottish members of the joint commission for the administration of justice which the Rump, again undoubtedly under his pressure, set up in 1652. These three, with one addition, reappear as the nominated Scottish members of the Barebones Parliament; and they continue as the Scottish members of the Scottish Council of State. In their common origin, as well as in their diverse past, these men illustrate both the consistent aim and the conciliatory method of Cromwell's policy.

The first three of these men, the commissioners for the administration of justice who, with four English colleagues, replaced the old Court of Session, were Sir William Lockhart of Lee, Sir James Hope of Hopetoun, and Sir John Swinton of Swinton. If we may use such terms in Scotland, the first was a royalist, the second a Presbyterian, the third an Independent. Lockhart, from a servant of Charles I, an ally of Montrose, whose anti-clerical views he shared, was to become a firm 'conservative' supporter of Cromwell, his best diplomatist, and a member, by marriage, of his family circle. The lands and offices with which he was rewarded in Scotland would draw sour comments from less yielding (or less tempted) compatriots. Hope was the son of Charles I's greatest law officer— the man who had framed the Act of Revocation, but then become a strong Covenanter. He was an enterprising and successful manager of his property, which included profitable leadmines in Lanarkshire, and he believed in the improvement

8

of Scotland untrammelled by English politics. He and his brother even urged Charles II to accept the English revolution and be content with his Scottish crown. To this the king replied that he would first see both brothers hanged at one end of a rope and Cromwell at the other, and he sent them both to prison. Hope continued to press his advice and service on Charles II, but after Worcester saw that reform would never be achieved through him, and became a Cromwellian. Pressed by Cromwell to attend the Barebones Parliament, he at first refused; he would, he said, 'own' the English government and act under it in Scotland; but he would not 'go out of Scotland or meddle in state affairs'. However, he was persuaded, and Cromwell afterwards regretted the persuasion. So Hope travelled up to London in the same coach with the third of 'our triumvirs' among the judges, Sir John Swinton. Swinton was a Berwickshire squire of radical views: an extreme Covenanter who refused any compromise with the Stuarts. After Dunbar, he, like several other extremists, had seen that the old politics were useless and turned to Cromwell. For this he had been excommunicated by the Kirk and condemned to death by the Scottish Parliament; but such sentences had now lost their effect. Swinton accepted cordially the new situation and became, in Burnet's words, 'the man of all Scotland most trusted and employed by Cromwell'.[1]

These three were the original nucleus of Cromwell's Scottish advisers. In 1653 they were joined by a fourth, Alexander Jaffray. Jaffray was provost of Aberdeen, a city and county which had never much relished the Covenant. In his youth he had studied the cloth-industry in England, and been educated (like many Scotsmen, including Sir James Hope) among the Huguenots of France. In 1649, and again in 1650, he had been

---

[1] For Lockhart's firm anti-clericalism see *The Diary of Sir Archibald Johnston of Wariston*, vol. iii (Scot. Hist. Soc., Edinburgh, 1940), p. 7. For criticism of him see John Nicoll, *A Diary of Public Transactions . . . 1650-1667* (Edin., 1836), p. 180; *The Diary of Mr. John Lamont of Newton 1649-71* (Edin., 1830), p. 90. For Hope see his *Diary*, 1646, ed. P. Marshall (Scot. Hist. Soc., 1958) and 1646-54, ed. Sir J. B. Paul (Scot. Hist. Soc., 1919); for Swinton, Burnet, *History of His Own Time*.

one of the commissioners from the Scottish Parliament sent to Holland to impose the Covenant on Charles II. Afterwards he was ashamed of the hypocrisy and compulsion involved: 'we did sinfully both entangle and engage the nation and ourselves and that poor young prince to whom we were sent, making him sign and swear a covenant which we knew from clear and demonstrable reasons that he hated in his heart'. Jaffray fought and was wounded at Dunbar, and after seeing 'the dreadful appearance of God against us' there, and conversing, as a prisoner, with Cromwell and his chaplain, John Owen, he decided, like Swinton, that Presbyterianism was 'not the only way of Christ'. He even ventured to say so in writing to the Rev. Andrew Cant, the presbyterian oracle of Aberdeen. This caused a predictable explosion, whose blast lodged Jaffray in the arms of Cromwell.[1]

Another whom Cromwell summoned to his Parliament in London was Alexander Brodie of Brodie, who had accompanied Jaffray to Holland. Jaffray urged Brodie to accept; but Brodie, a narrow, timorous spirit ('he is not a man of courage', he wrote of himself, 'but faint and feeble and unstedfast, wavering, unclear-sighted and impure'), after much introspection and a family conclave, accepted advice from the Lord that the Covenant was still binding and that he must 'eschew and avoid employments under Cromwell'.[2]

These were the Scotsmen with whose aid Cromwell sought to carry the English social revolution, as he understood it, into Scotland: a revolution, there too, of 'reformation of law and clergy'. And what did this mean in fact, in Scottish circumstances? First of all, it meant reducing the power of those who, in the civil wars, in Scotland as in England, had frustrated the expression and application of such a policy: that is, of the great lords, with their oppressive patronage, and the intolerant Kirk, with its monopoly of the pulpit. These were the men who, by

[1] For Jaffray see his *Diary*, ed. J. Barclay (Aberdeen, 1833).
[2] For Brodie see his *Diary* (Aberdeen, Spalding Club, 1863); also G. Bain, *Lord Brodie, his Life and Times* (Nairn, 1904). He refused office again in 1657 (*Thurloe State Papers*, vi, 351, 364).

these means, had first launched the National Covenant and made the English revolution possible; but by now they were the main obstacle to the progress of that revolution in their own land, and as such they must be broken. The English Commonwealth was determined to set up in Scotland as in England, a gentry-republic, where all land was free of feudal burdens, where the patronage of the nobility was destroyed, and where the Church had no coercive power over the laity. 'Free the poor commoners', was the cry of hopeful Scots after the battle of Worcester, 'and make as little use as can be either of the great men or clergy'.

The English Parliament did not need to be told. From the beginning, from the first proposal of union in the winter of 1651, this policy had been announced. 'Forasmuch as the Parliament are satisfied', ran the opening declaration of its purpose, 'that many of the people of Scotland who were vassals or tenants to and had dependence on the noblemen and gentry (the chief actors in these invasions and wars against England) were by their influence drawn into . . . the same evils', such persons who now put themselves under the protection of the Commonwealth were to be 'set free from their former dependencies and bondage-services' and to live as tenants, freeholders, and heritors, 'delivered (through God's goodness) from their former slaveries, vassalage and oppressions'. Thereupon the Republic declared the abolition of all jurisdictions other than those derived from Parliament. All feudal tenures and all heritable jurisdictions were cancelled. 'Justice', wrote a newswriter in the summer of 1652, 'was wont to be open and free for none formerly but great men; but now it flows equally to all; which will in short time make them sensible from what bondage they are delivered'.[1]

The Long Parliament declared; it was Cromwell who executed. In April 1654, in that first happy period of freedom from Parliament, so rich in legislation, the Protector's Council

---

[1] The Declaration of 28 October 1651 is printed in C. S. Terry, *The Cromwellian Union* (Scot. Hist. Soc., Edinburgh, 1902), p. xxiii. For the newsletter see *ibid.*, pp. 180-1.

issued the Ordinance of Union abolishing, among other things, all feudal lordships, heritable jurisdictions, military services, and wardship, and all forfeitures and escheats except to the Lord Protector. Over two years later, the ordinance was converted into an act by the second Parliament of the Protectorate, and the Cromwellians who knew Scotland foretold a new era of peace when 'all these unjust powers'—'the greatest hindrance to the execution of our laws' as James VI had called them—would be abolished 'and justice will flow in an equal channel'. From now on, they said, the great landlords would have to exchange patronage for wealth: instead of demanding from their tenants slavish personal attendance, they could demand improved economic rents, and so 'nobles and gentles', as well as their tenants, 'will be much happier than before'.[1]

Hardly less formidable than the despotism of the great nobles was the despotism of the Church. The English Puritans had no intention of breaking the established Church of Scotland. They would accept it, just as they would have accepted the established episcopal Church of England, just as they had accepted the presbyterian church system which the events of the civil war had imposed on England—but on the same conditions. Just as English episcopacy was to be 'moderate', and English Presbyterianism 'Erastian', so Scottish Presbyterianism must be mitigated by lay claims. The power of the church courts must be broken; the clergy must be under the civil law; the right of excommunication, which the English 'presbyterian' Parliament had absolutely refused to accept from its Scottish mentors, must now be reduced in Scotland; and there must be a large toleration. What Baillie had most feared from the restoration of the uncovenanted Stuarts in 1648—'ane weak Erastian Presbytery', with a large toleration beside it—was now to be set up by the Republic. On this point, the Republic was quite explicit. In its first declaration, it merely stated that it would promote the preaching of the Gospel in Scotland and advance

[1] Firth and Rait, *Acts and Ordinances*, ii, 871-5; T. Burton, *Parliamentary Diary*, i, 12-18. Cf. Firth, *Scotland and the Protectorate*, p. 333; James VI and I, *Basilikon Doron*.

the power of true religion and holiness, without defining who should be the preachers or what was true; but when its commissioners arrived in Edinburgh, they introduced, into this vagueness, an alarming clarity. Ministers, they said, whose consciences obliged them to wait on God according to the order of the Scottish Churches were to be protected and encouraged in their peaceable exercise of the same; but so also were others who 'not being satisfied in conscience to use that form, shall serve and worship God in other Gospel way'. That 'great Diana of the Independents', a toleration, was to be established in Scotland.[1]

To break the power of great lords and established clergy was a negative act. The positive policy of the Commonwealth consisted in building up in the vacuum thus created a constructive 'reformation of law and clergy' on the English model. The reform of the law was to take place in two stages. First, there was to be a restoration of law and order, which had collapsed at the time of Dunbar, and which every Scottish county petitioned the conqueror to restore. That was done, and done effectively. But the Commonwealth intended to go further than that. It intended to assimilate the law of Scotland to that of England and thereby not only to make the union complete, but also to effect in Scotland that same decentralisation of justice and simplification of law which was one of the most constant demands of the English country party and one of the greatest ambitions of Cromwell himself. In the earliest instructions given to the English commissioners sent to Scotland at the end of 1651, this aim is made clear. In order that the Scottish people may have right and justice duly administered to them, the commissioners were told to see the civil law of England put into execution 'as near as the constitution and use of the people there and the present affairs will permit'. For this purpose the commissioners could set up courts at will and appoint as law-officers both Englishmen and Scots.[2]

[1] The Parliament's *Declaration* is printed in Terry, *op. cit.*, p. xxi; the commentary of the commissioners, *ibid.*, p. xxvi.

[2] Instructions to Commissioners, 4 December 1651 in Firth, *Scotland and the Protectorate*, p. 395. Cf. the declaration of the Commissioners for regulating the universities, 1652, in which they state 'that they intend, God

Within a few months, the English Council of State itself set up, to replace the old, hated Scottish Court of Session, a mixed board of four English and three Scottish 'commissioners for the administration of justice'. This was the board on which Lockhart, Hope, and Simpson—'our three complying gentlemen', as Baillie called them—took their seats. Thereafter the particular reforms began. Legal fees, as in England, were regulated. The use of Latin in legal documents, as in England, was abolished. Legal language and procedure, as in England, was made easier. These were all measures of simplification. Decentralisation was represented by the restoration, by ordinance, of local courts-baron to try petty cases (but with provision, here too, against heritable jurisdictions), and by the sending of English justices on circuit through the country; also by the establishment, in 1655, of justices of the peace on the English model. These had been instituted before, by James VI, but it was only under the Protectorate, with the abolition of 'the regal power of their lairds of manors', that they began to 'take some life'. Finally, there were significant changes in the substance of the law. The severity of the law against debtors was mitigated, as in England. Church censures were frustrated. The burning of witches, that favourite sport of the Scotch clergy and judges, was interrupted. The Scottish diarists, who record with such lubricious relish the constant public executions for buggery, bestiality, and sorcery, are forced sadly to admit that the English not only pulled down the stools of repentance in the churches but also gave to supposed witches 'liberty to go home again upon caution'. They were, as Baillie complained, 'too sparing' in such matters; they even made inconvenient inquiries into the tortures which had made the poor women confess.[1]

---

willing, in convenient time, to alter and abolish all such laws . . . as shall be found inconsistent with the government of the Commonwealth of England'. (Firth, *Scotland and the Commonwealth*, p. 44.)

[1] For particular law reforms see Terry, *op. cit.*, p. 176; Firth, *Scotland and the Commonwealth*, pp. 276-85, *Scotland and the Protectorate*, p. xxx; Nicoll, *Diary*, pp. 93, 96; Lamont, *Diary*, p. 42; and, in general, Aeneas Mackay, *Memoir of Sir James Dalrymple, Viscount Stair* (Edin. 1873). For justices in

It was at the end of 1655 that the aims of the administration of justice in Cromwellian Scotland were most fully formulated. We can see them in the Protector's instructions to his Council in Edinburgh, and in that Council's instructions to the new J.P.s. We can also see them in the reports which the President of the Council sent home. Among instructions for raising men for his West India expedition, and securing the country, Cromwell insisted that justice be restored and extended throughout Scotland, that vagabondage be controlled, that the endowment of hospitals be investigated and their rents strictly applied, and that every parish maintain its poor, so that none go begging. The instructions to the J.P.s defined these functions in detail, and the President of the Council himself set an example by regulating Heriot's Hospital in Edinburgh, reducing the cost by £600 p.a., and putting it 'in as good a way for the end it was erected as ever'. This policy is of a piece with the policy applied in England in the same months by the major-generals: it shows that Cromwell sought to enforce the same social policy in both countries—that the English Revolution was, in his eyes, indivisible. That the policy was successful is shown by the testimony even of Presbyterians, lawyers, and patriots from John Nicoll to Sir Walter Scott.[1]

There remained the reformation of the clergy. Here, far more than in England, the problem was to find, encourage, and train liberal ministers. The existing ministers were divided by politics into 'Remonstrants' or 'Protesters' on one hand – men who refused any compromise with the Stuarts—and 'General Resolutioners' on the other, who (with the General Assembly, while it lasted) were prepared to believe that Charles II could be a 'covenanted king'. But whatever their

eyre see Nicoll, *op. cit.*, pp. 102-5; Lamont, *op. cit.*, p. 47. For J.P.s see Terry, *op. cit.*, pp. 180-1; Firth, *Scotland and the Protectorate*, pp. xxxviii, 98, 308-16, 403-5; *Thurloe State Papers*, iv, 741. For stools of repentance see Lamont, *op. cit.*, p. 44; for witches, Baillie, *Letters*, iii, 436; Lamont, *op. cit.*, pp. 44, 47; Firth, *Scotland and the Commonwealth*, p. 368.

[1] *Thurloe State Papers*, iv, 127, 129, 525; Firth, *Scotland and the Protectorate*, p. 483; Nicoll, *op. cit.*, p. 104. Scott's observations ('Cromwell certainly did much to civilise Scotland . . .' etc.) are in his notes to Dryden's Heroic Stanzas.

differences, the majority of both parties were rigid and intolerant Presbyterians, and the four universities of Scotland, where
they were trained, were crusted cells of orthodoxy. The English
Commonwealth was determined not only to 'laicise' the established Church, but also, as in England, to 'propagate the
Gospel' in undeveloped areas. For both purposes it needed to
capture control of the universities; and so, from the beginning,
it instructed its commissioners not only to promote preaching
and secure maintenance for sound ministers, but also 'to visit
and reform the several universities, colleges, and schools of
learning in Scotland', to alter, abolish and replace statutes, and
to purge and appoint professors. These powers, confirmed
afterwards to the Council of State in Scotland, opened the way
to a fierce struggle. It began in Glasgow, the very citadel of the
National Covenant, where (happily for us) the voluble Robert
Baillie was virulently recording the changes which he vainly
resisted.[1]

The key figure in the struggle for Glasgow was Patrick
Gillespie, the original leader of the Remonstrants, and now the
leader of that minority among the Remonstrants whose hatred
and distrust of the Stuarts drove them, in spite of their doc-
trinal purism, to welcome the English conquest. In both
capacities, both as a Remonstrant and as an Anglophil, Gillespie
was hated by Baillie and the other 'Resolutioners' in Glasgow.
Already, in the spring of 1651, Baillie and his party saw the
danger ahead. There were vacant places to be filled, and it was
essential to fill them with sound 'Resolutioners'. So they
appealed to the king and Scottish Parliament to send visitors
who would support them in making the appointments. But
events moved too quickly. Within a few months king and
Parliament would be scattered, the new English authorities
would intervene, and Baillie could only wring his hands and
wail at the successful 'impudence' of Gillespie who, thanks to
this backing and the support of the local 'Remonstrants', in

[1] Instructions to Commissioners, 1651, Firth, *Scotland and the Protectorate*,
p. 393; Declaration by the Commissioners 4 June 1652, Firth, *Scotland and
the Commonwealth*, pp. 44-5.

defiance of the rights of electors, soon got himself nominated principal of the university 'for the poisoning of our
seminary'.

Once in power Gillespie never ceased to outrage his rivals.
He introduced other professors—'young men', Baillie protested, of no learning or character, teachers of recondite
heresies and blasphemous opinions; he interfered in other universities; he exerted the patronage of the university to stuff
schismatic clergy into every position; he manufactured straw
votes to consolidate his power; and, worst of all, he was so
favoured by the English that he could never be defeated. In
vain the General Assembly had deposed him: the General
Assembly it was which perished. In vain the town council of
Glasgow denounced him for neglect of duty and misappropria-
tion of funds: his 'good friend' Cromwell's other great ally in
Scotland, Sir John Swinton, having shuffled off his own excommunication ('a strange enormity'), soon silenced such
complaints. In the end Gillespie, by means of 'his own silly
creatures', got Cromwell's English secretary of state, John
Thurloe, made chancellor of the university and himself vice-
chancellor—and then passed his office on to a creature 'to be
sure of a new vote'. And in any crisis, he would sweep off to
London, with outward pomp, live there in 'a high, vain and
sumptuous manner', beyond any bishop in Scotland, walk
ostentatiously with Major-General Lambert, preach publicly
before the Protector in an elegant velvet cassock, be closeted
with him in Whitehall, and then return to Edinburgh in
triumph, in a coach followed by twenty-five horsemen, with
increased powers, an enlarged salary, and a huge bill for
expenses to be met by the University of Glasgow.

The first of Gillespie's ominous visits to London took place
in 1653 and lasted eleven months. When he returned, he brought
with him a formidable document, which once again showed
the unity of policy in the two countries. It was an ordinance
'for the better support of the universities of Scotland and
encouragement of public preachers there'; and it set up, among
other things, a body of commissioners comparable with the

English 'triers' or 'approvers', whose agreement was necessary before any minister could be presented to any living, and who had power to provide 'out of the treasury of vacant stipends, or otherwise, as they shall think fit, a competent maintenance for such ministers who have gathered congregations in Scotland'. These commissioners, of course, had been nominated by, and included, Gillespie and his friends; and the ordinance, at which the established clergy were 'very much displeased', was known as 'Mr. Gillespie's charter'.[1]

Gillespie did not go alone to London. Cromwell invited with him five other clergymen; and although three of them refused to go (they belonged to the majority who would have no truck with the 'sectaries'), two did. One of these two was John Menzies, professor of Divinity at Marischal College, Aberdeen, whose excommunication by the Aberdeen synod had been stopped by the English garrison.[2] Through him, and through John Row, the intruded Independent principal of King's College, Cromwell's influence penetrated Aberdeen. There, according to Baillie, 'all in both colleges'—with the exception of the formidable Andrew Cant—'have avowedly gone over to Independency and Separatism'; and from 'Aberdeen's nest', 'the apostates of Aberdeen', Gillespie fetched new professors and new votes to increase his power in Glasgow. At the same time Edinburgh was also won over. While Gillespie was being imposed on Glasgow, the town council of Edinburgh was instructed to 'call', as principal of their university, a completely anglicised Scotsman who, suspiciously enough, had just returned from a visit to London, Robert Leighton. Like the Glasgow professors, the Edinburgh ministers tried to dissent. They said that 'they were not satisfied with the manner of the call'. They dissented in vain: Leighton was appointed. Only St. Andrews, the university of Andrew Melville, held

---

[1] The ordinance is given in Nicoll, *Diary*, pp. 164-7 and thence in Firth and Rait, *Acts and Ordinances of the Interregnum*, iii, pp. cxii-cxiv.

[2] The three who refused were the Remonstrants Robert Blair, and James Guthrie, and the leader of the Resolutioners, Robert Douglas. (See Firth, *Scotland and the Protectorate*, p. 102). The one who accompanied Gillespie and Menzies was the Remonstrant John Livingstone.

out; but, as Baillie wrote to a friend there, 'see to your colleges as you may: they are fully masters of Glasgow, Aberdeen, and almost of Edinburgh'.[1]

It is easy, reading Baillie's letters, to see the struggle for the Scottish universities as merely an attempt to intrude English puppets, 'Protesters' against 'Resolutioners' in the bitter struggles of the Kirk. But when we look below the surface, we see a far more deliberate policy. The Cromwellian intruders were not mere political creatures. They were not orthodox 'Protesters'—they were very different, for instance, from John Guthrie or Sir Archibald Johnston of Wariston. They were men who had come to believe that the Church of Scotland must admit the laity, not merely into the formal structure of the Church, as 'ruling elders', more clerical than the clergy,[2] but as an independent influence. To men like Baillie, such an idea was anathema. To them the structure of the Church was sacred, and to preserve it the laity must be firmly kept in place. They must not become like the English laity, 'very fickle and hard to be keeped by their ministers'. Baillie was a great inquisitor. He would have burned books if he could—'I am one of those', he wrote, 'who would gladly consent to the burning of many thousand volumes of unprofitable writers'; and we know what kind of books he would have burned: the 'insolent absurdity' of John Selden, the great advocate of lay

---

[1] For the capture of Aberdeen and Edinburgh see J. Kerr, *Scottish Education* (1910), pp. 122, 134; Sir Alexander Grant, *The Story of Edinburgh University in its first 300 years* (London, 1884); Baillie, *op. cit.*, iii, 244, 326-7.

[2] The idea that ruling elders represented the laity was indignantly repudiated by the Scotch Kirk. James Guthrie, in his *Treatise of Ruling Elders and Deacons* (published in 1699), refers contemptuously to those 'who either out of ignorance or disdain do call them *lay elders*, as if they were a part of the people only'; and cf. George Gillespie, *An Assertion of the Government of the Church of Scotland* ... (Edinburgh, 1641). Ruling elders, all insisted, were *jure divino* and part of the clerical structure. For this reason the whole institution was rejected by the English laity, who scoffed at 'that sacred beast, the ruling elder'. As a nineteenth century authority wrote: 'the term *lay elder* is itself a term of scorn. . . . There is no such office. The office of elder is an ecclesiastical one. He who holds it ceases to be a layman' (J. G. Lorimer, *The Eldership of the Church of Scotland* (Glasgow, 1841), p. 44).

sense in religion, the 'tridentine popery' of Grotius, and the trash of that 'very ignorant atheist', that 'fatuous heretic', Descartes. To him the intellectual fare of his flock must be as uniform, as monotonous, and as unpalatable as their unvarying daily diet of salt-beef and oatmeal. But the new Cromwellian churchmen were very different. Robert Leighton was a mystic who detested religious formalism, believed in toleration, and was accused of the usual heresies in consequence. He had already revolted against the intolerance of the church courts when he accepted the rule of Edinburgh University. Behind Baillie's bitter phrases we can see that the 'ignorant young men' whom Gillespie brought to Glasgow were similarly impatient of the old intolerance and formalism. Such, for instance, was Andrew Gray, fetched from St. Andrews, who disgusted Baillie by his 'new guise of preaching, which Mr. Hew Binning and Mr. Robert Leighton began'. Instead of 'exponing and dividing a text', and 'raising doctrines and uses', this young man 'runs out in a discourse on some common head, in a high, romancing, unscriptural style, tickling the ear for the present, and moving the affections in some, but leaving . . . little or nought to the memory and understanding'. The formidable list of heresies of which Baillie accused Richard Robertson, another of Gillespie's supporters in Glasgow, points the same way.[1]

Having installed such men in positions of authority, and empowered them to 'plant and dis-plant' ministers and teachers, Cromwell strengthened them in material ways. By 'Gillespie's charter' he granted to the Universities of Glasgow and Aberdeen a number of church lands from the dissolved Scottish bishoprics (granted but not conveyed by Charles I in 1641), and added 200 marks sterling *p.a.* from the local customs for the support of students in theology and philosophy. When the 'charter' was published in Scotland, Robert Leighton was sorry

---

[1] For Leighton see esp. W. L. Mathieson, *Politics & Religion*, ii, 218 *seq.* For Andrew Gray (whose sermons in 'the new guise', like those of Leighton and Binning, continued to be printed), and Richard Robertson see Baillie, *op. cit.*, iii, 223-4, 239-40, 258.

that he too had not been in London, with Gillespie and Menzies; so he hurried to repair the omission. Cromwell agreed to grant a like bounty to Edinburgh, and ordered the clause to be drawn; but afterwards, as Leighton reminded him, 'you did not think the time fitting for its insertion, as Parliament was sitting' —that tiresome English Parliament which always blocked the patriarchal administration of the Protector. Nevertheless, Leighton persevered, and in 1657, by another personal visit, obtained 'after Mr. Gillespie's example, some £200 sterling to the college out of some Church-lands; which in my mind', adds Baillie sourly, 'will be as soon obtained as the flim-flams of Mr. Gillespie's gifts'.[1]

Apart from endowments Cromwell made gifts to Glasgow University for its building programme. In 1633 Charles I had promised, but not paid, £200. Cromwell paid it.[2] Monck and the English officers in the North also subscribed to the building funds of Aberdeen. With this support, the new principals of both universities set to work. John Row at Aberdeen built 'Cromwell's Tower'; at Glasgow even Baillie had to admire the 'gallant buildings' which the hated principal raised 'as good as alone' with 'very great care, industry and dexterity'— though of course he grumbled at the daily din of masons, wrights, carters, and smiths, questioned Gillespie's 'strange ways of getting money for it', and afterwards worked himself into tantrums at the 'vanity and prodigality' of those 'vain-glorious buildings'. At Edinburgh, Cromwell went further: in 1656 he issued a patent setting up a College of Physicians with wide powers: a real contribution to lay studies. Like so many of Cromwell's reforms, it had abortive precedents: James VI and Charles I had projected such a college, but done nothing practical; and like all Cromwell's constructive work, it foundered at his death; but like Durham University and the

---

[1] Firth and Rait, iii, p. cxii; *Thurloe State Papers*, iv, 566. Leighton's application is printed in *Calendar of State Papers Dom.*, *1657–58*, p. 77; for its success see Baillie, *op. cit.*, iii, 366.

[2] Baillie afterwards disingenuously concealed this fact, partly no doubt in order not to give credit to the usurper, and sought to get the money paid over again, doubled, and with interest, by Charles II (*Letters*, iii, 413, etc.).

Royal Society, the Edinburgh Medical School owes something to the attempts of Oliver Cromwell.[1]

The Cromwellian reform of the universities was incidentally a reform of education, but it was primarily a means of evangelising the country. Once the basis had been established, the work went ahead. Loud and many were the complaints of Baillie as he watched the working out of 'Gillespie's charter'. Gillespie, he complained, had seized the purse; no minister could get any stipend unless he satisfied the new Independent triers: when a handful of Remonstrants or Independents called a man 'he gets a kirk and a stipend; but whom the Presbytery and well near the whole congregation calls and admits, he must preach in the fields, or in a barn, without stipend. So a sectary is planted in Kilbride, another in Leinzie' . . .[2].

But it was not only in Kilbride and Leinzie that the Cromwellian government hoped to 'plant' ministers. Ultimately the wild Highlands, beyond the settled organisation of the Kirk, must be evangelised. The need was there. The whole Highlands and Islands, the government was told, 'are all atheists, but their inclination is to popery'. From Orkney and Shetland came complaints of vacant livings and school-endowments swallowed up by the gentry. The power of the Kirk, so formidable and so exclusive in the Lowlands, did not reach to those waste lands. 'I have not yet met with any grandees of the Presbytery', a royalist agent wrote from Thurso; 'they keep in the warmer and fatter pastures, sending out their colonies of the younger fry to the leaner and more remote quarters'. But the opportunity was there too. 'A very precious people who seek the face of God' was reported from Sutherland and 'divers other parts beyond Inverness', and another evangelist wrote that some of the Highlanders, though often 'as brutish as heathens', listened to the new gospel 'with great attention and groanings, and seeming affection for it'. 'To get the Highlands planted with ministers', one of the English commissioners declared, was 'the only way to bring them to civility'. At

---

[1] Sir Alexander Grant, op. cit., i, 221-2.
[2] Baillie, op. cit., p. 244, cf. 248.

present, however, the Highlands were hardly attainable: the source of disorderly royalist risings, they were only held in awe by Cromwell's forts; and as in Wales, it was unorthodox missionaries who accepted the challenge. In 1657 George Fox crossed into Scotland, and saw the same opportunities which the 'Anabaptist' preachers had previously seen in Wales: 'as soon as ever my horse set his foot on Scottish ground, the infinite sparks of life sparkled about me, and . . . I saw the seed of the seedsman Christ'.[1]

Destruction of 'feudal' power and introduction of English law, reformed and simplified as in England; vigorous local administration of poor law and poor relief; destruction of clerical tyranny and liberalisation of the established Church by the infusion of lay influence in and alongside it; reform of education, endowment of universities, competent maintenance for the new, liberal ministers, and evangelisation of the neglected parts of the country—such was the puritan ideal for the Scotland which had been 'incorporated' in the new Commonwealth. But how was such a programme to be applied? Where, in Scotland, was a party to be found which would carry through such a work? The Scots had failed to carry out their social revolution in England because, in spite of solemn covenants and identical names, there was, in the social structure of England, no basis for a 'presbyterian' party in their sense of the word. Would the English, having conquered Scotland, find in that very different society, not merely individuals like Lockhart, Swinton, or Gillespie, but a party prepared to realise their ideal? By definition it must be an anti-aristocratic, anti-clerical party, and its basis should be found, as in England, in the independent laity, and particularly among their leaders, the educated gentry.

At first it seemed possible. The Scottish gentry might have

---

[1] *Thurloe State Papers*, iv, 401, 646; Terry, *op. cit.*, p. 124; Firth, *Scotland and the Protectorate*, p. 122; *Scotland and the Commonwealth*, pp. 31, 363-4; Swarthmore MSS., ii, 121, quoted by G. B. Burnet, *The History of Quakerism in Scotland, 1650-1850* (1952), p. 35. Cf. George Fox, *Journal* (Everyman), p. 163.

disappointed Charles I by supporting the Covenant, but they had soon resented the tyranny of the Church. In 1644 it was among the mutinous laity that Montrose, that former Covenanter who cared not for presbyters and present royalist who cared not for bishops, had found his followers. In 1648 it was the laity in the Scottish Parliament who had insisted, against the General Assembly, on fulfilling the 'Engagement' and going to the rescue of an uncovenanted king. In both those adventures they had failed. After Preston, as after Philiphaugh, the clerical tyranny had been sharpened; but so had the resentment of the laity; and when the Zealots were finally crushed at Dunbar, there were some Scotsmen who were disillusioned and others who had long sighed for release.

Foremost among those who had sighed for release were the old royalists; and indeed, once their own hopes were dashed at Worcester, they were the first to accept, even to welcome, English rule. It was 'those gentlemen whom they call malignants' who, in 1651, were found to be 'most free to serve the English interest', 'I find the old royalists generally throughout the country tendering their *devoir*', wrote an English agent in 1652, and added that the 'fiery kirkists cannot digest a thought of the loss of their infinite power and prerogative'. Already, before the Union was settled, the royalists were said to have done 'more real and visible services than the whole generation of Presbyterians' would ever do. Cromwell, with his eagerness to restore the old alliance of 1640, welcomed this ex-royalist support, which he found from some of the most distinguished of Scottish laymen. Apart from Sir William Lockhart, he drew towards him Sir Thomas Urquhart, the translator of Rabelais; Sir John Scot of Scotstarvet, the publisher (with Cromwell's aid) of the first maps of Scotland; and Sir Alexander Irvine of Drum, who was delighted to be able to defy the local presbytery, and the dreadful Andrew Cant himself, by appealing to the English commander. In vain the presbytery thundered excommunications; in vain it declared that any appeal from spiritual to secular tribunals was 'Erastianism', 'contrary to our Covenant and liberties of this Kirk'. 'I altogether decline their

9

judicature', declared the unabashed knight, 'as not being established by the Commonwealth of England', and having secured
the support of General Monck against 'the fury of a superstitious clergy', he wrote genially to his persecutors begging
them not to trouble him with any 'more such papers, that are
but undigested rhapsodies of confused nonsense'. Both Irvine
and Urquhart explicitly declared—indeed, it was one of the
charges against Irvine—what so many Englishmen had already
shown, that there was more natural sympathy between a
royalist and an Independent than between either and a Scotch
presbyter.[1]

Royalist support might be welcome to Cromwell, in Scotland as in England; but it could hardly be the basis of republican
policy. For that he looked elsewhere, and since the presbyterian laity were inarticulate, he had to look to the parties in
the Kirk. There the majority party, the party of the 'General
Resolutioners', was hostile on all counts: both in religion, since
it was the party of the General Assembly which Cromwell
dissolved, and in politics, since it was the party of Charles II,
whom he had beaten. Their rivals, the 'Remonstrants', might
be the extremists of the Kirk, but their primitive presbyterian
purity was at least counterbalanced by their hatred of Charles
II. It was the Remonstrants, in their previous incarnation as the
whiggamore Zealots, whom Cromwell had, in effect, put into
power after the defeat of the Engagers in 1648, and it was in
their broken ranks, after Dunbar, that he discovered his first
converts, including Gillespie, Menzies, and their companion
in London, John Livingstone. Unfortunately, these converted
Remonstrants were a minority of a minority; the majority of
their party listened to the last-ditch, anti-Stuart, anti-Inde-
pendent fanaticism of Johnston of Wariston and the hysterical
trumpet-blasts of William Guthrie: men whom the Cromwellian rulers of Scotland regarded as 'Fifth-Monarchy Pres-

[1] For royalist support of English rule see Terry, *op. cit.*, p. 7; Firth,
Scotland and the Commonwealth, pp. xxvi, 29-30, 339, 348-50. For Cromwell's help to Scot of Scotstarvet see *Calendar of State Papers Dom., 1654*,
p. 158; Firth, *Scotland and the Protectorate*, p. 45.

byterians', the irreconcilable foes of all government. It soon became clear that a wider basis must be found if Cromwell's policy in Scotland was to rest on a Scottish party.

Moreover, it also became clear that Cromwell's personal allies in Scotland, estimable though they might be in themselves, were not a reliable bloc. In the summer of 1653 Lockhart, Swinton, Hope, and Jaffray had all come south to sit in the Barebones Parliament. The Barebones Parliament did not concern itself much with Scottish affairs; but the Scottish members played a decisive part in the crisis which caused its dissolution. In the last division of that Parliament, when the radicals, to Cromwell's indignation, obtained a majority of two votes for the abolition of tithes, it was noted that 'the English in this vote were equal, and the Scots did cast it'. For although Lockhart voted with the 'conservatives', Hope, Swinton, and Jaffray all voted with the 'radicals'. What their motives were, whether English or Scottish, we do not know; but Cromwell evidently distinguished between Swinton and Jaffray, whom he continued to trust, and Hope whom, like the radical leaders, he never forgave. Next year Hope was dropped from the commission for the administration of justice and never again employed. The reason afterwards given was that he 'had not so well conducted himself to His Highness at the dissolution of the Little Parliament' and his post was offered to Jaffray (who refused). In future, Cromwell did not rely much on parliaments: he relied on administrators. It became the task of his President of the Council in Scotland to create there a party through which the Protector could realise his ideals: a party which must rest on a wider basis than a few royalists who used the Republic against the Kirk, the minority of a radical minority within the Kirk, and a few officials who went dangerously wrong in Parliament.[1]

[1] See Jaffray, *Diary*, pp. 51-2; Hope, *Diary 1646-54*, pp. 163-7. *Thurloe State Papers*, iv, 268-9; Firth, *Scotland and the Protectorate*, pp. 214, 385. Since Swinton and Jaffray both afterwards became Quakers, it is probable that the opposition of both was on religious grounds and respected by Cromwell as such. But the incident reveals, once again, Cromwell's inability to create a party in Parliament. (Cf. my essay 'Oliver Cromwell and his Parliaments',

Fortunately, by 1655, the President was fit for the task. In that year Cromwell sent to Edinburgh his ablest political adviser, another ex-royalist, the man who would nearly save the English revolution by making the Protector king: Lord Broghil. In his new post, Broghil used all his political skill and personal charm to make the Cromwellian settlement work. Beginning on the narrow basis of Gillespie and his friends, he sought to win over to them the most reasonable of the Resolutioners. But he soon gave this up as 'hopeless'. The spirit of party, he wrote, dominated the clergy and any sign of reconciliation between 'the honestest sort of public resolutioners and remonstrators' only caused such men to be disowned by their followers, who were determined to 'have that thread of distinction run through all their work'. Finally, he decided to shift his basis altogether. Since it was impossible to gain either of the two parties as a whole, he proposed to woo the Resolutioners, who at least were the larger and more united party, and then, having purged those of them whose laxity might be 'scandalous to conscientious Christians', to join to them 'Mr. Gillespie, Mr. Livingstone and their friends'. Thus a party would be gained of 'the most sober, most honest and most godly of this nation'; the Stuarts would lose the support of the Scotch ministers, 'whose power over the people has been such that hardly has ever anything been done without them, and all that has been done has been with or by them'; and Scotland might enjoy the same kind of moderate Presbyterianism as England might have accepted in 1647 and might still accept in 1657. For when the Scots had failed to unite the two countries under a rigid clericalism, and the English had failed to unite them under a godly Independency, might not a 'lame erastian Presbytery', in the end, prove to be the form which would divide them least?[1]

in *Essays Presented to Sir Lewis Namier*, 1954.) Since the Scottish members were generally regarded as mere government dummies, it is particularly ironical that, in this instance, they should have caused a significant government defeat.

[1] For Broghil's policy see *Thurloe State Papers*, v, 127, 222, 268, 460, 479, 557, 597, 700.

Broghil obtained Cromwell's sanction; he wooed the Resolutioners; he ended Gillespie's monopoly over appointments by securing an amendment to his 'charter': from now on, it was agreed, any minister could be appointed, and enjoy his stipend, if he undertook to live peaceably under the present government. Broghil even persuaded the ministers, by private treaty with the leading Resolutioners—'by his courtesies more than his threats', as Baillie wrote—to cease praying publicly for Charles II. Before long, he forecast, the Stuarts would be forgotten; every minister in Scotland would have obliged himself, 'under his own hand, freely', to own the government, 'and being engaged themselves, they will in interest, if for nothing else, engage the people'. On that Erastian basis the social revolution could go forward. 'If we manage these things well', Broghil wrote, 'the two parties in Scotland, *viz*. Remonstrants and Public Resolutioners, shall both court us, as too long we have courted them'. Indeed, the Remonstrants, in alarm, sent emissaries up to London to lobby the Protector; but their rivals had an emissary too, who appeared with a letter of personal recommendation from Broghil, and was briefed, as Baillie wrote, 'to mar the Protesters' designs and further ours'. This emissary was Baillie's friend—his candidate for the principalship of Glasgow University if Gillespie should die—'that very worthy, pious, wise and diligent young man, Mr. Sharp'.[1]

If ever there was a chance of saving the revolution, in Scotland as in England, Broghil was the man who might have saved it. A 'lame, erastian Presbytery' in both countries, with a large measure of toleration, under a reconstructed parliamentary monarchy of the house of Cromwell—such, it seems, was his ideal. And he was hastening towards it. On going to Scotland, he had stipulated that he should not stay there more than a year. In that year he secured notable results. 'If men of my Lord Broghil's parts and temper be long among us', wrote Baillie, 'they will make the present government more beloved

[1] *Thurloe State Papers*, v, 301, 323, 655; Baillie, *op. cit.*, iii, 321, 344, 352, 356-7.

than some men wish.' Then Broghil passed over to Ireland and
organised his patronage there so well that at the next Parliament he had a solid Anglo-Irish party ready to support his
plans for Cromwell's kingship. And yet, as we know, all
foundered. Shortness of time and the opposition of the Army
frustrated him in England. In Scotland there was also another
fatal flaw. Just as the Scottish party in England, which seemed
so strong in 1646, was found in fact to have no basis, so the
English party in Scotland, which he nursed into being in 1656,
lacked real solidity. In spite of everything, the only solid
organisation in Scotland remained that of the Kirk: the Kirk
which, widely hated though it was, nevertheless, in the universal
defeat, remained the one re-uniting focus of national feeling.[1]

We can see this at many levels. In the Church half the Scottish
triers refused to act. They declared that Gillespie's charter was
an encroachment by the state on the jurisdiction of the church
courts, and ministers had to be intruded by the English soldiers.
In the law there was the same reluctance. The Scottish commissioners resisted the legal reforms and the Council, who at
first had wanted Scotch judges, since they alone understood
their system, ended by recommending English judges, who
alone were reliable. Scottish justices of the peace also refused
office as 'a manifest encroachment on the liberties of the Kirk',
contrary to the Solemn League and Covenant, and incom-
patible with Malachi ii. 10. On the other hand the Kirk parties
grew confident. Broghil thought that he was using the Resolutioners to laicise Scotland, but the Resolutioners assumed that,
through this favour, they would reassert the old clericalism in
England. As usual, Baillie is the perfect barometer. As soon as
Broghil turned from the Remonstrants to the Resolutioners,
Baillie was back at his old trade, lecturing his English brethren
and rebuking them for the timidity of their ambitions. Why,
he asked, had they only 'a show of a Presbytery and Synod?'
'Why want you a General Assembly? Why have ye no power
at all to execute ecclesiastic jurisdiction?' He was not going to

[1] For evidence of the continuing hatred of the Kirk in the late 1650s see
Baillie, *op. cit.*, iii, 448; *Wariston's Diary*, iii, 27, 180-1.

be content with a 'lame, erastian Presbytery', even in England, let alone in Scotland. It was with some reason that Monck, unlike Broghil, continued to believe—until he too was disillusioned—that, for Cromwell's purposes, the Remonstrants were 'better to be trusted than . . . the General Resolution men'.[1]

So Broghil's policy quickly crumbled against the social facts of Scottish life. Cromwellian policy depended on the existence of a self-conscious, independent laity with gentry leadership. It was this class which had broken the Scottish attempt to impose Presbyterianism on England; it was the absence of such a class that rendered futile the English attempt to laicise Scotland. For where is the Scottish laity, the equivalent of that vocal, powerful estate of the realm which, in England, was transforming politics, religion, education? We read the private diaries which should reveal it, and what do we find? Here is Sir Thomas Hope of Craighall, that great lawyer, constantly making vows to the Lord and recording his superstitious dreams. Here is Sir Archibald Johnston of Wariston exuding page after page of rhapsodical bigotry. Here is Alexander Brodie of Brodie recording the remarkable providences of the Lord towards him, lamenting, occasionally, his own sins, such as impure thoughts in church and a 'sinful affection' (very rare in Scotland) for planting trees, and, more regularly, the sins of others, the 'gross inbreaking of idolatry, blasphemy, superstition, heresy and all manner of wickedness', denouncing Quakers and Jews, transcribing the scandalous activities of witches, and deploring 'the corrupt and dangerous principle of toleration and liberty'. Here is Andrew Hay of Craignethan, regularly recording, along with the weather, his freedom (or not) from temptation, calculating the days to the last Trump, nosing out witches, prying into cases of fornication, and reading, with unctuous relish, the dismal ends of heretics, whoremongers, apostates, atheists, witches, and Quakers.[2] Here are

---

[1] Firth *Scotland and the Protectorate*, pp. 211, 345; *Thurloe State Papers*, iv, 324, 480; Baillie, *Letters*, iii, 303.

[2] See, for instance, his record of 'a tolerable day', 22 January 1660.

John Lamont of Newton, gloating over the fate of Montrose and a long list of 'witches, adulterers, buggers, incestuous persons and such as had lain with beasts', and John Nicoll who, to an equal curiosity and zeal in these interesting matters, and a particular hatred of Lockhart, Swinton, and Gillespie, adds a devout conviction that a great storm in the neighbourhood was caused by the wrath of God at a new tax of a halfpenny per pint of beer in Edinburgh.[1]

All these were educated men. They read Greek, Hebrew, Latin, Italian; some of them had studied abroad; but they had no independent lay attitude, and reading their diaries we see why neither the ruling elders nor the Parliament of Scotland had any laicising influence on the Church. Nor were the Scottish merchants any better than the gentry. Monck regarded the burghs as 'generally the most faithful people to us of any people in this nation'. They were, he said, 'the very first that owned us and have ever since lived peaceably under us, and whose interest is most agreeable to ours, by reason of their trade and traffic'. For that reason he urged that their taxes should be kept down and their privileges kept up. But there is a difference between peaceable life and positive support, and it is clear that if the burghs gave the English no trouble, being 'impoverished through want of trade and the late troubles', they equally gave it no constructive help. In fact, Monck's defence of the burghs was elicited by Cromwell's proposal to interfere with their liberties in order to gain some support by putting the 'Remonstrant' minority in power in Glasgow— clear evidence that the 'Resolutioners' who actually represented them, and who persecuted Principal Gillespie, were unsatisfactory. Scottish trade was too slight and static to sustain a dynamic policy, and the royal burghs which controlled it were timid oligarchies. A glance at the eight or nine members whom they returned to Cromwell's Parliaments sufficiently

---

[1] See *The Diary of Sir Thomas Hope of Craighall* (Edinburgh, Bannatyne Club, 1843); *The Diary of Archibald Johnston of Wariston* (Scot. Hist. Soc., Edinburgh, 1911, 1919, 1940); *The Diary of Andrew Hay of Craignethan, 1659–60* (*ibid.*, 1901). The other diaries have already been cited.

shows their lack of independence. Most of them are English officers or officials: the burghs would accept anyone who would pay his own expenses. In 1656 only one of the burgh members was a known Scottish merchant, Sir Alexander Wedderburn of Dundee; and he had been a royalist.[1]

But perhaps the most striking evidence of the contrast between the social claims of England and Scotland is provided by the petitions of their counties. All through the civil war the English counties sent up petitions to Parliament. Sometimes these petitions were organised by gentry in grand juries or other meetings, sometimes by radical propagandists; but whatever particular interest may colour them, they represented local demands, and their positive demands were, in one form or another, for that decentralisation and laicisation summarised as 'reformation of law and clergy'. In Scotland there was no such initiative in petitioning;[2] but in 1652, when the English government invited the shires and burghs to assent to the proposed Union and express their particular desires, what was the result?[3] Meetings dominated by 'fiery kirkists' protested against the 'vast and boundless toleration' of all sorts of errors and heresies whose extirpation was a duty imposed by the Solemn League and Covenant; they repudiated the 'Erastian' subjection of the Church to the magistrate; then, after the natural demands for freedom from cess or confiscation, reduction of the army of occupation and release of prisoners of war, a few positive demands were made: 'that those who enjoy heritable privileges . . . may be protected and established in them'; 'that gentlemen's houses be exempted from quartering and that their gardens, parks or orchards and other policies may be protected from destruction'; and, above all, 'that the people of this land may be governed by our own law, though

---

[1] For Monck's support of the burghs see Firth, *Scotland and the Protectorate*, p. 195; *Thurloe State Papers*, vi, 529. For the list of burgh M.P.s see Terry, *op. cit.*, pp. lvi-lvii, lxiii-lxiv. For the conditions of their appointment see *Thurloe State Papers*, vii, 555, 616-17, etc.

[2] Cf. *Thurloe State Papers*, vii, 593.

[3] All the replies of the counties and burghs are printed in Terry, *op. cit.*

the power of administration be derived from the parliament of the Commonwealth of England'. From the outer fringes of the country, where the Kirk was not yet firmly planted, a faint voice might seem to welcome the Union for the social change it might chance to bring[1]; from the lower classes in the cities an even fainter voice might have been enlisted[2]; but from the men of substance in settled, historic Scotland the answer was firm: no reformation of law or clergy.

So the necessary basis for Cromwell's policy in Scotland was lacking. As an independent estate the laity simply did not exist. In that poor and backward country, the organised Calvinist church was the only institution which could rise, and raise others, out of ignorance and squalor. As such, it claimed a monopoly of salvation. It also claimed the right to crush down all those deviationists who, by individual effort or foreign example, sought to rise or to raise men higher. And in that society, aided by the fact of defeat and the destruction of national organs, it made good its claim. Monck himself, in a moment of despair, recognised its success when he declared, in 1657, that the only hope of Scottish support was in a drastic reduction of taxes, 'and then, in case they be not quiet, I think it were just reason to plant it with English'—in other words, to treat it like Ireland where also, in the ruin of all other organs, the Church had become the engine of nationality. The clergy might no longer pray openly for the king, but it was vain to hope, said Monck, that they would observe the day of thanksgiving for the Protector's narrow escape from assassination. 'This people generally', he wrote, a few months before Cromwell's death, 'are in as fit a temper for rising as ever I knew since I came into Scotland'.[3]

[1] I refer to the 'Assent and Desires of Orkney and Shetland', Terry, *op. cit.*, pp. 122-6.

[2] In 1659 Gillespie's party in Glasgow sought to use the craftsmen as a means of capturing control of the town council (Baillie, iii, 433), and two hundred 'well-affected persons in and about Edinburgh' petitioned in favour of toleration (Nicoll, *Diary*, p. 245; *Wariston's Diary*, iii, 126, 128). But I know no other or earlier evidence of participation by the classes which, in England, played so prominent a part in the democratic movement.

[3] *Thurloe State Papers*, vi, 330, 664, 762.

Scotland did not rise. Whatever its temper, it was physically apathetic, and all knew it. Its force was spent, and it simply waited on events. But as soon as the events had happened, and Monck, marching out of Scotland, had restored the Stuarts, all the Cromwellian reforms in that country were swept away. In this at least Scotland was not like Ireland. The hereditary jurisdictions returned. Cromwellian justice was denounced, even by those who had lately extolled it, as 'iniquity and oppression over a poor, distracted land'. The 'Independent' preachers and professors disappeared from Kirk and college. Robert Baillie himself replaced Gillespie at Glasgow, and being nominated by the king, forgot his former zeal for the rights of electors. Even if Presbytery did not recover its monopoly, at least the infamous doctrine of toleration was no more heard. And to signalise the victory of religion and justice, Kirk and Parliament were happily united in the greatest of all Scottish witch-hunts. As a Scottish historian writes, the number of victims can only be explained on the assumption that nine years of English mildness had left a heavy backlog of candidates to be despatched. The holocaust of 1661 was the reply of Scottish society to the English attempt at 'laicisation'.[1]

Meanwhile what of the Scottish Cromwellians? They had rejected the established Kirk parties and sought, by serving the usurper, to import a new form of society for which Scotland itself supplied no base. Now they were scattered. Some, indeed, though not the best of them, navigated the change. John Menzies was one of them. It was 'dangerous to slip a buckle', said this timorous Independent, and put his neck back, in good time, into the old presbyterian harness. Others sought niches, comfortable or uncomfortable, to the Left or Right of the new Establishment. Gillespie and Livingstone, the old Remonstrants, went Left: the restored Presbyterians rejected the first and were rejected by the second. On the other hand the

[1] Nicoll, *Diary*, p. 304; Mathieson, *op. cit.*, ii, 171-2. It is interesting to note that in Lorraine, freed at the same time from civilising French rule, there was a similar atavistic outbreak of witch-burning.

Cromwellian Resolutioners went Right. Robert Leighton[1] accepted episcopacy and became Archbishop of Glasgow. And as for Baillie's worthy, pious, wise, and diligent friend, James Sharp, he was able to prove yet again the infallible knack of the Glasgow professor for getting everything exactly wrong.

For in 1660 Baillie was confident once again that the glorious day of pure Presbyterianism had dawned, not only for Scotland, but for England too; and he intended to play his part. He had no intention of accepting the advice 'so oft inculcate from London' that the Scots should mind their own business. 'What is the Scots of this', he asked, 'but that we shall sit dumb and never open our mouth, neither to the King nor Parliament nor our brethren the ministers of England to request them to adhere to their Covenant and Petition against Books and Bishops? I fear we cannot answer for our miserable slackness herein already.' So Baillie once again threw his weight about. Did someone mention 'moderate episcopacy'? The good Scotsman choked at the thought: one might as well speak of 'moderate Papacy'! The forces of the Covenant must be mobilised to end this mismanagement in London. Offices in Church and State must be redistributed. Lord Chancellor Hyde must be dismissed. Church-patronage must be properly disposed. It was all perfectly simple. 'A few hours' treaty' would do it . . . And who should be Baillie's agent in all these matters but his reverend and beloved brother James Sharp? Sharp was to see Cromwell's *protégé*, 'that ass Lockyer', kicked out of the provostship of Eton and a learned friend put in; Sharp was to commission a team of English Presbyters to publish a manifesto 'for the crushing of that high, proud, malicious and now very active and dangerous party', the English episcopalians. But, alas, brother Sharp had other fish to fry. He was not wasting his time seeking to put back the shattered Humpty-Dumpty of Presbyterianism in England. As agent of the Kirk in London he was quietly selling out his

---

[1] Leighton was not, strictly speaking, a Resolutioner, but as he accepted membership of the General Assembly just before its dissolution, he can be counted as such.

employers as fast as he could and securing for himself, as his reward, an archbishop's mitre—and, afterwards, a somewhat dubious martyr's crown.[1]

These were the Cromwellian clergy. The Cromwellian laity faced the same choice. Lockhart, predictably, went Right, and found his way back from the protectoral to the royal court. So did Dalrymple, who became the greatest, most liberal of Scottish judges. The three 'radical' members of the Barebones Parliament, as predictably, went Left. Sir James Hope, 'laid aside' by a disgusted Protector, was, by 1659, known as a republican.[2] Death in 1661 saved him from defining his position in the new reign.[3] Swinton and Jaffray, like so many other genuine ex-Cromwellian laymen, became Quakers. Perhaps it was no accident that the strongest centre of early Scottish Quakerism was in Aberdeen, the area where the Covenant had always been weakest, where there was an old tradition of lay life, and where Cromwell had found most local support. In Scotland as in England, Quakerism was the ghost of deceased Independency sitting hatless in the seat thereof.

Leighton, Lockhart, Dalrymple, Swinton, Jaffray—these are among the most enlightened, most attractive spirits of mid-seventeenth century Scotland. In Scotland, as in England, Cromwell showed his genius for eliciting that latent talent which the Stuarts never failed to stifle or repel, and though the attempt ended in disaster, the men whom he discovered deserve to be remembered as distant precursors of the Enlightenment which dawned in Scotland a century later. For although England and Scotland were separated again in 1660, the Union of Crowns was as uncomfortable after as before the Great Rebellion. In 1707 a more cautious union of the two kingdoms

---

[1] Baillie, iii, 400-1, 408, 444-5.

[2] Firth, *Scotland and the Protectorate*, p. 385.

[3] I suspect he would have gone Left. His long verse-epitaph in Cramond churchyard dwells on his mineral interests and judicial virtues, but of his political ideals merely states that he pursued 'public peace and wealth'. The first editor of his diary, Sir J. B. Paul, dismisses Hope as 'wobbly' and 'pusillanimous', but all the evidence of his views seems to me compatible with a consistent policy: the material improvement of Scotland on a national basis.

was carried through. This time there was no assimilation of
Church or Law; but there was equal freedom of trade in a
large part of the world. Thanks to these mercantile opportunities, Scotland, in the next generation—it took a full generation
—gradually acquired, in a new independent laity, the social
basis for those changes which Cromwell had too hastily sought
to impose on it. In 1727 the last witch was burnt in Scotland.
In 1737 the great Secession relieved the Kirk of its fanatics.
Thereafter lay ideas transformed the 'Erastian' Scottish clergy,
whose liberal members, the champions of the lay Enlightenment, would be accused of the same heresies as Patrick Gillespie and Robert Leighton. From 1745 the Highlands were
opened up and kirks were 'planted' to civilise them as the
Cromwellian commissioners had wished. In 1748 the hereditary
jurisdictions were finally abolished, and the Scottish landlords,
as the Cromwellians had prophesied, exchanged old, barbarous power for new agricultural wealth.[1] By the end of
the eighteenth century, when English aristocrats sent their sons
to study agriculture in East Lothian, or politics in the Universities of Edinburgh or Glasgow, and used Scottish architects
to rebuild their country houses, the old difference between
the two countries, which had made their contact in the
previous century so explosive, had indeed changed.

[1] See H. G. Graham, *The Social Life of Scotland in the 18th century* (1901),
pp. 209-10, 494-7. In 1883 some of the greatest British fortunes from land
were enjoyed by the old Scottish aristocracy, whose poverty had been a
byword in the seventeenth century (see Bateman, *Great Landowners*, 1883,
quoted in G.E.C., *Complete Peerage*, vi. App. H., p. 713).

VI

SEVENTEENTH CENTURY AMERICA:
AN HISTORIOGRAPHIC VIEW

B. D. Bargar

THE writing of colonial history is presently enjoying a healthy maturity. By contrast, the earliest historians reveal certain childlike qualities. They were impressed with both the beauties and the terrors of the wilderness into which they had ventured, but they possessed an enviable confidence in Divine Providence. They never doubted the purposes of God the Father, whether they were writing of storms, starvation, or Indian warfare. The next stage, which we might term adolescence, was delayed in arriving and unduly prolonged. Generally speaking, historians who wrote in the nineteenth century demonstrate the characteristics of this phase. Their confidence, or in some cases over-confidence, stemmed from independence and self-reliance. Like so many individual youths experiencing growing pains, these adolescent historians were boastful, contemptuous, and immature. They were able to use the new 'scientific' method of research, which distinguishes their work from some of the historians of early settlements; but they were too quick to ascribe uniqueness to American institutions inherited from Europe or to frontier experiences duplicated in other parts of the world.

The mature stage of colonial historiography may begin as early as 1889, when Charles McLean Andrews and Herbert Levi Osgood received their doctoral degrees.[1] Although the

[1] Lawrence H. Gipson, 'Charles McLean Andrews and the Re-orientation of the Study of American Colonial History', *The Pennsylvania Magazine of History and Biography* (July, 1935), reprinted in Lehigh University's Institute

adolescent or 'patriotic' stage continues to influence historical writing in the twentieth century, especially in secondary school textbooks, Andrews, Osgood, and their students in the 'imperial' school have successfully challenged many theories advanced by their predecessors. It may be taken as a further sign of maturity that the new interpretation of the imperialists has not gone unchallenged. The influence of Karl Marx upon the writing of history has been so great that American colonial historiography could not escape it. Since the adjective 'Marxist' has unpleasant political connotations for some, it may reduce the area of controversy if we refer to the 'socio-economic' group of historians, who emphasise the importance of economic motives and the class struggle in colonial history.[1] There are, of course, other individuals, whose area of specialisation or whose approach defies classification. The fact remains, however, that the mature phase of colonial historiography is characterised by a healthy difference of opinion as to what constitutes the 'true' interpretation of the agreed-on facts. To carry the metaphor one step further, senility, the last stage, will not be reached until all historians agree that there is only one interpretation and that therefore no further research or argument is necessary.

It is common practice to conduct a survey such as this one chronologically. Several excellent studies are organised in this logical way, so that it would seem presumptuous on the part of the present writer to attempt to improve upon them.[2]

of Research, *Studies in the Humanities*. Professor Gipson, a former student of Andrews, is himself the *doyen* of the imperialist school and the author of a multi-volume study of 'The Great War for Empire'.

[1] E. S. Morgan, 'The American Revolution: Revisions in Need of Revising', *William and Mary Quarterly*, Third Series, xiv (January, 1957), pp. 3-15. Although the focus is the Revolution, the same schools of history can be observed at work in seventeenth century subjects, with the possible exception of the Namierist. A recent study of a colonial council employs Namier's technique, but falls outside the scope of this survey: M. Eugene Sirmans, 'The South Carolina Royal Council, 1720-1763', *ibid.*, xviii (July, 1961), pp. 373-92.

[2] Michael Kraus, *The Writing of American History* (Norman, Oklahoma, 1953). Richard S. Dunn, 'Seventeenth-Century English Historians of America', *Seventeenth-Century America* (James Morton Smith, ed., Chapel

Duplication, on the other hand, is even less desirable, so the plan of this essay will reflect its purpose: various topics and personalities in America's first century will be examined from the viewpoints of different historians, with special emphasis upon recent agreements or disagreements in each case. Among the many topics which have excited historical controversy, the following seem to be the more important: (1) the starting-point for American history, (2) the nature and significance of Puritanism, (3) the definition of democracy, especially in New England, and (4) the influence of Stuart despotism. Many colourful personalities cross the colonial stage, but among those who have succeeded in enlisting enthusiastic champions against their critics and detractors, the most interesting are: (1) Captain John Smith, (2) Roger Williams, and (3) Nathaniel Bacon.

American History: where to begin?

This question has been posed, implicitly or even unconsciously, by every historian of colonial America. The answer reveals a wide difference of opinion and also raises a secondary question: who was the first American historian? The historians who accepted a Providential purpose in history naturally began with a biblical approach. Thomas Prince believed that the proper starting-point for his *Chronological History of New England* (1736) was the creation of Adam: 'Year one, first month, sixth day . . .' Somewhat more realistically, William Bradford chose Scrooby (Notts.) as the starting-point for his *History of Plymouth Plantation*. Patriotic Virginians, however, are quick to point out that the *Mayflower* sailed a dozen years after the foundation of Jamestown, and even New Englanders admit that there were more strangers than saints on board. Thus, Scrooby cannot qualify as the starting-point and

Hill, 1959), pp. 195-225. David D. Van Tassel attempts a new, topical approach in his *Recording America's Past: An Interpretation of Historical Studies in America, 1607-1884* (Chicago, 1960), but only the first thirty pages deal with pre-Revolutionary historiography.

10

Bradford, charming though his history may be, cannot be regarded as the first.[1]

Captain John Smith is sometimes regarded as the 'Father of American History', owing to his impressive *Generall Historie of Virginia, New-England, and the Summer Isles* (1624). Even those who are prepared to overlook Smith's exaggeration and egotism hesitate to award him priority. Large parts of the *Generall Historie* were written by Smith's friends, although he himself certainly edited the whole work and gave credit to his collaborators. Since he spent only two years (1607-09) in Virginia, there are patriotic objections to considering him an American historian at all. Nevertheless, a recent biographer praises his 'unique contribution as historian' and compares his historical method with that of Xenophon.[2]

Others may be considered for the title 'Father of American History.' Richard Hakluyt is one possible candidate, even though he never visited the American continent, since the establishment of the first successful English colony in Virginia had to have its starting-point in England. Among those who promoted the project with both words and deeds, Hakluyt's name stands high on the list. A member of the Virginia Company, he expressed the strongest desires to visit Jamestown. Although this wish was never fulfilled, his great work, *The principall Navigations, Voiages and Discoveries of the English nation* (1589), together with its later and enlarged edition, assures his fame as a historian of English expansion.[3] His possible claim as first American historian, however, has not been widely accepted. A recent study of this problem establishes criteria, such as American residence and education, which disqualify all of the usual candidates. With such a rigid definition of what constitutes an American historian, no one older

---

[1] James Truslow Adams, *The Founding of New England* (Boston, 1921), pp. 98-9.

[2] Bradford Smith, *Captain John Smith: His Life and Legend* (Philadelphia, 1953), p. 262.

[3] Kraus, *op. cit.*, pp. 11-12, discusses Hakluyt's contributions without concern for the title for which I have nominated him in the present essay.

than William Hubbard, who died in 1704, can qualify.[1] Although his *Narrative of the Troubles with the Indians in New England* was published in 1677, his more important *General History of New England* remained in manuscript form until 1815, which makes it seem a little incongruous to regard him as the first American historian.

There are other, wider issues raised by this simple query. Some historians object to the Anglocentric approach to American colonial history, contending that other Europeans reached these shores earlier. Some Scandinavians maintain that Columbus knew of the Norse voyages. If this argument has validity, then the *Saga of Eric the Red* and the *Flateyjarbok* must be considered among our earliest sources. Adam of Bremen, whose *Description of the Northerly Lands* (c. 1070) first mentioned 'Vinland', might even be dubbed the 'Father of American History'. More seriously, the Hispanic group advanced a reasonable argument. After all, Spanish explorers marched through parts of the present-day United States. Since most of their earlier chroniclers concerned themselves with Mexico and Peru, however, it will not be necessary to nominate a Spanish 'Father of American History'.[2] James I may have recognised the King of Spain's dominion over part of North America when he drew the southern boundary for Virginia, but American institutions are predominantly English in origin, rather than Iberian or Icelandic.

The failure to answer this question authoritatively has had an unfortunate effect upon textbooks for American history classes in the tax-supported schools. While historians have

[1] Dunn, *op. cit.* The purpose of Dunn's article is to distinguish between Englishmen writing about America and the first Americans to do so, rather than to find the Father of American History.

[2] Kraus, *op. cit.*, pp. 5-11, briefly describes the Norse and Spanish accounts. Fortunately, since the Kensington Rune Stone proved to be spurious (Erik Wahlgren, *The Kensington Stone, a Mystery Solved* (Madison, Wis., 1958)), historians no longer concern themselves with the unlikely possibility of Norse voyages to the interior, but there is still a lively argument about which parts of the coast they visited. Samuel E. Morison doubts that Columbus heard about Vinland on his brief visit to Iceland in 1477; *Admiral of the Ocean Sea: A Life of Christopher Columbus* (Boston, 1942), p. 26.

argued about whether American history should begin in Eden, Iceland, or Scrooby, and whether American citizenship is necessary for the 'Father of American History', others have concentrated upon the period following the Revolution. A textbook author may devote 1000 pages to the history of the United States, compressing the first 176 years of our experience into approximately ten per cent of his study.[1]

Puritanism: good or evil influence?

There have been serious controversies about the nature of Puritanism. The Puritans themselves, of course, saw the guiding hand of Providence in their accomplishments, but later historians have accounted for their migrations by a wide variety of motives: from materialistic, land-grabbing greed to the desire for religious toleration. Patriotic historians of the last century were inclined to accept their ancestors' accounts at face-value. Puritanism was described as synonymous with religious liberty, civil rights, freedom of enterprise, and democracy—in short, the American way of life. The pendulum began to swing in the other direction, however, with the writings of Charles Francis Adams and his brother, Brooks Adams. Instead of describing Massachusetts as the source of religious liberty and political equality, the Adams brothers painted the portrait of Puritanism in darker tones. Rejecting the filiopietistic interpretation, they described a government by oligarchy and a religious intolerance which led to superstition.[2]

The battle lines were thus drawn before the turn of the century. The loudest salvoes were fired by amateurs, after-dinner speakers who reiterated the old 'truths' about the con-

[1] S. E. Morison and Henry Steele Commager, *The Growth of the American Republic* (New York, 1962, 5th edition, 2 vols.) is one of the best of several textbook accounts; in the first volume of more than 700 pages, the Revolution begins on page 178. Examples of this disproportion could be multiplied *ad nauseam.*

[2] George M. Waller, ed., *Puritanism in Early America* (Problems in American Civilization: Readings selected by the Department of American Studies, Amherst College, Boston, 1950), pp. vii and viii. This 'Amherst Series' publication provides a very useful edition of eleven different views of Puritanism.

tributions of the Puritans on the one hand, and by H. L. Mencken decrying their hypocrisy on the other. Serious historians have been compelled to examine this issue, but have not yet come to an agreement. Some of them continue the Adams interpretation, seeing puritan contributions to American development only after the defeat of the oligarchy which maintained intolerance and resisted change. Andrews believed that a continuation of seventeenth century Puritanism 'would have served no good ends either for Massachusetts or the world at large'.[1] James Truslow Adams emphasised the importance of the dissenting group within Massachusetts, rather than the oligarchs' conflict with the crown. Adams believed that the former, rather than the latter, were responsible for the triumph of the modern concepts of toleration and self-government.[2]

In recent years, a number of historians have re-interpreted the nature and contributions of the Puritans. They have tried to avoid both extremes: the filiopietism of the Patriots on one hand and the wholesale denunciations of extreme critics on the other. Samuel Eliot Morison has spoken in favour of the intellectual content and productivity of Puritanism, denying earlier contentions that it was sterile, superstitious, and morbid. The Salem witchcraft trials have provided both drama and horror for the opponents of Puritanism, but Morison prefers to emphasise the contributions of Harvard College and the members of the Royal Society who lived in New England. Critics may point to the accomplishments of European intellectuals in the age of Newton and Locke, but to be fair to the Mathers and the Winthrops, we should note the paucity of intellectual activity in the other colonies at the same time.[3]

Since Puritanism is primarily a religious, rather than an intellectual, movement, we should expect to find more agreement among historians in this area. Consideration of the nature of Puritanism in New England, however, presents us with several

[1] Charles M. Andrews, *Our Earliest Colonial Settlements* (New York, 1933), p. 84.   [2] J. T. Adams, *op. cit.*, pp. 155-6.
[3] S. E. Morison, *The Puritan Pronaos* (New York, 1936); cf. Amherst Series, pp. 68-79. Herbert Levi Osgood, *The American Colonies in the Seventeenth Century* (New York, 1904), i, 255.

dichotomies. Were the Massachusetts Puritans separatists or not? Was the Massachusetts church congregationalist or not? Did they expel dissenters for religious or other reasons? Historians who have examined these and related questions have produced a surprising variety of answers.

It is generally agreed that the Pilgrims of Plymouth were separatists, although some would argue that they were not Puritans.[1] The people who settled in Massachusetts, however, denied at the time of migrating that they were separating from the Church of England. Whenever they visited the homeland, they took communion in parish churches without fear of excommunication. Yet, they resisted Archbishop Laud and all other attempts to regulate their church government from outside the colony. A standard interpretation of this problem gives the credit to the Plymouth Separatists and especially Dr. Fuller, who visited the first settlers in the Bay area and explained the ordination of clergymen by the congregation. Professor Wertenbaker was one of the first to notice the weakness of this explanation. It is illogical to assume that a group of people as determined as the Massachusetts Puritans would remove themselves thousands of miles across the ocean without any idea of how to establish their own church.[2]

The Pilgrim Fathers present an appealing and attractive picture. Their many advocates give them credit for many concepts, including New England congregationalism, which objective research denies them.[3] Perry Miller's contribution is an analysis of the theological sources for a system of church policy which he calls 'non-separating congregationalism'.[4] This

---

[1] Charles A. Beard, 'On Puritans', *New Republic* (December, 1920); cf. Amherst Series, p. 3, says specifically that the 'Pilgrims were not Puritans. . . .' Edward Channing, *History of the United States* (New York, 1905), i, 271-2 and 272 note, among many other historians, regards the Pilgrims as part of the puritan movement.

[2] Thomas Jefferson Wertenbaker, *The Puritan Oligarchy* (New York, 1947), p. 29.

[3] S. E. Morison, 'The Pilgrim Fathers: Their Significance in History', *By Land and By Sea: Essays and Addresses* (New York, 1953), p. 233.

[4] Perry Miller, *Orthodoxy in Massachusetts, 1630–1650* (Boston, 1933; Beacon Paperback edition, 1959), ch. iv.

system, established in Massachusetts, owes nothing to Pilgrim example, but is firmly rooted in the writings and sermons of the English Puritans themselves. It differed from Anglicanism in dispensing with bishops, but it differed also from English Independents and Separatists in providing a provincial organisation which found expression in the Synod. Far from separating from the Church of England, the Massachusetts Puritans expected to demonstrate by their own example that a national church could enforce uniformity of doctrine and regulate its clergy and laymen in a satisfactory manner. When this lesson had been learned, the Church of England would become 'pure'.

Since the Massachusetts Puritans were Calvinist in doctrine, the use of the term 'synod' for their provincial meetings might lead one to assume that they were Presbyterians rather than Congregationalists. Yet, we have the example of Dr. Robert Child and the Remonstrants to prove how unwelcome avowed Presbyterians were in Massachusetts. John Winthrop's biographer points out several reasons why this was so.[1] Presbyterians accepted the idea of an inclusive church: everyone would be admitted to the sacraments and to membership, although a small group of elders would dominate the affairs of the congregation and might even cast out scandalous individuals. The Massachusetts church, however, was an exclusive church, denying the sacraments and the rights of membership to all but a few who could testify to their own conversion. Once admitted to membership, however, complete democracy governed congregational affairs. Also, the Massachusetts 'synod' was a meeting of clergy with only the force of public opinion to enforce its decisions. Whereas a presbyterian synod would enforce uniformity, Congregationalists in Massachusetts called upon the State, the General Court, to prevent Separatism. It would still appear that the two groups of Calvinists had much in common, but Professor Morgan has advanced a further reason for the refusal to tolerate Presbyterians in general and Child in particular. During the 1620s and '30s, when many

[1] E. S. Morgan, *The Puritan Dilemma: The Story of John Winthrop* (Boston, 1958), p. 77.

Puritans of different persuasions sought refuge in the Low Countries, a presbyterian clergyman turned informer and supplied Laud with information about the Congregationalists. Even after their flight to Massachusetts, many Puritans still carried bitter memories of this event and refused to allow Presbyterianism a foothold in their Bible Commonwealth.[1]

This attitude towards dissenters has presented the Puritans' chief advocates with a further dilemma. How can the patriotic historians claim that religious liberty is a contribution of the Puritans? One ingenious explanation can be found in the writings of Cotton Mather and traced, like a single thread in a fabric, through later historiography. Roger Williams was expelled, not because he disagreed with the religious concepts of the Massachusetts church, but because he questioned the legality of the Charter and the titles to land seized from the Indians. This banishment, like that of the Baptists and Quakers later, was not an example of religious intolerance; it was a political action taken by a state anxious to preserve itself from subversion and to maintain law and order. Quakers were warned not to preach in Massachusetts; if they returned anyway, they knowingly broke the law and deserved the punishment meted out to them. This interpretation has been questioned by one of the most sympathetic students of Puritanism. Perry Miller has pointed out that we are guilty of present-mindedness when we expect the Puritans to practice toleration. It was an evil thing to tolerate exceptions to the Truth and to God's will. They sought something different from religious freedom in Massachusetts: a pure church which would serve as an example to others. They were not hypocritical, but rather they practised what they preached, uniformity and 'Truth' as they understood it.[2]

Colonial Democracy: myth or reality?

Closely related to the problem of Puritanism is the question of democracy, especially in New England. To what extent did

[1] E. S. Morgan, *The Puritan Dilemma: The Story of John Winthrop*, p. 181.
[2] Miller, *op. cit.*, pp. 165 *et seq.*

the congregational practice of democracy within an exclusive church membership influence the political concepts of the town meeting and, on a wider scale, colonial government in general? Patriotic historians often described puritan New England as the seed-bed of American democracy. Later critics of Puritanism in general, however, have levelled some of their heaviest artillery at the restrictive franchise enforced in most of the New England colonies. Massachusetts and New Haven, in particular, have been designated theocracies, oligarchies and Bible-states regulated by the Mosaic Code. John Winthrop is often cited as the source to justify this criticism, especially his well-known sentiment that, 'The best part is always the least and of that best part the wiser part is always the lesser.'[1] In other colonies, where Puritanism was less influential, the franchise was generally restricted by property qualifications.

The question of voting rights in Massachusetts has excited the most controversy among historians, and paradoxically the most agreement. Mrs. B. Katherine Brown has pointed out (in an article which has itself generated more controversy) that a long list of historians who disagree with each other on many points of interpretation all agree that Massachusetts was undemocratic. The consensus is that only about twenty per cent of the population could vote, owing to the church membership qualification. There is disagreement about the relative democracy of the local and the provincial governments. Andrews, for example, maintained that a small group controlled both levels of government until 1648; afterwards, the town meetings became more democratic, but not the General Court. Mrs. Brown takes Andrews to task for saying that it is impossible to estimate the size of various groups within the population and then proceeding to do so. She also disagrees with Perry Miller's contention that the law of 1631, requiring church membership, was a trick perpetrated by the oligarchy. It is her opinion that the vast majority of the settlers were puritan in sympathy, so that there was no need to resort to underhand

[1] C. M. Andrews, *The Colonial Period of American History* (New Haven, 1934), i, 442.

politics. She also deals with the semantics of the term 'freemen,' but her principal conclusion is that there was a high degree of democracy in Massachusetts.[1] Neither church membership nor the later property qualification prevented a large number of men from participating in both local and provincial government. This interpretation has not been widely accepted, but it has caused historians to look for additional evidence. At a recent session of the American Historical Association, one young scholar announced that his research among the town records of Watertown failed to support Mrs. Brown's thesis. In fact, the older idea, best expressed in the works of J. T. Adams, was given new life. Instead of accepting Adams' figure of twenty per cent, however, Mr. Simmons suggested that perhaps forty per cent of the male inhabitants of Massachusetts were enfranchised.[2]

Few documents in colonial history have produced either higher claims for uniqueness and significance or more refutations and counter-arguments than the Fundamental Orders of Connecticut (1639). Patriotic historians saw in this document the first written constitution, the first democratic constitution, the first use of a constitutional convention, and a direct bequest to future generations culminating in the Constitution of 1789.[3] One of the self-assumed tasks of the imperial school was to analyse the Fundamental Orders and try to place them in proper perspective. Osgood devoted ten pages to pointing out similarities between practices in Connecticut and other colonies, thus destroying the claims of both priority and uniqueness. Andrews has dealt at length with both the document and its enthusiastic proponents. He brands most of the claims to priority and later influence on the national constitution as

[1] B. Katherine Brown, 'Freemanship in Puritan Massachusetts', *American Historical Review*, lix (July, 1954), 865 *et seq.* A similar interpretation will be found in Robert E. Brown, *Middle-Class Democracy and the Revolution in Massachusetts, 1691–1780* (Ithaca, 1955).

[2] Richard C. Simmons, 'Freemanship in Early Massachusetts: Some Suggestions and a Case Study', *William and Mary Quarterly*, Third Series, xix (July, 1962), 425.

[3] John Fiske, *The Beginnings of New England* (Boston, 1902), pp. 155-6.

fallacies. One luckless enthusiast is quoted only to be dismissed with the comment: 'There is not a word of truth in that statement.'[1] It should be noted that Andrews wrote his chapters on Connecticut in the midst of the filiopietistic atmosphere generated by the tercentenary celebrations. His own training at the seminar of Herbert Baxter Adams was 'scientific' *par excellence*, but in reaction to the patriotic oratory of the 1930s he may have gone to the opposite extreme instead of maintaining complete objectivity. He has also been accused of 'present-mindedness' (an even greater sin in the imperial school), in insisting upon a completely modern definition of the term democratic.[2] No colonial government, of course, could consult a majority of the population, since women and servants were unenfranchised.

Nevertheless, it is common practice for patriotic historians to refer to 'democracy in action' and the 'will of the people' in many anachronistic situations. When Governor Sir John Harvey was 'thrust out' of Virginia in 1635, what element of democracy was at work? According to Professor Wertenbaker, this was a clear example of 'the people' reacting to tyranny[3]— an early skirmish in the American Revolution, which was delayed 140 years. A re-interpretation of this event by Wilcomb Washburn points out that 'the people' had less to do with Harvey's expulsion than the Council. He views the quarrel as largely a political and constitutional struggle between two branches of the colonial government, each trying to assert its own domination over the other.[4] The most recent history of Virginia attempts to reconcile these two opposing views, but leans heavily in the patriotic direction. Professor Morton

---

[1] Andrews, *Colonial Period of American History*, ii, 142 note b.

[2] A. S. Eisenstadt, *Charles McLean Andrews: A Study in American Historical Writing* (New York, 1956), pp. 102, 217-18.

[3] T. J. Wertenbaker, *Virginia Under the Stuarts* (Princeton, 1914), ch. iii. In the Preface to the 1957 edition of this work, the author maintains his original interpretation: 'Attempts to defend Sir John Harvey are as unconvincing as those to belittle Bacon . . . Harvey's expulsion was richly deserved.'

[4] W. E. Washburn, *Virginia under Charles I and Cromwell, 1625–1660* (E. G. Swem, ed., Jamestown 350th Anniversary Historical Booklet #7, Williamsburg, 1957), pp. 20-9.

acknowledges, far more generously than Wertenbaker, Harvey's ability and accomplishments. His conclusion, however, refers to the event as 'one of the many instances in Colonial Virginia history when *the people* resisted arbitrary rule.'[1]

In fact, the concept of democracy provides the student of history with the most convenient touchstone for classifying new or unfamiliar historical works. The patriotic school did not die with George Bancroft. There are still historians at work who criticise colonial institutions for what they are not. Professor Morton and those who agree with him regard America's past as merely the proving ground for the development of our present democratic institutions.[2] The imperial school and its proponents attempt to see seventeenth century institutions as they were intended to be in their own period. In the latter case, one may judge their success or failure in proper perspective, rather than with hind-sight. Each student will wish to make up his own mind, but in view of the increasing volume of publication in the colonial field, it becomes more and more desirable to have some set of rules to guide one's judgment of a new contribution to the field. An author who credits 'the people' with great initiative and foresight in the seventeenth century deserves to be read—but with caution.

Stuart Prerogatives: divine or diabolical?

One of the most convenient phrases in patriotic historiography has been 'Stuart Despotism'. It has been employed by numerous historians to explain such diverse problems as: the emigration of the Pilgrims, the dissolution of the Virginia Company, the issuance of proprietary charters, the suspension of the New York Assembly, and the establishment of the Dominion of New England. Later research into these and other areas has generally failed to confirm the original explanation.

---

[1] Richard L. Morton, *Colonial Virginia* (Chapel Hill, 1960), i, 144. My italics.

[2] W. E. Washburn's review of Morton's *Colonial Virginia* in the *American Historical Review*, lvii (October, 1961), 150.

Writers who have depended upon Stuart Despotism have either misunderstood English institutions with which they were dealing or else they have simply begged the question instead of answering it.

King James I threatened the Puritans. They must conform or be harried out of the land. Thus, it is easy to explain the flight of the Pilgrim Fathers first to Holland and then to Plymouth. Patriotic historians failed to see the lack of logic in this explanation, since the Pilgrims were at first prevented from leaving the kingdom, rather than being hounded across the borders. The Archbishop of York, in whose province the Scrooby Separatists practised their non-conformity, was singularly lax in enforcing the royal threat. J. T. Adams has written that the 'persecution' of the Pilgrims was limited to jeering and taunting by their neighbours. When they encountered official obstruction to their plans, it was not because they had violated the Act of Uniformity, but because they were attempting to take their persons and property out of the realm without the necessary licences. In other words, it was administrative red tape, rather than religious persecution, which caused them the most difficulty. William Bradford recorded that the officials who prevented their first sailing treated them with consideration. Later, the Leyden group was willing to accept the king's word that he would not persecute them in the New World.[1]

The reasons for the dissolution of the Virginia Company in 1624 are also deceptively easy to find, if one is obsessed with Stuart Despotism. King James disliked both Sir Edwin Sandys and the policy which gave birth to the Virginia House of Burgesses in 1619. Two scholars, working independently on the problem, arrived at a new interpretation. Andrews emphasised the judicial nature of the dissolution of the company. Instead of acting by divine right, the king submitted evidence to the court, which acted with due process of law. Andrews concludes that the 'simple truth' of the matter is that the

[1] J. T. Adams, *op. cit.*, pp. 87-8 and 92, citing Bradford, *Plymouth*, pp. 12, 13-15, and 30.

company was bankrupt and that it was necessary for the crown to assume the receivership.[1] Wesley Frank Craven's conclusion is essentially the same, although his account reflects more of the economic interpretation and he is interested in correcting some of the praise bestowed upon Sandys in earlier accounts.[2] A recent biographer of George Sandys, the poet, takes exception to this aspect of Craven's account,[3] but whether one man is to gain credit is not the point of this discussion. No one man, much less James I, can bear all the blame and Stuart Despotism turns out to be no explanation at all.

The historian who is primarily interested in American national history generally regards the colonial period as merely the background to a more significant story. He sees in the mountain of information only a few veins of ore worth the trouble of mining. If he can trace the vein of democracy or federalism back to a colonial source, he will pay little attention to other characteristic institutions which fail to fit the national pattern. Thus, proprietary charters contribute little to the American national story and then only by emphasising the exceptions to the proprietors' powers. Palatine jurisdiction belongs to the Middle Ages, to a different civilisation, and is therefore difficult to interpret. One possible explanation, however, is Stuart Despotism. Charles I and his sons granted most of the proprietary charters with, no doubt, the intention of strangling the infant Democracy in its American cradle.

Osgood and Andrews were the first to examine the institution of the proprietary colony from an imperial, rather than a patriotic, viewpoint. They both discuss the proprietary grant as simply the normal, legal form for conveying both land and

[1] Andrews, *Colonial Period of American History*, i, 174.

[2] W. F. Craven, *The Dissolution of the Virginia Company* (New York, 1932).

[3] Richard Beale Davis, *George Sandys, Poet-Adventurer: A Study in Anglo-American Culture in the Seventeenth Century* (London, 1955), App. F, 'Sir Edwin Sandys and the Virginia Company'. Morton, who sometimes resorts to Stuart Despotism as a motive, nevertheless agrees that 'no one person or group was responsible for the Company's downfall'. *Op. cit.*, p. 109.

jurisdiction to an individual or to an unincorporated group of individuals.[1] Since the seventeenth century lawyers knew of no other way, they followed time-hallowed precedent in erecting palatinates in Maryland and elsewhere. Far from intending to perpetuate despotism, the earliest grants included provisions for consultations between proprietor and representatives of the inhabitants. Later charters demonstrate a trend in the direction of increased royal control, as in William Penn's grant. The proprietor of Pennsylvania was restricted in seven specific ways from exercising the degree of sovereignty granted to Lord Baltimore.[2] It was intended to enforce the newly formed mercantilist policy in proprietaries, but not to take away the rights of the inhabitants. It is sometimes regarded as sinister and significant that Penn's charter, unlike earlier ones, omits the customary clause guaranteeing the rights of Englishmen. Since this guarantee was intended to protect settlers from an arbitrary proprietor, it can be assumed that the seven restrictions on Penn's powers served the same end.[3] The Pennsylvanians, for example, were specifically granted the right of appeal to the royal courts.

The Duke of York's charter for a proprietary to be erected in New Netherland seems to give evidence of despotism. In an early draft of the grant, provision for an elected assembly was struck out, apparently at the express command of Charles II. New York became the exception to the policy which required an assembly in every English colony after 1619. The pressure of public opinion in favour of an assembly and the resultant decline in the duke's revenues caused him to grant an assembly in 1683, which had only a brief existence before New York was included in the Dominion of New England. Here,

[1] H. L. Osgood, *American Colonies in the Seventeenth Century*, ii, ch. i. Andrews, *Colonial Period of American History*, ii, ch. vi.

[2] *Ibid.*, iii, 283-4.

[3] Osgood, *op. cit.*, p. 12. Osgood and Andrews disagree about the significance of the king's promise not to tax the Pennsylvanians without the consent of Parliament. The former believes that there was an expression of intention to tax the colonies; the latter doubts that the intention existed in the minds of the lawyers who drafted the Charter. Andrews, *op. cit.*, iii, 285 note.

surely, is evidence of Stuart Despotism, perfidy, and greed. Andrews' interpretation of this series of events conforms with his attitude toward proprietaries in general. Viewed from the centre of the empire, rather than from the isolation of one colonial capital, the York Charter takes on a different perspective. Even the duke himself invites our sympathy, for as Andrews points out, he took a keen personal interest in his province, yet he did not establish a family interest like the Calverts of Maryland. Furthermore, he always acted on the advice of his commissioners (before 1685) and the Lords of Trade (as king). Although he omitted an assembly from his plan for the government of New York, he did not close his mind to the possibility and eventually accepted Andros' advice to establish one. The major accusation, however, is that James was perfidious enough to summon an assembly for purposes of raising revenue and then, as king, to incorporate New York into the Dominion of New England in order to rid himself of the assembly. Andrews, viewing this issue from the standpoint of imperial policy rather than patriotism, maintains that there were many reasons for erecting the Dominion. Dissolving the New York Assembly was not one of these reasons, but the larger policy engulfed the lesser one.[1]

The role of the Dominion of New England in this controversy is also interesting. Detailed investigation of this problem, especially from the imperialist point of view, shows once again the inadequacy of Stuart Despotism as an explanation. Miss Viola Barnes, a student of Andrews, has demonstrated that the new policy of consolidation was necessary both for the enforcement of the Navigation Acts and also for defence against the French, the Indians, and perhaps the Dutch.[2] Providing royal administrators for all the individual colonies of New England would have been too expensive, so one large jurisdiction with

---

[1] Andrews, op. cit., iii, 114-24. The footnotes in this section refer to older histories of New York by O'Callaghan and Brodhead, whom Andrews is at some pains to revise. His note on page 118 begins: 'I carry no brief for the Stuarts, but the facts speak for themselves'.

[2] Viola F. Barnes, The Dominion of New England (New Haven, 1923; New York, 1960).

one set of officials was the logical solution. Enlarging the area to include New York, and omitting representative government, may be considered errors of judgment, but not sheer despotism. Taxes were actually lower in Massachusetts under Andros than under representative assemblies. Mistakes were made, particularly in the way quit-rents were imposed, but the objective reader cannot agree with puritan critics of Andros' policies of religious toleration or suppression of piracy. Because he enforced the Navigation Acts, he was accused of being 'soft on popery'—a smear tactic which has a familiar but not congenial ring about it.

Examples could be multiplied, but in each case where Stuart Despotism was once used as an explanation, further research has shown that there are other, more significant, explanations. Members of the imperial school prefer to credit the exigencies of imperial policy for specific acts of the Stuart dynasty, while the socio-economic school prefer a more materialistic explanation. Whether they agree among themselves or not, it would seem that the older patriotic interpretation was completely discredited. Yet, even in the 1960s we find a detailed and authoritative history of Virginia referring to 'typical Stuart contempt for legislative bodies', 'the deadening hand of Stuart autocracy', and 'eighty-one years of Stuart despotism'.[1] Even more surprising and more revealing of the author's misunderstanding of English institutions is the opinion that: 'Had the spirit of the Glorious Revolution of 1688 been extended in full to the American Colonies, there might never have been a revolution of 1776'.[2] This is an incredible statement, considering that the recognition of parliamentary supremacy was both the principal result of the 1680s and the chief source of the problem of the 1770s. It only serves to demonstrate, however, that new interpretations may often be revised. So long as basic issues in colonial history are the subjects of this lively interest, our mature phase may be prolonged and senility postponed indefinitely.

[1] Morton, *op. cit.*, pp. 298, 306, 328.
[2] *Ibid.*, p. 354.

11

Captain John Smith: hero or liar?

Whether or not he is the 'Father of American History', Captain John Smith is certainly one of the most interesting and controversial personalities in early Virginia. Here is a man who bore three Turks' heads on his escutcheon, who survived the 'starving time' in Jamestown, who almost single-handedly infused new life and purpose into the expiring settlers, and who, as every schoolboy knows, was saved from a terrible death by the Princess Pocahontas. He appeals to both the romantic, who values derring-do and high adventure, and also to the pragmatic, who believes in getting things done. From the professional viewpoint, however, what can we make of Smith's *Generall Historie*? Is it a reliable source of information, or does Smith's obvious egotism render him an unreliable recorder of his own accomplishments? Before 1867 historians generally accepted Smith's account as true and drew upon it for their own chapters on early Virginia. In that year, however, Henry Adams[1] pointed out a number of inconsistencies in Smith's writings and the work of denigration began. The Pocahontas story has figured much too importantly in these attacks. Smith made no mention of his romantic rescue in his first account, *A True Relation* . . . (1608), but incorporated the story in his later *Generall Historie* . . . (1624), after the princess' death in England. Recently, historians have tended to excuse Smith's egotism and to value his history for its factual accuracy. Andrews, for example, doubted Smith's version of the romantic rescue, but nevertheless regarded his contribution to both the history and the historiography of Virginia as important.[2] W. F. Craven, willing to indulge a 'veteran in recounting his conquests of war and love,' corroborated Smith's account by his own research into the dissolution of the Virginia Company.[3]

As long as the lingering doubt about Smith's veracity

[1] Henry Adams' article appeared in the *North American Review* (January, 1867); cf. Bradford Smith, *op. cit.*, pp. 116 and 173-4.

[2] Andrews, *Colonial Period of American History*, i, 142.

[3] Craven, *op. cit.*, and also, *Southern Colonies in the Seventeenth Century* (Louisiana, 1949), pp. 72-3.

remains, however, historians will be concerned with proving or disproving various points in the controversy. One of his first biographers, Henry Wharton, tried to prove as early as 1685 that Smith was truthful.[1] The fact that he was only a commoner may have made his claims of knightly valour and chivalrous deeds unwelcome to class-conscious contemporaries. An interesting sidelight in this controversy demonstrates the lengths to which a scholar is required to go in establishing Smith's reputation. One of the more questionable periods in the captain's life concerns his adventures in Transylvania, his capture by the Turks, and his escape by way of Russia back to Western Europe. Scoffers, who doubted that Smith ever de-capitated three Turks, were quick to point out that none of the cities and rivers mentioned in his account can be found on a map. Philip L. Barbour, however, has painstakingly translated Smith's Elizabethan phonetics into contemporary Slavic, in order to demonstrate that these misspelled cities and rivers not only exist on the map of Russia, but are actually located in the order named by Smith in describing his escape route.[2] Granted, this episode has nothing to do with American historiography, but it should caution us when decrying other portions of Smith's career. The consensus now is that he was certainly an egotist and possibly an exaggerator, but that his account of Jamestown and the Virginia Company must be accepted as essentially true, whether Pocahontas rescued him or not.

Roger Williams: democrat or theocrat?

Roger Williams provides us with another personage who has been the subject of historiographical controversy. Less active and more contemplative than John Smith, Williams neverthe-less had some adventures of his own in founding a colony. His

---

[1] Henry Wharton, *The Life of John Smith, English Soldier* (Laura P. Striker, trans., Chapel Hill, 1957).

[2] Philip L. Barbour, 'Captain John Smith's Route through Turkey and Russia', *William and Mary Quarterly*, Third Series, xiv (July, 1957), 358-69. See also, L. P. Striker's 'Captain John Smith's Hungary and Transylvania' in Bradford Smith's biography, Appendix I. (Note 2, p. 134 above.)

persecution at the hands of the Massachusetts authorities has often been cited as proof of puritan intolerance. On the other hand, Williams was also a Puritan and his concept of 'soul liberty' might be taken as an argument in favour of Puritanism. Rather than enter this labyrinth again, however, let us consider Roger Williams as a political thinker. Of his many biographers, S. H. Brockunier has credited him with the most modern concepts of social democracy. At the risk of oversimplifying Brockunier's thesis, it would appear that he attributes great importance to Williams' attachment for a young lady of higher social rank. The frustration of this engagement by her parents supposedly turned Williams' thoughts in an egalitarian direction. From this youthful bitterness blossomed the modern concept of political and social democracy which Brockunier believed to be practised in Rhode Island.[1]

Two scholars disagree with this interpretation, but characteristically (and one almost comes to expect it by this time) they disagree with each other. Perry Miller has expressed his scepticism about Brockunier's thesis, but is more interested in Williams the prophet than in Williams the political thinker.[2] Alan Simpson, however, has made a more positive statement in refutation of the Brockunier thesis. In all the voluminous writings of Roger Williams, not a single pamphlet considers the nature of civil government. His only revolutionary statement was a denial of the state's responsibility for the soul. Where then is the concept of political and social democracy attributed to him by Brockunier? Judging from his correspondence with Governor Winthrop, Williams did not consider the civil constitution of Massachusetts obnoxious, except in so far as it interfered with religious freedom. Conversely, he had no dealings with the Levellers on his various missions to England. If the frontier had any profound effect on Williams, it made him less democratic than those left-wing Puritans who

---

[1] S. H. Brockunier, *The Irrepressible Democrat: Roger Williams* (New York, 1940).

[2] Perry Miller, *Roger Williams: His Contribution to the American Tradition* (Indianapolis, 1953). Cf. his review of Brockunier's book in *American Historical Review*, xlvi (July, 1941), 921-2.

remained in England. What he desired for Rhode Island was not social democracy, but rather a higher degree of civil liberty than he found in Massachusetts. Freedom of conscience was not exclusively Roger Williams' idea.[1] Andrews, considering this aspect of Rhode Island history, has demonstrated how toleration was growing in the minds of many persons as the only alternative to the religious stalemate of the seventeenth century.[2] Although Roger Williams certainly occupies an important position in colonial history, his contributions to our political heritage are not unique nor are they the exclusive product of the frontier.

Nathaniel Bacon: torchbearer or incendiary?

In 1676 Nathaniel Bacon was undoubtedly the most controversial figure in colonial America. In spite of the large amount of literature written about him since that date, he remains the subject of controversy. His supporters in the historiographical debate maintain that he was a valiant young man, who demonstrated bravery in conflicts with the Indians and sincerely desired political reforms of a democratic nature. Ranged against him was the tyrannical governor, Sir William Berkeley, and the aristocratic elements of Restoration Virginia. T. J. Wertenbaker has advanced an extremely democratic interpretation.[3] As implied in the title, *Torchbearer of the Revolution*, he regards the issues in 1676 as essentially the same as one hundred years later. This attitude, originating in the works of Bancroft and other patriotic historians is still current, although critics have not been found wanting to challenge many of its details. Bacon's reputation as an Indian fighter has been ridiculed by one recent scholar,[4] who points out that Bacon's men fought only

[1] Alan Simpson, 'How Democratic was Roger Williams?' *William and Mary Quarterly*, Third Series, xiii (January, 1956), 53-67. *Puritanism in Old and New England* (Chicago, 1955), pp. 46-50.

[2] Andrews, *Colonial Period of American History*, i, 494-5 note.

[3] Thomas Jefferson Wertenbaker, *Torchbearer of the Revolution: The Story of Bacon's Rebellion and Its Leader* (Princeton, 1940).

[4] Wilcomb E. Washburn, *The Governor and the Rebel: A History of Bacon's Rebellion in Virginia* (Chapel Hill, 1957), ch. iii.

'friendly' Indians or those who were not expecting an attack. Governor Berkeley, who has often been accused of protecting his own interests in the fur trade, was apparently trying to isolate the hostile natives and preserve a working alliance with others. The frontiersmen of the seventeenth century obviously agreed with their successors two hundred years later: the only good Indian was a dead Indian.

The controversy over 'Bacon's Laws' is more significant. The assembly which met in June 1676, is traditionally described as 'Bacon's Assembly' and its enactments are generally regarded as the corpus of his reform movement. Yet, Bacon himself was either sitting strangely silent in the council chamber, or else absent on the frontier, while the House of Burgesses discussed these so-called reforms. Craven, for example, doubts whether these laws should be considered Baconian reforms, since some of them seem to be aimed at Bacon rather than Berkeley.[1] The governor had appointed the troublesome young man to his Council soon after his arrival in the colony. The first of the reform laws specified three years' residence as a qualification for such a post. Other laws do seem to remedy abusive practices which had developed in Berkeley's administration, but many of them were re-enacted by the succeeding Assembly which was dominated by the spirit of reaction. Can such laws be considered Bacon's? Perhaps the solution is to be found in the most recent history of Virginia, where Professor Morton analyses both the role of Bacon in the legislature and the significance of the later re-enactment of 'Bacon's Laws' by the governor's faction. His conclusion is that these statutes are definitely Bacon's and are also reform statutes. As for the later re-enactment, Morton maintains that the omissions are more significant than the duplications. To take only one example, a law of 'Bacon's Assembly' prohibited plural office-holding and required rotation in the office of sheriff. Berkeley's friends omitted the latter provision, so that the sheriffs, 'the chief tools of the Governor in fixing elections', could be employed and the effective control of local government by

[1] Craven, *Southern Colonies in the Seventeenth Century*, p. 383.

'the people' reduced. When viewed from Morton's standpoint, the reactionary Green Spring faction succeeded in emasculating Bacon's reform programme.[1]

What was Bacon's ultimate goal? Was he merely seeking personal prestige? Did the cry 'A Bacon! A Bacon!' turn his head? Was he trying to avenge the death of his overseer as a result of an Indian raid? Were his motives only those of personality or did he have some sort of constitutional reform in mind? Those who praise 'Bacon's Laws' for their reform content consider them merely the first step in an abortive revolution. Evidence in favour of this view is usually adduced from a conversation between Bacon and one John Goode. The rebel leader asserted on this occasion that he would fight against royal troops, if necessary. Some historians have interpreted this dialogue as proof that Bacon desired the independence of Virginia and therefore deserves the title 'Torchbearer of the Revolution'. Because there was also unrest in Maryland and Carolina (although the causes were different), it has also been assumed that a form of union might have been possible in resisting the crown. Other historians, especially those who consider the colonies economically dependent upon the imperial connection, discount these claims as unrealistic. W. F. Craven, for example, points out that Virginia's population of 40,000 was hardly equal to the task of resisting imperial forces. If the possibility of foreign aid entered their minds, what other empire could have offered American colonists liberties comparable to those they enjoyed? Craven's conclusion is that 'the parallel sometimes drawn with the American Revolution seems to be without real justification.'[2]

[1] Morton, op. cit., i, 285.
[2] Craven, *Southern Colonies in the Seventeenth Century*, p. 388. Cf., Morton, op. cit., i, 263-4; Washburn, *Governor and Rebel*, p. 156; Wertenbaker, *Give Me Liberty: The Struggle for Self-Government in Virginia* (Philadelphia, 1958), pp. 92-3. Professor Wertenbaker remains unimpressed with Washburn's thesis, as indicated in both the patriotic tone of the last-named volume and the 1957 edition of his *Virginia Under the Stuarts* (see Note 3, p. 143 above). Morton, who published his two-volume history of Virginia after Washburn's study appeared, favours Wertenbaker's interpretation on this and other issues. A curious reader may wish to compare Morton's comments

Finally, what were the causes of Bacon's Rebellion? Some historians have represented it as the struggle of 'the people' against tyranny; others as the sectional quarrel of frontiersmen versus tidewater settlers; but most writers agree that a whole complex of motives was involved in the rebellion. Washburn, in searching for the one factor which acted as a spark in this inflammatory situation, suggests that it was the frontiersmen's attitude toward the Indian. He credits Robert Beverley, whose history of Virginia was first published in 1705, with being the first to notice this factor. Furthermore, he states, 'Beverley probably came as close to a successful interpretation of the rebellion as anyone since his time'.[1] This statement represents one of the most surprising trends in recent historiography of colonial America: recent scholars tend to find 'Truth' in the contemporary or nearly contemporary accounts of the problem which they were investigating. This tendency has been noted in the case of John Smith's account of the dissolution of the Virginia Company, but it is even more obvious in accounts of the American Revolution, which do not come within the range of this survey. It is understandable that present-day writers should wish to revise their predecessors, especially those of the nineteenth century, but if this trend is carried to its logical conclusion, the whole shelf of colonial history books can be reduced to a few contemporary accounts and all the more recent writings can be discarded. We began this essay with the observation that historical writing on colonial America has reached a state of maturity. The number of controversies engendered in recent years is adduced as evidence of this phase of development. The same spirit of investigation and healthy disagreement is likely to continue and to stave off both second-childhood and senility for many decades to come. It is less important that historians fail to agree than that they continue to search for the truth.

on Washburn's research (232 note) with the latter's review of the former's *magnum opus* (Note 2, p. 144 above).

[1] Washburn, *Governor and Rebel*, pp. 154 and 162. The most recent edition of Robert Beverley's *History of the Present State of Virginia* was edited with an introduction by Louis B. Wright (Chapel Hill, 1947).

VII

CLAYWORTH AND COGENHOE[1]

Peter Laslett and John Harrison

WILLIAM SAMPSON, Rector of Clayworth, began keeping his *Register* on 27 March 1676 and his entries continued until 8 March 1701. He had held the benefice of this Nottinghamshire village, five miles to the north of East Retford, since the year 1672 and had resided there since November 1675. For exactly a quarter of a century, therefore, from the beginning of one year in the Old Style until the end of the twenty-fifth year after that, this shrewd, intelligent clergyman recorded everything of importance which happened to the little community under his spiritual care.

The Rector's Book, Clayworth, Nottinghamshire, as this document has come to be called, was published in full in the year 1910.[2] It is a remarkable record, well known to the local historians of the county and quoted by ecclesiastical, social, and economic historians of Stuart England. Here was a man who well understood why it should be that barley from the clay soils should fetch a better price than barley from the sand soils

---

[1] John Harrison has undertaken the detailed research on the Clayworth documents, and has prepared all the figures for that village. He is at present engaged in an attempt to reconstitute families from the registers there over the years 1660 to 1760, according to the methods of M. Louis Henry and the French school of historical demography (see below). We plan a further article on Clayworth. For the research on the record at Cogenhoe (pronounced Cooknoe), and for the suggested theses in this essay, Peter Laslett is alone responsible. All dates are in the Old Style.

[2] Transcribed and edited by Harry Gill and Everard L. Guilford: Henry B. Saxton, Nottingham, publisher. The original is still in the safe in Clayworth church, and comparison shows the transcription to be fair.

which lay side by side in the seven great fields of Clayworth, fields which here and there were already enclosed. Sampson was an improver and an encloser himself, and quite aware of the importance of drainage of those parts of the village which were waterlogged all year or liable to flood in winter. He husbanded his rectory glebe with notable skill and economy; an implacable, not to say aggressive, champion of the rights of the Church, financial and social, as well as religious, but also a faithful and painstaking shepherd of souls.[1]

'Sparrows of the Spirit' is the extraordinary title of the only book which has tried to make Sampson a figure of popular interest. A strange misnomer this, even if satirically meant, for a man who could record, without sign of emotion or regret, that George Richardson, blacksmith's apprentice of some years standing in the village, was hanged at Tyburn in March 1695 for stealing two horses out of the rectory stable. In 1679, at the very rails of the altar, and in sight of nearly fifty of their neighbours, Sampson withheld the communion cup on Palm Sunday from Ralph Meers and Anne Fenton, 'upon a common fame that they lived & lodged together, not being married'. Both of them had been servants in the largest house in Clayworth until a little time before, and within a few months they themselves were householders.

In 1682 Ralph Meers, labourer, was a churchwarden, but we know that his first child was conceived several months before marriage. This is one of the few pre-nuptial pregnancies we can trace at Clayworth. The improvement of the minds and the manners of his people was the evident object of Sampson's pastorate. When he died he left the means to the village to set up a regular school, the necessity and importance of which had been felt for many years. In *The Towne-Booke of Claworth* are still to be seen the proud, clumsy signatures of the poor

[1] See the *Rector's Book*, throughout: it contains annual accounts of the income of the church land, rising satisfactorily over the years. See also W. A. Tate, 'The Clayworth Memorial Map', *Transactions of the Thoroton Society*, 1940, for the intermediate, enclosed mixed with unenclosed, fields of the village as it was in Sampson's time, and for a reproduction of a manorial map of the year 1749.

boys of the village who had learnt to write from Sampson's benefaction.[1]

Sampson gives us twelve separate reasons why it was important to keep this *Rector's Book*, which he evidently thought of as in some sense belonging to the registration of baptisms, marriages, and burials. Apart from these events, or acts as the French would say, the record should contain the names of office-holders in the village, everything to do with tithe and with parish funds, details of the weather, the price of crops, and 'all differences and controversies of note' which affected the Church. The ninth of his reasons is the one which interests us most. It ought to set out, he claims:

> All the names of the Inhabitants of the Parish by a yearly Poll, and out of them to be noted the Communicants at every Sacrament.

It cannot be said that the *Rector's Book* does contain such yearly lists of the villagers, any more than an entirely complete series of high and low prices of their produce, valuable as his price recordings are. He may have been persuaded that it would be a good thing to have an up-to-date list of his parishioners because in that very month of April 1676 he received from the Archbishop of York the questionnaire for a religious census, generally called the Compton census.[2] This inquiry, and Sampson's own response, recalls an ancient and, alas, it seems a faint and ineffective tradition of the Christian Church of the West. The historian of English parish registers, J. S. Burn, has this important statement to make about it:

> Among the general canons set forth in some old Rituals is a direction for four books to be kept by the clergyman in every parish;

[1] *The Towne-Booke of Claworth containing the Names and accompts of all Parish Officers Beginning in the Year of our Lord 1674* contains details of Sampson's benefaction, which was particularly designed for the teaching of poor children, who sometimes signed the book if they won one of the prizes. We are grateful to the present Rector of Clayworth, the Rev. Cyril Blomeley, for allowing us to photograph this book and to work on the parish registers. For earlier attempts to found a school at Clayworth, see *Rector's Book*, p. 53. *Sparrows of the Spirit* is a paperback by F. West (London, 1961).

[2] A study of this census, which is potentially of the highest importance for the demography of Stuart England, is being made by Miss Anne Whiteman of Lady Margaret Hall, Oxford.

one for baptisms, another for marriages, a third for burials, and a fourth, the *Liber Status Animarum*.

In this fourth book, Burn continues in the original Latin:

> singulas familias suae parochiae, cum omnibus qui in ea vivunt diligenter conscribat, annotabitque qui ad Communionem apti, qui ad scholam catechisticam aut Confirmationem.[1]

'He must carefully inscribe in this book'—the *Liber Status Animarum*—'every family in his parish, with everyone living in it, and take note of those fit for Communion, and those fit for catechistical instruction or for Confirmation.' If all the beneficed priests of the English church had in fact kept all these four registers, above all if even some of them, a very small proportion would suffice, had kept a *Liber Status Animarum* to hand down to us, then the task of the historian of social structure would be transformed. We should have the chance of reconstructing the population of our country as it was during all those generations which went by before the census began in 1801, of doing it swiftly, accurately, and completely.

But the first sad lesson learnt by the beginner in the historical study of the social structure of Western Europe is that no such body of evidence seems to have been transmitted for any country, not even so far as I know for any community in any country. No document headed *Liber Status Animarum* seems yet to have come to light, at least, in England or in France. Perhaps the present description of what to search for may come to the attention of someone who can report the existence of an English example. But if the Roman priests who had care of the 30,000 parishes of France before the Revolution, a body of men so faithful and meticulous in maintaining the *état civil* for their parishioners that they put our own Anglican priesthood entirely to shame, if even the careful curés left behind

---

[1] *History of the Parish Registers in England* (1st ed, 1829, 2nd ed. 1862), p. 212. We have not been able to find these 'old rituals' and ecclesiastical historians have no immediate knowledge of them. Earlier in his book (p. 11) Burn refers to these four registers being enjoined by the Roman ritual printed in 1617.

them no document with this title in the marvellously stocked
Archives Départementales,[1] then the chance of an English one
coming to light seems very small indeed.

But to return to Clayworth in 1676. On 9 April Sampson
read a 'brief' to his congregation, an appeal that is enjoined to
be read by every parish priest in aid of a charitable purpose, in
this case relief and repair at Northampton after a disastrous fire.
Not content on this occasion with taking up coins in church,
the rector 'went with the Churchwardens from house to house
to collect it'. The entry continues thus:

> Whilst they were collecting this brief, I took occasion to enquire
> at the same time the names of all my parishioners which were these
> that follow Nominatim et (ad evitandam invidiam) alphabeticé.

Then follows the list,[2] household by household, in alphabetical
order—it was typical of Sampson to do all he could to avoid
invidiousness between neighbours—and within the household

---

[1] Or in the *mairie* of a Commune, which officially retains the pre-
Revolutionary parish registers, leaving the copies to go to the *Archives*,
though the Commune may be legally obliged to give up its documents to
the *Archives* if it betrays carelessness in preserving them. The immense
superiority of French over English registers, and the much greater care now
taken of them, together give French historical demographers a marked
advantage over others. Any user of the English registers will find it almost
impossible to believe that it is usual to find in France the maiden name of
the mother, as well as the names of godparents, in the case of baptisms; the
parentage of both bride and bridegroom as well as the names of witnesses
in the case of marriages; the age, parentage and the names of witnesses, with
once more the maiden name of the widow (where appropriate) in the case
of burials. Occupations of all parties are standard additions. The one
advantage of the English registers is that the three series together (baptisms,
marriages, and burials) go back to the sixteenth century, whereas in France
all three are not often present until after the middle of the seventeenth
century.

[2] *Rector's Book*, pp. 14-18. See E. S. de Beer, 'The Revocation of the
Edict of Nantes and English Public Opinion', *Proceedings of the Huguenot
Society* (1950), for an ingenious use of Sampson's record of collections for
briefs at Clayworth in relation to an assumed estimate of the wealth of the
village. The *Towne-Booke* shows that the practice of house-to-house collection was not all that exceptional, and was used in aid of the French Protestants as well as for Northampton and for the Christian captives in Algiers.
Sampson himself gave half of the money collected for the French and was
far and away the largest subscriber in all cases.

according to function. The head of household had his calling registered, and widowers and widows were so described. Wives, children, servants, kinsfolk, mothers-in-law, apprentices, journeymen, all were specified.

With this exhaustive list in his hand Sampson gave his answers to the questions put by his archbishop. There were 401 persons living in Clayworth in April 1676, and 236 of them were of an age to communicate, that is had attained the age of sixteen. No less than 200 of the 236 did actually take the sacrament during the Easter festival in that year: there were no popish recusants or dissenters in the village.[1]

A remarkable tribute to the still-persisting power of the Church over the inhabitants of a rural parish, it will be thought, and another lucky circumstance for the historian of population. For with no Roman Catholics or dissenters to worry about we can be the more confident that every inhabitant had his child baptised by the Rector, was married in church and buried in the churchyard, so that the totals of baptisms, marriages, and burials entered yearly in the *Rector's Book* can be relied upon. Even then Sampson tells us of two persons who apparently escaped registration, one a child baptised privately who died before his name was entered and another an adult seeking baptism who had been brought up a dissenter. But these details must not be allowed to draw attention away from the outstanding importance of this list of all the men, women, and children alive in the village of Clayworth in the month of April 1676. At the present time it must undoubtedly be regarded as the earliest authentic census of an English community.

Only three earlier listings, or sets of listings, have so far come to light, and none of them can claim to be authentic in the technical sense which historians of population have had to lay

---

[1] Pp. 18-19. Sampson actually reported 'under 400' to York as the population, but examination shows that seven names were overlooked at first, including the parson's own household. They were added later, presumably after he had sent his answers. Easter communicants rose to the notable figure of 212 in 1677, but they went down in the 1680s and '90s; during the last five years of Sampson's ministry the number was steady at 125.

down.[1] The purpose of the Clayworth census is known, the collection for Northampton which was quite unlikely to lead to evasion. It was drawn up by men who knew the community intimately, by the churchwardens in fact who happened that year to be two of the most substantial men in the village.[2] It was compiled neither by sitting at a desk and counting heads, nor by attempting to assemble the people, nor by asking them to report themselves, all of which ways of taking a census are likely to lead to omission, but by house to house inquiry, the most reliable method. Above all it was written down at the time and on the spot, except, it seems, for one afterthought, by an exact and experienced man, precise in business of this sort. Until he came to live at Clayworth, William Sampson had been president of Pembroke College, Cambridge, in charge of accounts and estates. In 1693 he was actually elected into the mastership, but he declined to serve.

Though of peasant stock from the neighbouring village of South Leverton, he was the brother of an eminent dissenting minister turned medical doctor and related by marriage to Nehemiah Grew, F.R.S., the botanist.[3] He undoubtedly belonged with the high intelligentsia of that great age of scientific and social inquiry, and it would be tempting to see in his statistical interest in his parishioners something of the attitude which was giving birth to demography in the work of Graunt, Petty, and King. But this can only be presumption. What is quite certain is that in the document which he left behind him from the year 1676 he gives to the sociological historian certain ground, or as certain as is ever likely to be found in Stuart

[1] Ealing, 1599 (complete with ages, a century before any other such record; PRO E/163/24/35, an article on this list is in preparation by Peter Laslett and K. J. Allison), Stafford, 1622 (County Record Office, W.S.L. D.1721/1/4); Cogenhoe, 1618–28, see below.

[2] Thomas Dickonson and Christopher Johnson, who may however have acted through a deputy in the actual progress from house to house, since both were gentlemen.

[3] See Dictionary of National Biography as corrected by E. S. de Beer, in the Bulletin of the Institute of Historical Research, 1943, pub. 1947, pp. 47–8. A John Sampson founded a school at South Leverton in 1691 and the Rector of Clayworth was made one of the visitors: Rector's Book, p. 97.

England. What is even more remarkable, what may in fact prove the statistical records of the village of Clayworth to be unique in England before the time of the census, is the fact that exactly twelve years later he wrote out the names of his parishioners all over again. We can be certain of who was living at Clayworth for two separate years, 1676 and 1688, and therefore we can compare the community over time.

Unfortunately we cannot be quite so certain that on this second occasion the numbering was as accurate as it was on the first. All Sampson tells us about it under the year 1688 is as follows:

> About May-Day I took the names of the Inhabitants of this my parish of Claworth, and placing them according to the Order of Houses and Families, down the North side of the Town, and up the South-Side, and lastly those of Wyeston.[1]

The purpose of this numeration, then, is known by assumption only, that it was due to the interest of the rector in having a precise count of his parishioners; we have to assume also that he himself did the counting, and take the hint provided in the passage just quoted that it was by house to house survey. But Sampson himself wrote it out and by 1688 he is so securely established as a reliable recorder, and he so clearly knows his parish like the back of his hand, that there must be a very strong presumption in favour of the quality of this list being as high as that of 1676. It is even more detailed in its descriptions of the households and their members, down to the particulars of the number of times individuals had been married.

Sampson himself makes six comments on the listing, and one of them is a remark on this last point: remarriage had been particularly common amongst the inhabitants of the hamlet of Wiseton. When we fully reconstruct from the information he gives us the marital state, as it might be called, of the whole of this English community in the year of the Glorious Revolution the result is truly astonishing. No less than twenty-six of

[1] The list follows on pp. 84-7. Wiseton is a second settlement in the parish of Clayworth, an independent manor.

the sixty-seven couples there had one partner or more who had been previously married, and two of the widowed had had more than one spouse, which makes twenty-eight. Of these marriages thirteen were second marriages, three were third marriages, four were fourth marriages and one a fifth marriage: the number is not given for the seven others. We have discovered from other sources that up to one-third of all marriages in Stuart England were second or later marriages for at least one of the partners, but this is the only opportunity we have found for examining the effect of this on a village society, perhaps the only one we shall ever have.

The marital history of the men and women of Clayworth is exemplified in the history of John Brason, who in 1676 was a servant and of course a bachelor. He married in that year, and his wife died in 1681. He married for a second time five months later and lost this wife in 1683, shortly after her child was born. We do not know when he married his third wife, but we do know that by 1688 he was established as the village butcher living now with his fourth wife, but with no children of his own; the only child in his family was a son of his wife's by a former husband. Widowhood, orphanage, living with step-parents, sometimes on both sides, adoption into the families of relatives or even of strangers, all these things were lamentably common in Stuart times. In 1688 no less than 28 per cent of the youngsters in Clayworth came from homes broken by death. This perhaps should make us a little less sorry for ourselves when we think of broken homes and parentless children in our own time.

We have filled in John Brason's intervening history from the parish registers, which were kept by Sampson with his usual carefulness alongside the *Rector's Book*.[1] But it may seem a

---

[1] He obviously originally intended to enter in this record all baptisms, weddings, and burials by names of the persons, but did so only for the years 1676 and 1677, after that recording only the annual totals. The ordinary parish registers are missing for the years before 1681, so that we have had to rely on the Bishop's Transcripts at Southwell for the years 1678–80 (made by Sampson himself). In 1681 he started a new volume for the parish registers (see p. 41) and this is still in the church.

12

little arbitrary to begin our consideration of the significance for social structure of this extremely rare double census by picking out the most unexpected of all its surprising items of evidence. Sampson tells us, which is interesting from several points of view, particularly that of the housing of the people and its effect on the constitution of the household, that there were eight empty houses in the village in 1688. He also re-capitulates the fact that there were ninety-one households in 1688, and that the population was 411. It was in precise fact 412, and this provides a certain figure for the mean size of the house-hold, a figure of critical significance for the historian of popu-lation as well as for the historical sociologist. It was 4·43 in 1688 and 4·09 in 1676; in this rural village, that is to say, over these twelve years the average household size ranged between 4 and 4½. This may seem small to those who think of our ancestors as living in great familial groups of grandparents, parents, and children, but its importance to the historian is that it confirms with exactitude what is known with fair reliability from coarser evidence. The household in Stuart times was surprisingly small, smaller than it became under the Georges, much smaller than it was under Victoria and smaller than it was to be again until the reign of George V.[1]

But it can easily be shown from Clayworth and from all the other evidence that a considerable part of the population at that time was not living in small households at all, but in large ones, in groups consisting of six persons and above. It can be shown also that the numbers of persons living outside families, living alone that is to say, or in institutions, was really very small indeed. This is a point which is raised by an interesting differ-ence between Clayworth in 1676 and Clayworth in 1688. In the earlier year all households were also families, though six of

---

[1] Size of household at Stafford 1622, 4·02: at Cogenhoe 1618, 5·61; 1624, 5·33; 1628, 5·45: at Lichfield 1688, 4·55: in Stoke-on-Trent 1701, 4·39: in Kent, thirty-three villages, 1705, 4·47. The proportion of persons living in households of six and above varied in these places between 40 and 60 per cent. See Addendum for the distribution of persons among households at Clayworth.

them consisted of solitary persons, two widows, two widowers, and two spinsters. By the later date something which might possibly be called an institution, an institution of the only type which was then at all common, had come into existence for the poor and solitary: they could now live 'in the common-Houses on Alms', and nine of them were doing so.[1] Joan Bacon and her daughter Anne were amongst them. Now in 1676 Francis Bacon, cooper (or barrel-maker), his wife Joan, and their children Nicholas, Anne, and Francis had been an independent household. So indeed was the family of Nicholas Bacon, cooper, the son, in 1688; himself, his wife Elizabeth whom he had married in 1686 after his father died, two children by her former husband. Apparently Nicholas had turned out his mother and his sister when he became head of the household and left them to live on alms in the common-houses, not willing or not able to give them shelter or sustenance.

We can only hope that such a woeful story was rare amongst the villagers of the old world. But it will serve to illustrate some of the principles which governed social and domestic relations, the principle that households did not ordinarily contain more generations than two, that living with in-laws or relatives was on the whole not to be expected and that orphans were normally the only persons who often found themselves living with relations. Most important is the rule that it was unusual, very unusual, to find two married couples within the same family group.

There were only three households containing grandchildren in 1676 and only five in 1688; only two mothers living with married daughters in 1676, and none in 1688; out of the ninety-eight households in 1676 and the ninety-one in 1688, three

---

[1] P. 86. No mention of the foundation of the common-houses, whatever they were, is found in the *Towne-Booke* or in the *Rector's Book*. They contained three widows, all of whom had been wives of householders with children in 1676, and two of whom still had children; a married couple, also ex-householders, and a spinster, not present in 1676. All are disregarded by Sampson in his totals for families and above in calculations of size of household.

contained 'kinsfolk', three nephews or nieces, one the husband's brother, one two sisters and two various relatives. No household at all contained two married couples, either a married son or daughter living with parents, or married brothers or sisters living together, or even a married couple living in service with another married couple. Far and away the most usual household, over 70 per cent in both years, was the household we are now accustomed to—man, wife, and children—but with the interesting addition in one household out of three or four of resident servants. Of those not headed by a married couple, most had widows in charge and a sprinkling had widowers; only eight out of the combined total of 189 were headed by unmarried people.

These details may seem wearisome, and cannot be said to belong to traditional historical inquiry. But the precise study of the situation at Clayworth in these two years and comparison with what can be more inexactly known from the other communities we can now examine makes it possible to put forward a general thesis about the structure of Stuart society. It suggests that what the anthropologists and sociologists call the nuclear independent family, that is man, wife, and children living apart from relatives was the accepted unit of society. It suggests, therefore, that the more generally accepted impression, that the independent nuclear family came into existence with industrialisation, is not in fact justifiable—living with in-laws and relatives may indeed be commoner now than it was then because of our enormously lengthened expectation of life. Households of one or two unmarried persons living on their own, childless households, are very much more common now than they were then. But the one really telling difference between the family in Stuart England and the family as we know it is, as we have already hinted, that servants were then counted as belonging to it.

A discussion of this sort obviously cannot be pursued in such a restricted context, and again the importance of the Clayworth evidence is to give a certain, precise sanction to what we know in general. We must reserve the demonstration of all this to a

more appropriate occasion,[1] but we must examine servants and
their function a little further, together with the proportion and
distribution of children and young people.

Servants, in the language of that day, the language we shall
use here, covered men and women, boys and girls, working
for their living at every agricultural, commercial, and industrial task, as well as the personal domestics our own parents
once employed. Apprentices, journeymen (when living with
their masters, as often they did), 'servants in husbandry',[2] even
sometimes secretaries and clerks, were intended, as well as men-
servants and maids. In 1676 there were sixty-seven servants at
Clayworth, in 1688 there were sixty-five; first 16·7 per cent
and then 15·8 per cent of the whole population. Men out-
numbered women (forty-three to twenty-four, then thirty-
three to thirty-two), and some of them were journeymen
(three and one), or apprentices (five and four). Servants were
found first in 33 per cent, then in 29 per cent, of all households,
so that they were by no means confined to the rich: still in both
years most servants belonged to groups of three or more, and
in 1688 there were two groups of six servants, two of four,
seven of three, and seven of two. Though the proportion of
men amongst them may have been a little high, the servants at
Clayworth seem to have been typical enough. Once more the
Rector's Book tells us precisely for one community what is
suggested more approximately for a number of other Stuart
towns and villages.[3] Something like one person in eight in the
countryside (and at least 80 per cent of the population was rural)
was living in a household other than the parental one, and
working there day and night.

[1] A general study of *The Social Structure of England in the Seventeenth
Century* is in preparation by Peter Laslett.

[2] A phrase which must be sharply distinguished from 'labourer', or
'agricultural labourer', never called servants under the old order because
they did not ordinarily live in. This distinction, and the crucial importance
of servants generally, will be discussed at length in the work referred to.

[3] Proportion of servants at Stafford 1622, 14·8 per cent; Cogenhoe 1618–
1628, *c.* 11 per cent–*c.* 17 per cent; Lichfield 1688, 8·6 per cent; in Stoke-on-
Trent 1701, 5·7 per cent; in Kent 1705, 18·3 per cent: the proportion of
servant-keeping households varied between a quarter and a third.

Clayworth must have been a forbidding village for servants, however, for their meagre wages were liable to tithe. A farthing in the shilling was due to the church, and a servant usually only earned between 50s. and 100s. in a whole year. The custom was dying when Sampson came, but he was not the man to let it drop. He frightened the servants so much that by 1679 he received £1 17s. 5d. from this source, out of a total receipt of nearly £250. Isabel or Elizabeth Bett died in 1677, and Thomas Bett, her son, a servant, came and paid 'fully for his wages at one farthing in the shilling. The occasion of his mother's death brought him to an honest mind.' But the rector had to proceed against the others in the spiritual courts, and even then they told him 'that all I could do was to excommunicate them, which was only their not going to Church &c.'. So he actually took the case to the Exchequer Court in London; it became the bitterest 'controversy of note' recorded in his book. Not until the gentlemen in the village, fearful that they would find themselves unable to get servants, combined against the embattled rector, did he give up this part of his tithe in return for other concessions.[1]

Servants were young people: at least they must be reckoned amongst those not old enough and lucky enough to find an opening to allow them to marry and become householders. But children, children not old enough to be described as sons or daughters, were the most numerous of the young. We have seen that 165 out of 401 people in Clayworth in 1676 were, in the opinion of their parish priest, too young to communicate, that is, under the age of sixteen. 'Children' were indeed a considerable proportion of the whole Clayworth community; there were 127 in 1676, or 31·5 per cent of the whole population, and 133 in 1688, or 32·5 per cent. These figures, not anything like as exact as the others we have quoted, nevertheless serve to illustrate another general feature of Stuart society, that so large a part of its resources in time, energy, and materials went in supporting the young and immature. In 1676 fifty-two

[1] *Passim*, especially pp. 59–62. This is a rare record of servants acting as a body in self-defence.

out of the ninety-eight households at Clayworth had children, so described, and in 1688 fifty-one out of ninety-one, that is well over half; if 'sons and daughters' are included, the proportion is nearer three-quarters. The average number of children in a household was 2·45 and 2·61, though in both years two-thirds of all children lived in sibling groups, as the psychologists say, of over three.[1] There is an interesting contrast with our own childhood experience, and the sibling group, we are told, is of the first significance in the formation of personality.

This is as far as we can go in the pursuit of the study of the historical structure of society from the evidence provided in these successive listings. Nothing has been said about the distribution of the land and wealth, nothing about the division by occupation, of these 400 people: how there were twenty-one freeholders at Clayworth in 1688, though six of them, the rector says, possessed less than £40 a year; how there were about twenty husbandmen, ten labourers, three or four gentlemen, three or four weavers, two or three shepherds, blacksmiths, and wrights, a butcher, a tailor, a cooper, a cutler, a bricklayer, a thatcher, sometimes a shoemaker, a spinner, a badger (corndealer), and still more callings amongst the heads of households, an astonishing variety, commercial and industrial as well as agricultural, in one single village. These details belong to the better-known features of Stuart society. The work done, and to be done, on Clayworth between 1676 and 1688 may perhaps come to be regarded as the ideal type of static community analysis, examining every constituent group and its structure, relations between groups and between individuals within each group. This is a type of social analysis which seems to be new to historians everywhere, at this level of realistic detail. Perhaps it may form an English counterpart to the dynamic analysis of peasant society over time, which is so advanced in France.

If we can find a way to apply French methods to English

---

[1] These figures are close to those of Lichfield in 1688, but the comparison is complicated by the issue of sons and daughters. If these are included at Clayworth, the mean size of sibling groups is changed to 2·09 and 2·23.

parish registers there is a great deal we shall be able to add to what we have begun to describe here. The birth rate, marriage rate, death rate, infantile mortality, fertility of mothers according to age, all these things could be recovered and they would tell us a great deal of why the community of Clayworth was as it was between 1676 and 1688, of how and why Stuart society as a whole was so different from our own. So also would the age of marriage, and the expectation of life, even such things as the rate of pre-nuptial pregnancy and illegitimacy. So above all would some convincing estimate as to whether the peasantry of England, like the peasantry of France before the middle of the eighteenth century, was liable to periodic starvation. With both types of analysis open to English historians, then, historical sociology could indeed be said to have made a beginning in our country.

But though we have come late to this study and though our evidence is so much inferior, we already know something in much more approximate ways.[1] And we can undertake in

[1] The crude exploitation of our defective English registers has yielded indications which seem to imply a higher rate of illegitimacy and pre-nuptial pregnancy in England than in France, for example. We have fairly reliable estimates of the age at marriage and of infantile mortality for a number of communities. All this rough information will be summarised in the work in preparation. For the methods of historical demography in use in France see the publications of l'Institut National d'Études Démographiques (I.N.E.D.) in Paris and its journal *Population*, and for the parish registers and the reconstitution of families in particular, see Michel Fleury and Louis Henry, *Des registres paroissiaux à l'histoire de la population. Manuel de dépouillement et d'exploitation de l'état civil ancien* (I.N.E.D., 1956). Though almost unknown here, this little book is a classic of documentary and numerical ingenuity, and the English student of parish records has nothing which remotely compares with it. The recognition that the harvest year was the proper unit for arranging these figures and that conceptions, not baptisms, are the events which have to be compared with fluctuations in burials, in marriages, and in the price of food is due to a remarkable article by J. Meuvret, 'Les Crises de subsistances et la démographie de la France d'Ancien Régime', *Population*, 1946. For examples of individual French communities, and whole groups of them, studied by the use of these methods, see Étienne Gautier and Louis Henry, *La Population de Crulai, paroisse normande, étude historique* (1958), Pierre Goubert, *Beauvais et les Beauvaisis* (2 vols., Paris 1960) and recent articles in *Population*. No work on English parish registers which takes into account these advances in method made in France since 1945 has yet been published. Even the

Clayworth, in the village of Cogenhoe in Northamptonshire also, dynamic study of a type which has not been done even in France, presumably because no documentary opportunity has yet occurred. We can study the turnover of population, the change in composition of the community in Clayworth over these dozen years, and even, in Cogenhoe, from year to year.

We know the birth rate, marriage rate, and death rate in Clayworth between 1676 and 1688: this is one of the important advantages of having its exact population and also a reliable register of baptisms, marriages, and burials. Since the population at the beginning was 401 and at the end 412 it seems reasonable (though we shall find ourselves being cautious about this) to assume a steady total over the years of some 400. The birth (baptismal) rate was 37·2 per thousand, the marriage rate 6·9, and the death (burial) rate was 41·25.[1]

Now these are crude rates, so crude and so likely to mislead that demographers no longer use them very much, although this is the accepted way of expressing the liability of a community to produce children, to marry, and to die. The numbers in this case are so small that very big variations can be expected from year to year, and the figures as a whole could be unrepresentative over so short a period. Nevertheless it must be said that the birth rate at Clayworth was obviously very high indeed as compared with what it is now in England and Wales, and the death rate even higher; the marriage rate was much the same. The birth rate reached thirty-five over the whole country at the height of Victorian fertility, but the death rate was in the twenties; nowadays they vary between twelve and seventeen. Another striking feature of the vital rates in the village is that there were more deaths than births, and there was a net loss from this of seven over the twelve years. Though

recent article on fluctuations in baptisms, marriages, and deaths in a group of Yorkshire parishes, 1540–1699 (Michael Drake, 'An Elementary Exercise in Parish Register Demography', *Econ. Hist. Rev.*, 1962), records baptisms, not conceptions and does not use the harvest year. It is, therefore, of little use in helping to decide whether crises of subsistence can be traced in England as well as in France.   [1] See Addendum for totals, etc.

this cannot have been normal for the whole of Stuart England, and though vital rates were probably high at Clayworth and especially the death rate, they were not abnormal for French communities at that time.

A net movement into the village of eighteen persons must have happened to bring about that increase of ten (really eleven) persons in 1688 over 1676 which the rector comments upon. Other reasons for people coming and going must be allowed for and with these high vital rates we should perhaps expect that the turnover of persons in the two lists might be rather high. It turns out to have been 61·8 per cent. John Harrison has discovered that 254 of the 412 people registered as being resident in 1688 were not there in 1676. If we put it the other way round, we find that only 158 of the 401 persons living in the community in 1676 were still to be found in it in 1688: 244 of them had disappeared, that is 60·86 per cent.[1] Now only ninety-one of these 244 who disappeared are recorded in the parish register as dying, so that all or practically all of the rest must have moved away. The startling fact is that a settled, rural, perfectly ordinary Stuart community could change its composition by well over half, getting on in fact for two-thirds, in a dozen years. So surprising is it that we do not yet know quite what to make of it.

Indeed the very uniqueness of the Clayworth record is itself baffling: it leaves us without adequate means of appreciating its significance. No doubt as studies of this sort become established, comparable documents will be found, and work will be done on the question of how much turnover we might expect to find under given conditions. We are very fortunate that the recognition of the possibility of so much change of this kind has very recently led to the recovery of a record which does do something to provide a context for the Clayworth evidence. Acting on a hint from Burn's *History of Parish*

---

[1] John Harrison's figures are summarised in the Addendum to this paper. There is still room for error in these calculations, arising for instance from unmarried women or servants present in 1676 who married outside Clayworth and were there again in 1688 but under a different name.

Registers[1] we found that the earliest of those preserved at Cogenhoe, a village a few miles on the Bedford side of Northampton, contained no less than six listings of the inhabitants, family by family, and name by name, dating from the decade 1618–28, and less useful earlier listings too. They were made by Christopher Spicer, Rector of Cogenhoe during those years.[2]

[1] 1862 ed., p. 212, mentioning the Cogenhoe register immediately after describing the *Liber Status Animarum* as 'the one best answering the description', though the year of the list (sic) is given as 1640, and no list for that date is to be seen in the document.

[2] A documentary description of this record is of some importance to the exact student of demographic evidence. It is a parchment register book, presumably supplied as the Act of 1597 required, by John Spicer, then Rector of Cogenhoe, and with its earlier pages filled with entries dating from 1545 onwards copied from the older paper books. This new register was in use till 1636, and before or about 1610 Christopher Spicer, presumably a relative, who had succeeded John as rector, began to use the two paper flysheets at the beginning of this parchment book to write out lists of communicants. There are several such lists before 1612, one headed 'Ester Day Communicants', and in that year he compiled a much longer one headed 'Communicants upon Ester Day, 1612'. He used the next page to record a terrier of his glebe, and these flysheets are also scribbled over with baptisms, marriages, and burials subsequently copied fair into the parchment pages, a frequent practice in register books. In 1615 he turned to the end of the book, and on the first page of the two flyleaves there wrote out a list of what seems to be all of the inhabitants in order of Christian name. He did this again in 1617, though in the intervening year he simply listed the households in the parish, giving names of heads and a total for each, with the population at the end. Next, overleaf, comes the 1618 census, leaving a wide margin to the right; as in all that follow, households are listed alphabetically, the name of each member given, though not relationships with the head (wife, son, servant, etc.), nor occupations, nor personal descriptions (widow, bachelor, etc.). No date is present for this first list, the heading having perished, but the second, on the facing page, is headed: *The register of the names of the parishioners. 30 May 1620. A note of the names of all parishioners 29 June 1621* follows, and overleaf, on the last page of the book, comes the 1623 list, heading perished. *A note of the names of all the parishioners 1624 15 August* was written next, but back on the final page of the flyleaves at the beginning of the book. The last list, headed simply *1628*, appears in the margin alongside the 1618 census. Totals for all six listings are given by the author, and numbers in each household except in 1618 and 1623. Only the 1628 list is quite free from the effects of the rotting away of the corners and edges of the manuscript and the dates of those lacking headings have had to be discovered by inference. But it is a remarkable record, and we are very grateful to the present Rector of Cogenhoe, the Rev. Mark Meynell, for allowing us to work on it. Unfortunately we have as yet been unable to

One of the notable features of this extraordinary series of recordings is the variation in the totals of persons and households. It must be remembered that all these figures are approximate, because only preliminary work has yet been done on the document and because all the listings except the last are in some degree affected by the state of the manuscript, but the figures in the following table are accurate enough to demonstrate this surprising fact.

COGENHOE 1616-28

	Total Population	Numbers of Households		Total Population	Numbers of Households
1616	187	32	1623	174	34
1618	185	33	1624	176	33
1620 (30 May)	150	30	(15 Aug.)		
1621 (29 June)	154	31	1628	180	33

Perhaps the population of Clayworth went up and down in the same way, which would make our vital rates less convincing. At Cogenhoe with an average of 5·2 baptisms, two marriages and 2·7 burials a year from 1611 to 1635 the registered birth (baptismal) rate was something between twenty-six and thirty-five per 1000, the marriage rate ten to 13·3, and the death (burial) rate 13·4 to 17·9. Birth and death rates, then, were lower than at Clayworth, the death rate so much lower that it looks as if there must have been under-registration.[1] But, and

find out anything further as to why or on what occasions Christopher Spicer compiled these listings. Peter Laslett and Susan Ault are preparing an article on Cogenhoe, with more accurate figures.

[1] Also to be suspected, especially for deaths, from the lists themselves which contain instances of people apparently dropping out without their deaths appearing in the register, for example the head of a household being replaced by his widow or his son. There are less obvious signs of births not being recorded, and these possible omissions do little to confirm Christopher Spicer as a competent registrar. Nevertheless the preliminary analysis of the households themselves as successively described by him reveal no patent discrepancies. The low figures in the above rates are for a population of 200: the high for a population of 150.

here is the critical point of comparison with Clayworth, the turnover of population was of the same order in both villages. Of the 180 individuals living at Cogenhoe in 1628, some 94 had come to live there since 1618. The turnover at Clayworth in the twelve years from 1676 to 1688 was 61·8 per cent: in Cogenhoe in the ten years from 1618 to 1628 it was about 52 per cent.

The turnover of population at Clayworth may, then, not have been abnormal for seventeenth century England, and the facts we have examined should persuade us to look very carefully at our assumptions about the settled immobility of persons in pre-industrial times. But it might be easy to exaggerate the importance of the rate of *structural* change which these figures imply. A 60 per cent turnover of persons in twelve years is after all only 5 per cent a year, and we should probably overlook the replacement of one person in twenty every year in an organisation which we belonged to, just as Sampson did at Clayworth. The birth rate and death rate in his village over these years was so high that they might by themselves have required a high proportion of this replacement of persons if the community were to stay at full strength.[1] Given that there was migration on a surprising scale in and out of these communities, it may nevertheless have been very local migration. If we had recovered evidence from groups of neighbouring villages and not from single villages, much less turnover might have shown up.[2] Some of the turnover, moreover, could perhaps have been due to seasonal movement of persons in search of work, and so should not count as change of settlement.

Some of these considerations may finally make this turnover

[1] A death rate of forty per thousand might seem to bring about a reduction of the original population by 48 per cent in twelve years, but in fact so many of the deaths were of infants (infantile mortality rate near 300 per thousand births 1680–88) that this does not follow, and the deaths of those who came in after 1676 have to be reckoned with also.

[2] Work on the registers of neighbouring parishes might show where some of these people came from and went to: this will be undertaken for Clayworth and Cogenhoe.

of persons seem less startling than it does on its first discovery. It seems doubtful, however, whether in these particular cases seasonal employment explains very much. The enormous variation in the demand for labour over the year in agriculture was undoubtedly one of the governing influences on the life of our ancestors, and on the structure of their society. The number of people wanted to work the land may have been three or four times as many in late summer as in midwinter, or even more. Important as this is, and it will have to be discussed at length elsewhere, it cannot affect the Clayworth counts because each of them was taken well before harvest-time. Even in mid-August at Cogenhoe it is difficult to discern any sign of a temporary influx of labour. The migration we are examining seems to be of a different character.

There are four distinct elements in the turnover of persons in these two villages. The first is the appearance and disappearance which came about through births and deaths; this we have already discussed. The second and statistically most important is the annual movement of servants in and out of the community to take and leave jobs in the households of employers. The third, not quite distinct from the second, is the movement of other individuals, and the fourth is the movement of whole families and their vicissitudes. Let us take these in order.

The fact that the total turnover over a number of years is nothing like what it would be if turnover had been cumulative shows that one section of the community was changing much more rapidly than the rest. Everything goes to show that this section was the 10 or 15 per cent of servants. Anne Bingham was the solitary servant in Clayworth in 1688 who had been in service there in 1676, and she had changed her place. The other sixty-six had either ceased to be servants or left the village, or both. Only Elizabeth Stocking of the twenty-six servants at Cogen-hoe in 1628 had been amongst the thirty-one there in 1618; even she was absent in 1621 and changed households between 1624 and 1628. The numbers went down as low as seventeen in 1620 and 1621, yet about a hundred different names of servants

occur in Spicer's six lists.[1] and they make it clear that a servant
tended to stay in one household for one or two years, and then
move on. Of this hundred, seventy-one appear only once in
the lists and only ten more than twice: in 1624, for example, ten out of twenty-three servants were new, though
two of them had been in the village as servants at some
time since 1618: of the thirteen who had stayed from
1623, three had changed households. Between 1618 and 1620
over three-quarters of the servants left their places and the
village.

Servants then were the most mobile members of the community, though not all of them came from outside it, and some
of their movements took place within it. Perhaps a sixth of the
servants at Clayworth, perhaps twice that proportion at Cogenhoe, had names borne by the established families. Not infrequently when they left their places they married and settled
down as householders, like John Brason and Ralph Meers at
Clayworth. This is one of the reasons why the movement of
servants cannot be separated from that of individuals generally,
for brides and bridegrooms coming into a village might have
been servants elsewhere, just as sons or daughters leaving a
village might well be going to be servants in another. The
migration which took place because of marriage, though of
considerable social significance, was relatively small: only five
of the 244 people who disappeared from Clayworth between
1676 and 1688 were brides certainly known to have left on
marriage.

Independent movement of individuals may be difficult to
separate from the movement of servants, but its extent and
importance must not be overlooked. At Cogenhoe between
1618 and 1620, for example, twenty-three individuals disappeared and fourteen arrived, quite apart from the movement

---

[1] It will be remembered that these are rough figures, and that at Cogenhoe servants are not always easy to distinguish from members of the family
of kin. In this village of, say, 175 souls on the average, some 450 names of
residents are registered by the rector in the various lists he wrote out
between 1610 and 1628, and it will be recognised that many more would
appear if he had kept an absolutely complete record.

of households and servants: the full lists show sons and daughters coming and going, there one year, absent the next. When such an arrival or departure was final it might mean a definite change in structure. There can nevertheless be no doubt that the important and unexpected source of structural change was the transfer of whole households. Over the same interval 1618–1620 at Cogenhoe no less than four out of thirty-three households left the village, taking thirty-one people with them, including ten servants: a fifth household disappeared on the death of its head and the marriage of his only child, whose mother went to live with her. This formed a new household at Cogenhoe, but only one other appeared during the two years. The enduring, familial structure of the village community had changed quite suddenly and not inconsiderably, because one of the households to leave was the biggest in the villlage, the family of Edmond Norwood, gentleman, with his wife, four children, and nine servants. Two substantial working households moved away also, and the removal was final for everyone. At Clayworth in 1688 something like twenty-three of ninety-one households were new since 1676, and ten of these were entirely novel: the thirteen others may possibly show some continuity, or the movement of relatives into the village to take over existing establishments.

We have perhaps spent too long on this phenomenon of the turnover of population in our two villages. We could go on to show that in spite of sudden change of this sort, and of the more gradual change which came about through the succession of son to father, nephew to uncle, kinsman to kinsman, the impression of permanence in the constituent households which composed a Stuart community is easy to understand. Nearly half of the heads of households at Clayworth had either died or had left the village by 1688, nevertheless their successors presided over units of persons which were mostly recognisably the same. And at Cogenhoe, where eight out of thirty-three households failed to survive a decade of change, it is still true that over three-quarters of them did survive, often with different heads, with a membership sometimes extensively

revised, but still the same households, inhabiting the same
buildings, working the same fields. The system, that familial,
patriarchal system which dominated and gave structure to pre-
industrial society, had succeeded in maintaining permanence
in spite of the shortness of life, the fluctuations of prosperity,
the falling in of leases, the wayward habits of young folk in
service, and the fickleness of their employers.

The institutions of the old world must be looked upon in
this way, as expedients to provide permanence in an environ-
ment which was all too impermanent and insecure. The respect
due to the old and experienced, the reverence for the Church
and its immense, impersonal antiquity, the spontaneous feeling
that it was the family which gave a meaning to life because the
family could and must endure, all these things helped to reconcile our ancestors with relentless, remorseless mortality, and
mischance. But they must not deceive the historian into sup-
posing that the fixed and the ancient were the only reality: an
unchanging, unchangeable social structure may well be essential
to a swiftly changing population.

The historical observer in an inquiry of this sort can only
feel himself to be in the position of the scientist in his bathy-
scope, miles beneath the surface of the sea, concentrating his
gaze for a moment or two on the few strange creatures who
happen to stray out of the total darkness into his beam of light.
Where have they come from, and what will happen to them?
he cannot help asking himself. What did happen to poor little
Copperwhite Mastin, son of Elizabeth Mastin, spinster, and
seven months old in May 1688, the only bastard alive in Clayworth? Or to the Coles household, thirteen strong, which
appeared at Cogenhoe in 1623, no doubt as tenants of the
leased-out manor, was there in 1624, but had disappeared by
1628? Even more puzzling and challenging is to ask whether
these two communities are in fact typical of the whole. On this
the historian can only talk as the scientist might. Here are two
samples of communities in motion, two tiny globes of light
disposed at random a little way down into the great ocean of
persons who lived and died in our country before records of

13

persons in general began to be kept. These samples may be ordinary enough, but they may be quite extraordinary. We cannot yet tell: we may never be able to tell.

ADDENDUM TO CLAYWORTH AND COGENHOE

SOME FIGURES FOR CLAYWORTH 1676–88

I. *Distribution of Persons between Households*

Persons per Household	1676		1688	
	Households	Persons	Households	Persons
1	6	6	4	4
2	10	20	12	24
3	31	93	20	60
4	16	64	20	80
5	16	80	11	55
6	7	42	7	42
7	3	21	5	35
8	7	56	6	48
9	1	9	5	45
10	1	10	1	10
	98	401	91*	403*

* Excluding Common-houses

In households of 1–3	47	48%	119	29%	36	39·5%	88	21·8%
In households of 6 and above	19	19·5%	138	34·5%	24	26%	180	44·5%

II. *Baptisms, Marriages, and Burials*: 1st May, 1676–30th April, 1688.

	Baptisms	Marriages	Burials
Total	190	33	197
Annual Mean	15·88	2·75	16·41
Rate per 1000 at a population of 400	37·2	6·9	41·25

The loss by excess of burials over baptisms was 7: the year 1679 was exceptional for burials (33) and if this is reduced to the mean for other years the overall mean is almost exactly 15.

III. *Turnover of Persons*: Totals

	1676	1688
Persons	401	412
Households	98	91 and Common-houses
Servants	67	65

Registered in 1676 but absent in 1688

244 persons, 60·86% of population.
> 91 (22·5% pop.) known to have died.
> 53 servants who presumably left the village.
> 40 (approximately) who left the village as members of 10 complete households.
> 74 (approximately) unaccounted for.
>> *The above categories are not all exclusive.*

Present in both 1676 and 1688

158 persons, 39·4% of 1676 population, 38·35% of 1688 population, including 1 servant, in a different household, and 8 other servants who had themselves become householders, 6 of them marrying each other.
> 6 children in 1676 were servants in 1688.

Of these 158, 79 are known to have died in the village by 1714.

Newcomers in 1688

254 persons, 61·8% of population.
> 92 baptised in Clayworth 1676–1688.
> 58 had come to the village as servants.
> 35 (approximately) had come to the village as members of 10 novel complete households.
> 68 (approximately) unaccounted for.
>> *The above categories are not all exclusive.*

Heads of Household

Of the 98 heads in 1676, 47 had disappeared by 1688.
> 34 by death in Clayworth.
> 10 by migration with their households.
> 2 by being absent from 1688 list, though apparently subsequently dying in the village.
> 1 by going to the Common-houses.

Of the 91 heads in 1688, 50 had been head in 1676 and 41 were new.

18 of new heads had been present in 1676 but not as heads, 4 had been servants.

23 of new heads thereafter appear in Clayworth for the first time.

Of these 10 headed households with surnames apparently new to the village.

11 headed households with surnames present in 1676 but with no other sign of continuity.

2 headed households which seem different but could perhaps be continuations of 1676 households.

Of those head in 1688, 75 are known to have died by 1730.

VIII

KING JAMES II AND THE REVOLUTION OF 1688:
SOME REFLECTIONS ON THE HISTORIOGRAPHY

Maurice Ashley

THE object of this essay is to investigate one aspect of the historiography of the revolution of 1688 in England.

It has been generally agreed by modern historians that the revolution should first be set in its international frame. One of the earliest historians to stress this was Lawrence Echard, Archdeacon of Stowe, who, writing in 1725, said:[1]

> The Revolution . . . seems not so much to be the Cause as the Consequence of the . . . great Confederacy and War against France, or rather an Incident intermix'd with it.

Later Leopold von Ranke and Onno Klopp developed the point and in the chapter which he has contributed to *The New Cambridge Modern History* Dr. Esmond de Beer devotes particular attention to it.[2] Unquestionably the Dutch rulers of the time were perturbed about the possibility of a new Anglo-French alliance against them, constituting, as it would have done, the most formidable naval combination in the world; but equally King James II was anxious to avoid provoking the Dutch by concluding such an alliance. That was why as late as the end of September 1688 the English ambassador in the United Netherlands was assuring the States General that no secret Anglo-French treaty existed.[3] But naval preparations had by then been made by both nations and these created as much a situation of mutual distrust as Anglo-German naval building

---

[1] *The History of the Revolution and the Establishment in England in the Year 1688*, p. 43.

[2] Dr. de Beer kindly allowed me to read his chapter in proof.

[3] *Recueil des Instructions: Angleterre, ii, 1660–1690* (1929), 411.

did before 1914; it was because of this fear that Prince William of Orange, husband of James II's elder daughter, was allowed by his Dutch compatriots to invade England that autumn in order, as he said, to restore her 'ravished liberties'.

But the invasion would not have been tried unless Prince William had first been convinced that a substantial number of influential people in England would welcome his arrival. Since 1066 no military assault had been successfully launched on Britain from oversea except when partisans of the invader stood ready to receive him. Even during the Interregnum when the Spanish monarchy was aware that King Charles II had many active supporters in England it refused to send an amphibious expedition on his behalf against the Commonwealth unless it was first assured that a port of debarkation had been seized by royalists. So in considering the causes of the revolution of 1688 the question still needs to be asked why King James II had become so unpopular that William of Orange was able to achieve a bloodless triumph.

In studying the reign of King James II one asks oneself three questions:

(1) What were the character and aims of King James?
(2) What were the aims of William of Orange and when precisely did he decide to move against his father-in-law?
(3) What part was played by the man who was King James's chief minister until the very eve of the revolution—Robert Spencer, second Earl of Sunderland?

The third question has already been largely answered in Dr. J. P. Kenyon's brilliant biography of Sunderland, although one is not entirely convinced that, like so many statesmen of that and the succeeding age, Sunderland did not attempt to 're-insure' himself with William through the agency of his wife.[1]

---

[1] *Robert Spencer, Earl of Sunderland, 1641–1702* (1958), chs. 4 to 6; in 'The Earl of Sunderland and the Revolution of 1688', *Cambridge Historical Journal*, No. 3 (1955), pp. 297 *seq.*, Dr. Kenyon discusses the historiography in detail. Anne Sunderland's letter to William of Orange of 7 March 1687 begging him not to help James II by supporting the repeal of the anti-

The second question depends on a more careful examination of the Dutch sources than has hitherto become available; but there can hardly be any doubt that Prince William made up his mind to intervene several months before the birth of the Old Pretender and perhaps as early as the spring of 1687.[1] Moreover, it is reasonable to assume that William knew the character of his father-in-law sufficiently well to realise that once he moved against him James would obstinately refuse any compromise or concession and rather abandon his throne than his principles.

On the first question or questions historians have been much divided. Was King James really a dense bigot who 'blew the lid off the stove'? Or had he a reasonably long-term thought-out policy for religious toleration, embracing his fellow Roman Catholics which followed logically upon the 'liberty of conscience' instituted under the Cromwellian Protectorate and the declarations published by his brother, King Charles II? Was it his subjects' prejudices and his tactless methods which cost him his throne?

One of the first historians to discuss King James II's policy was White Kennett, Bishop of Peterborough, who wrote his *Complete History of England* in 1705 and himself had been an Anglican vicar aged twenty-eight when the revolution took place. The Earl of Danby, who had played a prominent part in the revolution, read this book with close attention;[2] Sir Charles Firth called its author a careful and laborious writer.[3] And he had certainly lived through the events he was describing,

Catholic laws, was first printed by John Dalrymple, *Memoirs* (1790), ii, App. to Book V, pp. 58-61; the original in her handwriting is in the Public Record Office, K.W.C. 8. Neither Dr. Kenyon nor Professor Lucile Pinkham, *William III and the Respectable Revolution* (1954), pp. 40-1, believes that Sunderland had any hand in his wife's letter: Dalrymple suspected that 'the letter was her husband's diction'. My own feeling is that Sunderland might have known of this letter and been willing to accept this little piece of re-insurance in case things went wrong.

[1] Cf. Pinkham, *op. cit.*, ch. 3. This book has been severely criticised, but the arguments on this point are plausible.   [2] B.M. Add. MS. 28042.

[3] C. H. Firth, 'The Development of the Study of Seventeenth Century History' in *Transactions of the Royal Historical Society* (1913), discusses Kennett and other early historians.

having refused, among other things, to read in his pulpit King James II's second declaration of liberty of conscience published in April 1688.

Kennett wrote that 'whether by his own Zeal or the Importunity of Others' James had from the beginning of his reign been set upon 'arbitrary measures' for 'promoting Popery'.[1] He also thought that if at the outset members of the Church of England had followed the advice of the court the dissenters would have been 'entirely destroyed'. An example of the king's attitude to the dissenters was the case brought against the ageing Richard Baxter in May 1685 for having committed sedition in paraphrases of the New Testament which he had published. He was bullied by Chief Justice Jeffreys and sentenced to a fine of 500 marks and to be bound over for seven years. About 1686, however, the king in order to achieve popularity and protection for the papists resolved to show indulgence to the dissenters. But, added Kennett, 'it is very plain that if King James could have got the Bishops and Clergy and Body of the Church of England to have Persecuted and Extirpated the Dissenters he would have chosen that Way of utmost Severity much rather than Indulgence and Toleration'. In fact as late as 1687 'their Meetings were frequently Disturb'd both in City and Country'. Fines were levied and many were prosecuted. Later dissenters 'caught greedily at the Bait' offered by James's declaration of liberty of conscience, 'without discerning the Hook in it'. Kennett nevertheless admitted that the king was generous to the Protestants who escaped to England from France after the French monarchy had revoked the Edict of Nantes in October 1685.

Writing some twenty years after Kennett, Rapin de Thoyras, who himself had been a French Protestant, while repeating a story that James had told a Jesuit that 'he would either convert England or die a martyr', noted that the king had proclaimed liberty of conscience (except for field conventicles) in Scotland at an early stage of his reign; that he had received and protected French Protestants fleeing from the wrath of King Louis XIV;

[1] Ed. of 1719, pp. 442, 450, 486.

and that they had praised James's virtues: 'I myself remember to have heard a preacher in the church of the Savoy launch into the profanest flattery'. Later the king used absolutist methods to attain his ends. 'It was evident that the King no longer pretended to govern by the laws of the land, but according to his own will and pleasure.' In the end, according to Rapin, it was not upon an army of thirteen or fourteen thousand men that the Prince of Orange relied but upon the disposition of the exasperated English who impatiently awaited his arrival.[1]

Lawrence Echard wrote a little earlier than Rapin and is quoted by him. Echard thought that Charles II had died 'with the Liberties of England at his mercy' and that his brother, King James, though 'a kind husband and indulgent father', who restrained his pleasures, was under the influence of priests, Jesuits and the Earl of Sunderland. His aim was to obtain far-reaching advantages for the Roman Catholics with the backing of a large standing army; it was not until the third year of his reign that he courted his old enemies, the dissenters; they then 'snatched at the bait without thinking of the hook in it'—Kennett's phrase; Sunderland and the Spanish ambassador in London were responsible for making James imagine that there was no danger of interference with his plans from the United Netherlands; so that when at last he finally realised on 23 September 1688 William's design to invade he 'turned pale' and ultimately fled.[2]

Other contemporary historians included James Welwood, a physician, who wrote his memoirs after having conversations with King James II's daughter, Queen Mary II. Welwood stressed the constitutional aspects and thought that the dissenters were never inclined 'to swallow the Bait of Toleration'. Men's eyes, in his view, had been opened more and more every day to the dangers to their liberties and 'the Monster of the Dispensing Power.' The dissenters were being used as 'tools'; William and Mary were therefore obliged to repudiate the

---

[1] *The History of England* (trans. N. Tindal), xii (1742), pp. 65, 68, 80, 115, 130.   [2] *The History of the Revolution*, 1725, pp. 63, 79, 181.

idea of taking off the penal laws and the tests.[1] But King James was urged on by his fate. Abel Boyer, writing his *History of William III* in 1702, on the other hand, thought that King James had all along been 'of a facile, manageable disposition, easily led on by Jesuits and his high-spirited, bigoted Queen'.[2] This 'easy credulous Prince' even ignored the advice of the Spanish ambassador. But Boyer also stressed the king's generosity to the Huguenots; he had given them money out of his privy purse and permitted them to establish a church in Soho Fields. The nonconformists eagerly accepted the opportunity he offered them for freedom of worship and sent daily addresses of gratitude to him. But the Jesuits who advised him wanted him to re-establish popery.

When one turns to Gilbert Burnet's *History of His Own Time*, first published in 1724 but written much earlier in draft form, one reaches an entirely different class of contemporary history. For Burnet knew personally the people concerned, even though he spent much of King James II's reign out of England: he had conversed with James on several occasions, as well as being on intimate terms with Queen Mary and in the confidence of William of Orange. Writing in 1683 of an interview he had with James before he came to the throne, Burnet observed that though he was very firm in his religion and very much devoted to his priests, 'yet when I knew him he seemed very positive in his opinion against all persecution for conscience sake'.[3] Burnet also quoted Marshal Turenne's tribute that James was the 'greatest prince' and 'like to be the best general of his time'. Burnet added, however, that 'he quickly ran into amours and vice' and so at the end of his life came to lose the reputation of 'a brave man and a good captain'. Burnet emphasised that at the beginning of his reign King James was resolved not to be governed by French counsels. He states that the king strongly disapproved of Louis XIV's persecution of French Protestants, which he blamed on

---

[1] *Memoirs of the Most Material Transactions in England* (1736), pp. 156, 169, 189.   [2] Pp. 37-8.

[3] H. C. Foxcroft, *A Supplement, etc.* (1902), pp. 51-2.

Mme de Maintenon and the Archbishop of Paris, and illustrated in some detail how good he was to the forty or fifty thousand refugees who came to England. As soon as the aftermath of Monmouth's invasion was over in 1685 the dissenters were in 'high favour' with the court. Though the Anglican clergy began to preach against popery, the dissenters did not. On the whole, Burnet seems to have regarded the king's kindnesses to the dissenters as a real danger to William of Orange's plans for intervention in England. Though in June 1688, at the time of the trial of the seven bishops for seditious libel and at the time of the birth of the Old Pretender, the opportunity for William to intervene was considered to be most propitious, William himself was unwilling to take the risk of coming over without a large army and fleet. If he had not come when he did, Burnet thought, the chance might have been missed and the alliance already achieved between King James and the dissenters might have contributed to the holding of a Parliament favourable to King James's religious policies.[1] (Recently Dr. Kenyon has argued that James's policies, as executed by Sunderland, stood a good chance of succeeding early in 1688 and that was why those who invited William to come over begged him to do so urgently lest the opportunity be missed.)[2]

John Oldmixon, the Whiggish historian, whose history of England also appeared in the first half of the eighteenth century, read Burnet but evidently preferred to ignore much of what he said; Oldmixon described James as 'sanguinary and cruel', asserted that James had gone on persecuting dissenters as long as he could, and strongly criticised Lawrence Echard for saying that they 'caught at the bait of toleration' while denying James Welwood's suggestion that they might have supported the king in Parliament. Since King James had 'subverted' the constitution, Oldmixon thought that the nation had every right to appeal to the Prince of Orange.[3]

One can pass rapidly over the historians of the mid-eighteenth

---

[1] *History of My Own Time* (1823), iii, 4-5, 81-2, 153, 248.
[2] *Cambridge Historical Journal* (1955), p. 278.
[3] *The History of England* (1730), pp. 704, 721, 723, 740.

century, who, unlike their predecessors, had no direct contact with the events. James Ralph, a conscientious compiler, wrote that it was proper to recollect the prosecution of Baxter at the beginning of the reign of James II 'and in what Manner the Dissenters in a Body were treated in the first Memorial set forth in the name of the Church of England . . . to illustrate the real Designs of the Court'. Ralph follows Burnet in saying that the king was 'very kind' to the Huguenot refugees and notes that it was 'not to be supposed that such a Politician as the Prince of Orange would neglect any Opportunity of Advancing his Interest'.[1] David Hume, for whose merits as a historian the present Regius Professor of Modern History at Oxford has recently put in a good word,[2] concentrated on the unconstitutional character of King James's policies: 'Almost the whole of this short reign', he wrote, 'consists of attempts, always impudent, often illegal, sometimes both, against whatever was most loved and revered by the nation.' Yet the king 'was become a great patron of toleration and an enemy of those persecuting laws which, from the influence of the church, had been enacted both against the dissenters and catholics'. James had strong historical precedent on his side for the use of the dispensing and suspending powers and was 'more unfortunate than criminal'. His domestic life, Hume thought, was 'irreproachable', but he was 'infected with Catholic superstition'.[3]

It is with the publication of Sir John Dalrymple's *Memoirs of Great Britain and Ireland*, 1771–73, a year or two after David Hume's *History of England* appeared, that one reaches a striking change in the historiography of the revolution. For Dalrymple had access both to the papers contained in King William's chest, notably the correspondence between King James and his son-in-law and the letters relating to the Dutch envoy, Dykveld's mission to England in 1687, and to the dispatches of Paul Barrillon, the French ambassador in London throughout the

[1] *The History of England* (1744), pp. 948, 958.
[2] *The Listener*, 28 December 1961.
[3] *A History of England*, viii (1818), 256, 258, 305.

reign.[1] Barrillon's detailed reports were also printed in part in
Charles James Fox's unfinished *History of the Early Part of the
Reign of James II*, published posthumously in 1808 and were
used in F. A. J. Mazure's *Histoire de la révolution de 1688 en
Angleterre*, published in 1825. Fox had also investigated the
question of the authenticity of James II's own 'memoirs' which
had earlier been examined in France by Thomas Carte and
James Macpherson during the eighteenth century, both of them
publishing extracts. Fox was sure that Macpherson had never
really seen James's 'original journal'—which he said had been
burnt in 1802—and Macpherson said that Carte had never seen
it. During the Napoleonic wars the Prince Regent had purchased a narrative compiled by Jacobite scribes from James's
papers (consisting, according to Fox, of four volumes folio and
six volumes quarto) and this was published in 1816 by the
Reverend James Clarke, the historiographer royal, under the
title of *The Life of James II*.[2]

All this new material threw fresh light on King James's
policy and character. Barrillon's reports were interpreted to
mean that at the outset of the reign the king's aim was, with
the aid of the French king, to get rid of all the penal laws and
Test Acts which prevented full equality of citizenship for
Roman Catholics and also to abolish the Habeas Corpus Acts
which detracted from an absolutist system of government. As
early as 6 July 1685 Sunderland had told Barrillon that the
king was anxious to establish the Roman Catholic religion, but
admitted that this would be difficult without French support;[3]

[1] One hundred and seventy years after Dalrymple the Public Record
Office is publishing the *Calendar of State Papers Dom.* for the reign of
James II. One volume was published in 1960. Mr. E. K. Timings who is
engaged on this work tells me that Dalrymple missed nothing of importance.

[2] For the latest examination of the complicated question of the authenticity of James's memoirs see *The Memoirs of James II* (1962), introduction,
by A. Lytton Sells, p. 25 *seq.*: in my view the MS. published by Clarke is a
fair representation of what James II thought and was based on James's own
papers. It is clear from what Fox saw and what James told Burnet and
Cardinal Bouillon that he left behind him a great many papers of different
kinds, though I agree with Dr. Kenyon that James did not himself do much
literary composition.

[3] Printed in C. J. Fox, p. cv.

that is to say, he wanted to reverse the Reformation settlement, not simply to impose toleration either by prerogative means or with the aid of a 'packed' Parliament. The king had no sympathy with the dissenters whom he regarded as 'republicans'. 'Partly to gratify the natural vindictiveness of his temper,' wrote Charles James Fox, 'he persevered in a most cruel prosecution of the Protestant Dissenters upon the most frivolous pretences':[1] the prosecution of Baxter was a case in point. Mazure, who had made use both of Barrillon's reports and those of Bonrepaus, the intendant general of the French Marine, who twice carried out special missions to England during James's reign and was a voluminous correspondent, described James as 'a feeble and vain King', absolutely governed by his Roman Catholic camarilla. It was true that James repudiated the idea of being a French vassal and strengthened his army and navy. But he alienated the Dutch, and his nonconformist subjects did not trust him, fearing his later concessions to them were a trap. In the end James would neither call Parliament, prepare for war, nor accept the help of Louis XIV and so he laid himself open to being deposed by William of Orange who had marched '*froidement, mais constamment à son but*'.[2]

Mazure also studied Clarke's *Life of James II*. From that book the impression derived was that King James attributed his fall to fate and the Earl of Sunderland. This 'cunning lord', according to the *Life*, 'thrust the King forward towards the precipice, to gain an interest with him he saw was about to supplant him'. In the *Life* it was argued that James had been the consistent supporter of 'liberty of conscience' which he thought was not only right in itself but beneficial to trade. Before he withdrew from England to France he appealed 'to all who are considering men and have had experience whether any thing can make this Nation so great and flourishing as Libertie of Conscience. Some of our Neighbours dread it'.[3]

In 1834 another valuable contribution was made to the

[1] C. J. Fox, *A History of the Early Part of the Reign of James II*, p. 101.
[2] F. A. J. Mazure, *Histoire etc.*, 1825, ii, 127, 165, 265.
[3] Clarke, pp. 72, 269.

accumulation of historical material on the reign of James II when Sir James Mackintosh's *History of the Revolution of 1688* was posthumously published. For Mackintosh had got hold of letters written by the papal nuncio, Ferdinand D'Adda, and by the Spanish ambassador, don Pedro de Ronquillo, who had been in England during the reign. Mackintosh had been a Whig and was the friend of Charles James Fox and Canning, but he was an indolent philosopher, lawyer, and historian. He scarcely seems to have taken notice of his own manuscripts. He thought that 'none of the most discerning friends or opponents of the King seem to have doubted that he meditated no less than to transfer to his own religion the privileges of an established Church'.[1] James's 'Declaration of Indulgence' was intended merely to divide the Protestants. He welcomed the Huguenots only because they would be of service to trade and increase the population. His real purpose therefore was the full catholicisation of England: through Barrillon King James II assured King Louis XIV in May 1687 that 'we shall, in concert, do great things for religion'.[2]

Such were the materials that were already at his disposal when Lord Macaulay wrote his powerful best-selling *History of England*, published in the middle of the nineteenth century. Macaulay had few doubts about James's character or policy. From the beginning James had shown himself a sycophant of the French king, apologising to him for calling a Parliament and shedding tears when he offered him a small sum of money. James had no real sympathy for the nonconformists: 'the manner in which Baxter was treated by a judge [Jeffreys] who was a member of the Cabinet and a favourite of the Sovereign indicated, in a manner not to be mistaken, the feeling with which the government at this time regarded the Protestant Nonconformists'. After the failure of Monmouth's invasion the dissenters were 'cruelly' treated: 'through many years the autumn of 1685 was remembered by the Nonconformists as a time of misery and terror'. Relying on Barrillon's reports,

---

[1] *History of the Revolution* (1834), p. 209.
[2] Barrillon to Louis XIV 2/12 May 1687, cit. Mackintosh, p. 207.

Macaulay argued that James's public attitude to the French Huguenots arriving from France had been hypocritical. In his heart he approved of what Louis XIV had done: he insisted that Huguenot ministers 'speak with reverence of their oppressor.' He ordered the burning of a pamphlet condemning the persecution; he was 'mortified' by the large amount of money collected for the Huguenot refugees; and he gave instructions that the money should be paid only to those who joined the Church of England. In Scotland Presbyterians were persecuted by James's orders and he refused to give way over his demands for open worship for the Roman Catholics there: 'concession had ruined his father'. Macaulay makes mention of the king's mistress, Catherine Sedley, Countess of Dorchester, and remarks that 'she was, however, only one of several abandoned women who at this time shared with his beloved Church the dominion over his mind'. Though towards the end of the reign the king granted concessions to the dissenters when he found that he could not rely on the Anglicans to assist his catholicising policy ('for a time he meditated a plan to gain the Dissenters in order to persecute the Church of England') still in his heart, according to Barrillon, he would have preferred to obtain entire liberty for the Roman Catholics and yet maintain the penal laws against the nonconformists.[1]

Some ten years after Macaulay's *History* was published, Leopold von Ranke published the volumes in his *Englische Geschichte* covering the revolution of 1688. Macaulay is reckoned the supreme exponent of the 'Whig interpretation of history', Ranke the father of modern 'scientific history'. Both of them used much the same materials; both of them depended largely on Barrillon for their views of James's character and policy; and though Ranke was sometimes critical of Macaulay, their conclusions were not widely different. Ranke thought that throughout his life King James was 'very dependent on priests and women', that he was more closely attached to France than Charles II had been, and that Louis XIV en-

[1] *History of England*, i (1857 revision), pp. 328, 366, 389, 401, 429.

couraged him to conceal his real convictions. He had been reluctant to protect the nonconformists whom he had long regarded as his bitterest enemies. He 'approved at bottom of the proceedings of Louis XIV in revoking the Edict of Nantes'. It was not until the spring of 1687 that he decided to put into practice 'what he had said at the beginning of his reign—that if the Episcopal Church did not comply with his wishes he would turn to the Nonconformists'. Confidential relations never existed between King James and William of Orange and in effect James agreed in the spring of 1688 to commit himself to full military and diplomatic support of France: 'No prince has ever had less thought for the balance of power in Europe than James II'. William of Orange came to England to redress the balance of power.[1] William, as Lord Acton once pointed out, was, in Ranke's view, 'neither the friend of popular liberties nor the champion of the Protestant religion'.[2] His enterprise was directed against France, and it had the approval of Spain, the pope, and the emperor.

The Macaulay-Ranke portrait of King James II and his policies remained basic for historians of two or three generations and Barrillon's dispatches continued to be a principal source. Yet even before those two famous historians had written, the Roman Catholic historian John Lingard had queried how reliable that source was. Paul Barrillon d'Amoncourt, who belonged to the class of administrators and diplomatists most favoured by Louis XIV, was undoubtedly a rich and able man of vast experience; he was a friend of Mme de Sévigné, La Fontaine, and Mme de Maintenon, of whom he was said to have been enamoured. The French historian Jusserand says that he was highly conscientious, sane in his judgments, and careful of the truth; but he admits that he was a born flatterer.[3] Another French historian, Henri Forneron, wrote that Barrillon was 'a master of the art of corrupting men

---

[1] *History of England*, iv (trans. 1875), pp. 218, 227, 282, 312, 382, 384.
[2] Cit. H. Butterfield, *Man on his Past* (1955), p. 229.
[3] *Recueil des Instructions: Angleterre*, ii, 223 *seq.* Barrillon came to England as ambassador in 1677, but he had held administrative posts since 1657.

and of hiding his contempt for those whom he corrupted' and
thought that he was both cynical and unscrupulous.[1] Lingard
suggested that the pressure which Barrillon exerted on the
French king at the beginning of James's reign to provide him
with a substantial sum of money for the purposes of bribery
was part of an endeavour to increase his own importance in
the new reign.[2] Another Roman Catholic writer considered
that Barrillon was careful not to tell Louis XIV what he thought
might offend him.[3] As things proved, James did not really need
money nor did he get it from France. Barrillon, Lingard
believed, was 'acting a part' and put language into King
James's mouth which he did not in fact use.[4] A careful reading
of Barrillon's dispatches[5] neither sustains the view that James
was sycophantic to France—in fact it is now plain that he was
less, not more, pro-French than Charles II—nor that he
approved the methods employed by Louis XIV to convert the
French Huguenots.

Is it true that at the beginning of his reign James adopted a
policy of violence towards the dissenters, as Macaulay wrote,
only abandoning it when he was unable to help his fellow Roman
Catholics to power with the aid of the Anglicans? This is a matter
for research. But one of James's first actions as king was to
order the release of all persons imprisoned for religious
reasons, including 1200 'Quakers': Lingard noted that. This
question may, to some extent, be linked with James's attitude
to the French government's treatment of its protestant subjects.
Lingard thought that after the revocation of the Edict of Nantes
in October 1685 James 'openly declared his disapprobation of
religious persecution and promoted with all his influence
measures devised for the relief of the refugees'. Both Lingard
and later Roman Catholic historians have pointed out that the
relevant quotations from Barrillon's dispatches lend no sub-

---

[1] *Louise de Kéroualle* (trans. 1897), pp. 193–4.
[2] *History of England* (fifth edition, 1869) x, 130–1.
[3] M. V. Hay, *The Enigma of James II* (1938), p. 181.
[4] *Loc. cit.*
[5] Most of these can be read in the Baschet transcripts 31/3 in the Public
Record Office. Cf. Pinkham, *op. cit.*, p. 95 note.

stance to the view that James approved of the 'dragonnades', the deliberate policy of billeting French soldiers in protestant homes to enforce conversions, while Mackintosh in 1834 quoted a dispatch of Ronquillo dated 12 August 1686 in which he said that what Louis XIV had done was neither Christian nor good politics and that he himself 'would force no man's conscience but only aimed at the Roman Catholics being no worse treated than the rest instead of being deprived of their liberties like traitors'.[1] In fact Barrillon was at pains to assure James that the stories of cruelties in France were false and unjust and James was at first misled because he seemed to imagine that the mass conversions were achieved without extreme pressures being used.[2]

One further point is worth noting about Barrillon and the religious question. After the books by Macaulay and Ranke were published the Public Record Office commissioned M. Armand Baschet to make transcripts of French documents bearing on British history and about 1875 full transcripts of the dispatches of Barrillon (and Bonrepaus) were acquired. Neither of them was all that well informed about English affairs: their source of information was court gossip. For example, they devoted a great deal of attention to the movements of the Countess of Dorchester. But Barrillon himself states that as early as the beginning of 1686 rumours were rife that the king was aiming to introduce liberty of conscience for nonconformists.[3]

It it also worth noting that the often-repeated story about the prosecution and punishment of Richard Baxter at the beginning of James's reign was given disproportionate importance by Macaulay and by some of his predecessors and was scarcely a reflection of the king's general policy. The punishment of Baxter, his modern biographer noted, was principally owing to the prolonged antagonism of Roger L'Estrange, but even

---

[1] P. 678: the translation by M. V. Hay, *op. cit.*, p. 185 is misleading.
[2] Cf. Hay, p. 186.
[3] Barrillon to Louis XIV, 7 January 1686 and 7 February 1686. P.R.O. transcripts 31/3/163, fo. 237 and 31/3/164, fo. 260.

then it was relatively lenient for those times; Baxter was never
sent to the King's Bench prison and the mildness of his treatment may well have been due to the effect of letters that
Baxter himself wrote to the king.[1]

There is not room in this essay to pursue the historiography
of the revolution in detail into modern times.[2] It is remarkable,
however, that modern historians are by no means in agreement
about all its aspects. The best of King James II's recent biographers, F. C. Turner, has expressed the view that at the time
of his accession James 'was suffering from a premature mental
decline' and suggests that the sexual excesses of his youth had
resulted in 'a fairly common mental disease'.[3] Lord Acton
thought that because he was well over fifty when he came to
the throne he was 'in a hurry' to win arbitrary power and
suppress Protestantism.[4] He was not, Acton thought, 'a sinister
tyrant but an unintelligent absolutist', yet he urged Louis XIV
'secretly to pursue the work of revocation and was reluctant
to allow collections to be made for Huguenot fugitives'. Sir
Richard Lodge, in contrast to Acton, thought that learning
from Charles II's experiences King James was 'cautious' at
first, though afterwards he 'embarked on a policy of such
blundering ineptitude as to suggest in later days the suspicion
that Sunderland must deliberately have guided him to his
undoing'.[5] H. W. V. Temperley opined that the influence of
the great William Penn was decisive on him;[6] Acton attributed
a late change of heart to 'the famous Rancé';[7] Mrs. F. M. G.

---

[1] F. J. Powicke, *The Reverend Richard Baxter Under the Cross 1662-1691*
(1927), pp. 136-50.
[2] I have not discussed Henry Hallam who in his *Constitutional History*
relies on Barrillon for the belief that James's aim was to destroy the Protestant Establishment (ed. 1832, p. 74). It is disappointing that two of the
most brilliant writers of the pre-war years, Hilaire Belloc (*James II*, 1928)
and Dr. G. M. Trevelyan (*English Revolution*, 1938) had so little new to
contribute.
[3] F. C. Turner, *James II* (1948), p. 234.
[4] Review of Ranke in H. Butterfield, *loc. cit.*
[5] *The Political History of England*, viii (1912), chs. xi-xiii.
[6] *Cambridge Modern History*, v (1908), ch. x, p. 237.
[7] *Lectures on Modern History*, p. 221.

Higham pointed out that James had an illegitimate daughter who became a Quaker;[1] David Ogg quotes contemporary tributes to James's 'moral qualities', though with a justifiably ironical aside.[2] Andrew Browning wrote that 'James was by no means a complete fool', that he refused 'slavish subordination to France', but was advised by 'a small and strange collection of adventurers'.[3]

As to his policy, the universities of the world are also not at one. Professor Lucile Pinkham of Minnesota in 1954 wrote in her book *William III and the Respectable Revolution* that King James II's 'aim was religious toleration for all faiths, including Protestant dissenters no less than Roman Catholics' and that he was 'appalled by the revocation of the Edict of Nantes'.[4] Professor Gerald R. Cragg of Montreal in his *Puritanism in the Period of the Great Persecution, 1660–1688* (1957) observed that 'the accession of James II promised no substantial improvement in the lot of the nonconformists', that 'for nearly two years persecution continued unabated', and that 'no one'—overlooking Professor Pinkham—'believed that James II was genuinely concerned about religious liberty'.[5]

When I was a pupil of Mr. Ogg many years ago I learned the adage: 'history does not repeat itself, but historians repeat one another'. This is clearly less true of the history of the revolution of 1688 than of much history; but that some historians have repeated completely false accounts of King James's character and policies is, I think, clear from the above examination, which speaks for itself. My own conclusions are tentative. I doubt whether King James II can be altogether white-washed, but I find it hard to believe that he was mad, the pliant tool of the French king, his second wife, his mistresses, or his priests, or even of the ingenious Sunderland, or that he was inconsistent

---

[1] *King James the Second* (1934), p. 246.
[2] *England in the Reigns of James II and William III* (1955), p. 140 *seq.*
[3] *English Historical Documents, viii, 1660–1714* (1953), p. 15 *seq.*
[4] P. 13. Mr. Christopher Hill in his *The Century of Revolution* (1961), p. 241, also appears to take the view that this was a 'respectable revolution'.
[5] P. 28.

in his attitude to religious toleration[1] or that he was blatantly hypocritical in his dealings with the Huguenots. He was the victim of his own strengths and weaknesses: his devotion to his co-religionists, his elephantine methods of pressure politics, his over-cautious diplomacy that generated mistrust—and the implacability of his political foes. The papers of religious devotion that James compiled in his final exile show him to have been a deeply convinced Christian, sincere, humourless, and rather stupid, but a believer in toleration and one who came to accept that the loss of his throne was not due so much to the machinations of his enemies as a punishment from God for his immoral life.[2] There are, I have heard, historians who will be satisfied with that.

[1] Since this essay was written I have read *The King and the Quaker* by Vincent Buranelli (University of Pennsylvania Press, 1962.) He writes (p. 203): 'Penn says that he has long been acquainted with James Stuart, first as Duke of York and then as King, and has uniformly found him an advocate of toleration theoretically and always willing to act on the theory by favoring the persecuted of other religions than his own. The record runs from 1673 to 1688, a very impressive record in Penn's judgment.' It is interesting that both William Penn and Gilbert Burnet (*supra*, page 190) testify to James's opposition to persecution for conscience's sake. The treatment of dissenters during the early part of James II's reign would be a good subject for a thesis.

[2] *Papers of Devotion of James II* (ed. Godfrey Davies, Roxburgh Club, 1925). Lord Acton stressed James's continued belief in toleration in his exile; H. Butterfield, *op. cit.*, p. 231.

IX

THE FRENCH PRIVATEERING WAR, 1702–13

J. S. Bromley

AMONG the massive, miscellaneous, and insufficiently appreci-
ated prize papers of the High Court of Admiralty, in the Public
Record Office, there survives a note to David Strang, London
merchant, dated Lisbon, 15 February 1706, about his ship
Abraham: 'Dear Uncle', it runs, '. . . 'tis ill news of poor
Captain King . . . who has been four times taken and retaken
about six leagues from Lisbon.' The *Abraham* had been first
lost to a French privateer, recaptured by a Zeelander, then
retaken by three French privateers, and recaptured again by
one of Queen Anne's men-of-war.[1] After that her case is lost
to sight, but it was not unusual and will serve to strike the note
of common war-time experience on seas where rode not only
the privateering hosts of France and the maritime powers, but
Biscay and Galician privateers, Catalans and Majorcans, Maltese
and Corsicans, the Savoyards of Oneglia and Finale, Neapoli-
tans and Ostenders (who in 1706 perforce changed sides), to
say nothing of the continued vitality of Caribbean *flibustiers*
and of the Algerine corsairs, whose flag, whether legitimately
flown or cunningly assumed by others, explains why so many
Mediterranean vessels were found without a soul on board.
Much might also be feared from a character who, though
commonly called a privateer, is better described as an armed
trader—commissioned as the French term had it, *en guerre et
marchandises*, sometimes deliberately 'pour faire la course en
chemin faisant'. His business was with transportation or fishing,
but he often went more powerfully armed than most privateers.

---

[1] P.R.O., H.C.A. 32/49: prize papers, *Abraham*, J. King. Unless otherwise
stated, dates are given in new style.

Nearly all the West India and slaving ships of Nantes, for example, and the codfishers of Saint-Malo and Bayonne were of this breed; and so, apparently, except for the Channel Islanders, were most of the English vessels for which more than fifteen hundred letters of marque were issued from June 1702 to August 1712,[1] notably for Mediterranean and African voyages. Even when the great powers had concluded their hostilities, indeed especially then, open piracy was not confined to the Indian Ocean and the slaving coasts.

It is never easy to assess the economic impact of war. We are still at a stage where each war, each belligerent country, and perhaps each of its main trades, seem to demand separate notice. The task is doubly difficult when wars occur in an expanding world economy, such as was that of the late seventeenth century, and accepted judgments on the direct and still more on the indirect effects of the European wars of 1689–1714 are likely to require revision as more quantitative information comes to light. For a period when European and above all colonial economies were highly sensitive to fluctuations in seaborne commerce, such inquiries may well include a more thoroughgoing effort than has yet been made to assess losses and gains by capture at sea. The crude numbers of these, in European waters at least, can with patience (and a fair approximation to accuracy) be extracted from the records of the prize courts, which also yield much detailed information about the composition and ownership of the ships and cargoes condemned (in part or whole) as good prize, or sold pending judgment, or simply ransomed at sea. Even when the estimated ('appraised') or actual auction price of every prize ship and cargo is unknown, other sources may be available for ascertaining the gross yield of prize sales, year by year, for certain

---

[1] The precise figure was 1540, as compared with 490 for the Nine Years War: Letter of Marque Declarations in P.R.O., H.C.A., 26/1-3 and 13-21. The small-scale but intensive privateering of Jersey and (especially) Guernsey bears many resemblances to that of Calais and the lesser French bases: see my article, 'The Channel Island Privateers in the War of the Spanish Succession', *Transactions of the Société Guernesiaise*, xiv, pt. iv (1950), pp. 444-78.

ports.[1] If all this tells us more about activity in the privateering business itself than about its success in dislocating the map of commerce—so palpably subject to fluctuation from other causes and in any case still so far from being statistically understood even in time of peace—we can reasonably retort that privateering deserves study for its own sake, whether as a field for speculative investment which could bring windfall profits and so finance other enterprises, or as an outlet for resources otherwise dammed up by war, or humbly as an expression of local poverty. At different times and places, over many centuries, privateering has been all these things and more. Thus for Flushing and Middelburg the *commissievaart* of the wars of William III and Marlborough remained what it had been throughout the Dutch War of Liberation, at once a principal means of livelihood and the focus of an intense provincial patriotism, often to the detriment of the Dutch navy.

In France, the later wars of Louis XIV are remembered as the apogee of the *guerre de course*, the heroic age of Jean Bart and the chevalier de Forbin of Dunkirk, René Duguay Trouin of Brest and Saint-Malo, Jean Doublet of Honfleur, Jacques Cassard of Nantes and Marseilles, the d'Iberville brothers of La Rochelle and Hudson's Bay and the nursling Louisiana. These names have ministered to national pride when those of Jean Ango's captains—Drake's true predecessors and peers in the Habsburg-Valois struggle—have unjustifiably been forgotten, in part no doubt because these last were often Protestants or pirates or purely private officers, or because England and not Spain had become the mortal enemy in French naval circles. Another reason may be suggested. Louis XIV's 'grande guerre de course' was a good deal more than a privateering war waged by syndicates of private individuals for private profit. Naval ships and personnel took part in it. Some of the most notable armaments were led by commanders of the king's own choice, to attack objectives of his choosing. They were

---

[1] A readily accessible series, for the Zeeland ports, is to be found in G. N. Clark, *The Dutch Alliance and the War against French Trade, 1689-1697* (1923), p. 148.

organised in close collaboration with his naval intendants, who supervised the fitting out of fourth-rates and frigates, drawing on masts, stores, and victuals in the royal arsenals, making full use of the standing machinery of the *inscription maritime* for recruitment of sailors and of the *compagnies franches de la marine* for the sizeable proportion of soldiers required, at the same time keeping the secretary of state for the navy informed of every step in the whole elaborate process, much as if the enterprise were wholly the king's business, except that working capital came from private pockets and articles of agreement were negotiated with the directeur or principal *armateur* of the syndicate that provided it. In such cases, it was the king's ships and guns which were at risk and he took a fraction (usually a fifth) of the net proceeds of any prize; crown influence might also be decisively exerted to procure the most advantageous sale of prize cargoes; and a big attraction of these arrangements to the private *armateur* was that they enabled naval discipline to be imposed on the seamen, who were notoriously prone to decamp with an advance of wages and to force the premature closure of a cruise. These *prêts de vaisseaux* became increasingly common in the years of acute financial distress in France, from 1707 onwards, when unemployed naval officers themselves took the initiative in proposing armaments and negotiating subscriptions for them, when the naval authorities saw their ships rotting in harbour and their dockyard labour melting away for lack of wages and bread,[1] when the only hope of offensive action was an appeal to the profit motive of a speculative generation. Nevertheless, the system of royal partnership, of which instances are recorded as early as 1689,[2] was not the mere product of necessity. It also implied a positive strategic plan for the application of naval power to the special circumstances of bringing two world trading powers to their knees.

By 1695 it was argued, notably by Marshal Vauban, in his

[1] For an account of this distress see M. Giraud, 'Crise de conscience et d'autorité à la fin du règne de Louis XIV', *Annales (E.S.C.)*, 7e annee (1952), pp. 172–90.

[2] Henri Malo, *Les Corsaires dunkerquois et Jean Bart*, 2 vols. (Paris, 1913–1914), ii, 177–8.

often-quoted *Mémoire sur la Caprerie* of 30 November,[1] that the correct way to do this was by the systematic destruction of the enemy's sea-borne commerce. In itself, of course, this was neither a very new nor a peculiarly French notion; but it was plausible to argue that the war potential of the English and Dutch depended very much more than did that of the French on the maintenance of overseas trade, and from this argument Vauban and others drew a ruthless inference for naval policy. A navy, they argued, was good only for the protection and destruction of commerce unless it enjoyed such a mastery of the seas that it could transport troops wherever the higher military strategy required. By 1695 it seemed evident enough that the French navy no longer justified its keep in this last respect. Accordingly, why not spend it in small change by deploying its manpower and such of its units as were suitable—chiefly *vaisseaux* of forty-eight to twenty-eight guns, light frigates, and galleys—in order to place privateering on a firmer and more scientifically organised basis? The use of small but fast-sailing squadrons, under enterprising commanders like Jean Bart (in whom Vauban discerned the fighting qualities of a De Ruyter), against carefully selected objectives, could do more than inflict economic losses on a scale for which French oceanic commerce hardly offered similar scope to the enemy: they might force him to adopt ruinously expensive measures for the defence of his life-lines. The geographical distribution of French ports, in relation to the focal zones of enemy trade in the North Sea and Channel Soundings, seemed destined by Providence to invite such a strategy; from Brest, in particular, profitable sallies could be launched whatever the set of the wind. And all this with every prospect of more than covering the costs of armament, into which it would not be difficult to attract private capital. Above all, in the thought of Vauban, who had seen something at first hand of the Dunkirk 'capers', the development of a quasi-naval *course* would encourage many

---

[1] It is printed in Rochas d'Aiglun, *Vauban. Sa famille et ses écrits. Ses oisivetés et sa correspondance: analyse et extraits*, 2 vols. (Paris-Grenoble, 1910), i, 454-61.

more wholly private armaments, upon which was bound to fall the main task of harrying enemy trade in detail—in 'une guerre libre et de caprice qui se fait pour le Roi aux dépens des particuliers'—but which in themselves were unequal to the enemy's cruisers, seldom willing to risk their crews in combat, and rather quickly wound up in default of early successes.

Vauban's classical exposition of privateering as a war-winner undoubtedly found ready acceptance in some naval circles as well as at court. This was not simply because so many members of both already had a stake in privateering syndicates (*sociétés d'armement*), or because the business was already flourishing: Vauban feared indeed that it might languish unless something were done to speed the judgment of prizes and lessen the duties on prize goods levied by the general farms: he claimed in his *Mémoire* to know of entrepreneurs who had given it up for these reasons, at both its most vigorous bases, Saint-Malo and Dunkirk (although we now know that the number of corsairs commissioned at Saint-Malo in 1695, and in 1696, was well above previous levels—seventy-one against an average of fifty for 1692–94).[1] Far more significant was the background of debate about the merits of navies which had continued since Colbert's time. It is well known that Louvois, whether from personal or higher motives, had opposed the policy of a big navy, and after Seignelay's death in 1690 his arguments seem to have gained ground; a full year before the disaster of La Hogue, the naval party was having to defend its position.[2] On the other hand, the anti-navalists, with whom Mme de Maintenon came to be identified, can hardly be said to have triumphed as a direct and immediate consequence of La Hogue. Their moment came with Chamillard's budget of 1695, which

[1] See the lists in Anne Morel, *La Guerre de course à St-Malo, 1681-1715* (Paris, Académie de Marine, n.d.), pp. 106 *seq.*

[2] See the *mémoire* by Bonrepaus, dated 20 June 1691, in A[rchives] N[ationales], Marine K, carton 1360. I owe this reference and the next to Dr. Lionel Rothkrug, of the University of Pittsburg, who generously placed at my disposal much of the documentation for his thesis on reform movements under Louis XIV.

drastically cut back expenditure on the navy, on the ground that some of its ships would be better turned over to the *course* than left idle 'on the pretext of a glory that is purely imaginary'; and even then the elder Pontchartrain (who had charge of the navy until succeeded by his son Jérôme in 1699 and who himself invested in privateering armaments) is described by Chamillard as reluctant 'to abandon the king's ships to adventurers'.[1] Contrary to what is often supposed, it was not the experience of La Hogue that persuaded a navally apathetic Louis XIV to lay his fleet, as it were, under cellophane. A year later, in fact, after the scattering of the 'Smyrna' convoy off Lagos in June 1693, the French Atlantic and Mediterranean squadrons united again, to form a grand fleet exceeding ninety of the line—far more than fought at Beachy Head, let alone La Hogue—and in June 1694, off Catalonia, Tourville's combined forces were still more than half as large as this.[2] What was lacking, down to 1695, was not a fleet, but any clear idea of how to use it aggressively, once the battle of Ireland had been lost; minor operations on the Catalan coast and the persecution of enemy commerce did not require these formidable concentrations of manpower and firepower. It was the two strategically unrewarding campaigns of 1693 and 1694 that clinched the argument of the anti-navalists. Even then, it would be absurd to describe their victory as definitive or to regard the strategic thought of the French government, always the resultant of a parallelogram of divergent forces and personalities, as a set of clear convictions. It is significant that ships of the line were under construction not only in 1694 but in 1702, 1704, 1706, and 1707;[3] and after all it was with fifty line-of-battle ships, not to mention the incidental usefulness of galleys, that the admiral of France, Toulouse, claimed the tactical victory of Málaga in

---

[1] G. Esnault, *M. Chamillard . . . correspondance et papiers inédits*, 2 vols. (Le Mans, 1884), i, 5–9.

[2] C. de la Roncière, *Histoire de la marine française*, 6 vols. (Paris, 1899–1932), vi, 147, 150 n.

[3] A.N., Marine G¹³, fos. 1-10, and B⁵, no. 3. Cf. estimates of the French line-of-battle in 1700, 1703, 1706, and 1710 in J. H. Owen, *War at Sea under Queen Anne, 1702–1708* (1938), pp. 278-80.

July 1704. He did so in an effort to recover Gibraltar, the significance of whose recent capture was at once appreciated in France
and Spain. During the remainder of the War of the Spanish
Succession, however, except for the 'Alarm from Dunkirk' of
1708, French naval units were employed only in the humbler
offices of trade protection—Spanish as well as French—and in a
grand offensive against Allied trade, perhaps the most intensive
ever waged by the French nation. Now, at any rate, Vauban's
strategical theory was to be seriously tested.

The miscellaneous character of privateering operations and
the wide dispersion, by capture and otherwise, of the sources
which record them make it very difficult to form any clear
notion of their general shape and total effect. The large French
literature on the subject is rich mainly in narrative, often rather
breathless, hagiographical, and bewildering. Charles de la Roncière's synthesis of 1932,[1] while seriously documented and
vigorously written, does justice only to the highlights of the
campaigning—to such episodes as Duguay's Spitzbergen cam-
paign of 1703, the heroic death of Saint-Pol-Hécourt, the
rewarding St. Helena cruise of the chevalier des Augiers in
1706, the capture of H.M.S. *Nightingale* by de Langeron in
1707, the memorable attacks on Anglo-Dutch convoys to
Portugal and from the Baltic and Archangel in 1706–07, Cassard's victorious romp through the Dutch Caribbean at the
very end of the war. The historians of the Malouins and
Dunkerquois[2] have gone further into the everyday routine
substance of privateering, whose institutional framework in
Brittany was admirably surveyed many years ago by H. Bourde
de la Rogerie in a somewhat austere format.[3] Much fundamental

---

[1] *Op. cit.*, vi, 160-295, 406-546. Cf. Owen, *op. cit.*, ch. 4, for the activities
of the Brest and Dunkirk squadrons in the Channel Soundings, 1704-05, and
Le Nepvou de Carfort, *Histoire de du Guay Troüin, le Corsaire* (Paris, 1922).

[2] Morel, *op. cit.*; the sequel to Henri Malo's two volumes on Jean Bart
and his period is *La Grande Guerre des corsaires: Dunkerque, 1702–1715* (Paris,
1925).

[3] *Inventaire sommaire des Archives Départementales: Finistère*, vol. iii (Quimper, 1902), introduction.

research remains to be done, however, on the French prize system as a whole, on the capital structure and 'rentability' of armaments *à la course*, on the *armateurs* themselves and the varying social milieu behind and below them. In this place no more is attempted than to rough out the broad contours of the phenomenon as it was experienced in 1702–13, as a basis for a few tentative conclusions as to the elementary magnitudes and fluctuations involved.

Such a limited inquiry is made practicable by the preservation in the Archives Nationales of twenty-two folio volumes of abstracts of the judgments of the *Conseil des Prises*,[1] the prize court of fifteen members constituted in 1695 to assist the newly installed admiral of France, Louis Alexandre comte de Toulouse (1678–1737), the king's son by Mme de Montespan who presided over it and in whose house it met every Wednesday. To this *Conseil*, more properly a *Bureau* in the strict language of the *Almanach Royal*, all prize depositions and other proceedings were transmitted from the *sièges d'amirauté* at the ports, and it gave judgment subject only to appeal to *le Roi en son Conseil*—in practice, to the *Conseil des Finances*, which was attended both by the admiral himself and the secretary of state for the navy when it sat in prize causes. Doubtless we owe the excellent record-keeping of the *Bureau des prises faites en mer* to the good method of Henri du Trousset de Valincour, secretary-general both of the navy and of the admiralty jurisdiction. The judgments contained in the abstracts are preceded by a summary of the nature of the prize ship, its cargo and voyage, a rough indication of the place of capture, the name of the captor (ship and captain), the port into which the prize was taken or the amount of ransom if not worth bringing in, and the date on which proceedings were registered by the local *amirauté* (or consul or governor if taken into a European port outside France or to a French colony). By 1691, when the seven Breton *amirautés* were definitively created, there were

---

[1] G5 234-255: 'Dépouillement des jugements des prises', June 1702–December 1713. For a sketch of the genesis and functioning of the *Conseil* see A. de Boislisle (ed.), *Mémoires de Saint-Simon*, vii, 413-4.

over fifty seats of admiralty somewhat unevenly distributed round the French coasts, many of them in tiny and decaying places with little or no prize business. Only in Brittany were there any important privateering bases or prize markets without an *amirauté* of their own, with the result that the prize litigation of Roscoff was handled by admiralty officers from Brest, and that of Port-Louis and Lorient (until 1782) by those of Vannes—a common cause of delay in the liquidation of prize business which led the naval authorities in Lorient to claim a jurisdiction of their own, unsuccessfully, in 1709. Elsewhere,[1] prizes were almost invariably proceeded against at the ports into which they were brought, and there too they were auctioned if condemned by the *Conseil des Prises*.

There is much to suggest that the judgments do not record all the prizes taken into colonial ports, either because the formalities were not always observed in the colonies or because the written *procédures* were lost on their way to France; it is scarcely credible that no prizes at all should have been taken into Martinique in 1705 and 1706, whereas eighteen are recorded in 1703 and as many as seventy-five in 1711, and an even greater mystery surrounds the mostly blank returns from Saint-Domingue, whose *flibustiers* had certainly been very active in the previous war.[2] On the other hand, it is unlikely that the returns from the principal non-French ports in Europe—mainly Spanish, but also Malta and Leghorn—were seriously deficient; whatever concealment went on in such compara-

---

[1] Bourde de la Rogerie, *op. cit.*, p. x. For a complete list of the *sièges d'amirauté* (to which Sables d'Olonne should be added), and for the boundaries between the Breton *amirautés*, see *ibid.*, pp. xi-xiii.

[2] According to an English prisoner-of-war out of Martinique, writing to the Commissioners of Sick and Wounded on 17 April 1705 (O.S.), that island then had 23 privateers and 1400 men wholly dependent on privateering; they had taken 240 prizes since the beginning of the war and 2000 prisoners, of whom 500 joined the French (P.R.O., S[tate] P[apers] 42/119, fo. 106). Warre gave Burchett a figure of 250 prizes on 9 September 1704 (O.S.), according to 'the last Advices to France from Martinico' (P.R.O., Adm[iralty] 1/4089, fo. 615). The surviving dispatches from Martinique in 1705-6 (A.N., Colonies C8A 15 and 16) point to enemy naval pressure as a more effective deterrent; expeditions against St. Kitts and Nevis in 1706 absorbed 1400 and 1000 privateersmen respectively.

tively out-of-the-way and lawless haunts as the Ionian Islands or the Greek Archipelago, French consular correspondence at this time leaves an impression of regularity and efficiency, while the corsairs generally had too much need of consular protection and technical services to seek to evade jurisdiction.[1] While further work is required on the critical sifting of Valincour's abstracts,[2] they offer a reasonably reliable basis for indicating the crude statistical outcome of the *guerre de course* outside American waters.

Disregarding such oddities as the ransoms of Fort Gambia in 1702 and 1704, of Nevis by d'Iberville in 1706, of Rio de Janeiro by Duguay in 1711, of Surinam and Curaçao by Cassard in 1712-13,[3] and confining the calculation to waterborne prizes—from English men-of-war to the herring-busses of the Maas—we arrive at a total of 7220. Eliminating 245 recaptures and 312 releases (mainly of neutrals), this total is made up of 2118 ransoms and 4545 other condemnations.[4] The proportion of ransoms is surprisingly high, but most of them are accounted for by the depredations of Dunkirk and Calais privateers on fishermen and coasters: 726 ransoms to Dunkirk (mainly in Dutch florins) and 793 to Calais (mainly in sterling). Saint-Malo (190) and Brest (149) bring the total— chiefly at English expense—to 1858, leaving only 262 to other bases (a fair number of these bills being expressed in Spanish

[1] These observations are based primarily on a reading of the consular correspondence preserved in the archives of the Marseilles Chambre de Commerce, series K, and on the articles of agreement (*projets et escrittes d'armement*) found in the A[rchives] D[épartementales], Bouches-du-Rhône, Amirauté IX B 4-5. My thanks are due to the custodians of these archives for their courteous assistance.

[2] A more refined account requires, in particular, the pursuit of cases on appeal which circumstances have not permitted me yet to undertake.

[3] The most lucrative hauls were those of Duguay (La Roncière, vii, 538) and Cassard (*ibid.*, p. 546). D'Iberville demanded an indemnity of £42,000 or 1400 slaves as the price of quitting Nevis (R. Bourne, *Queen Anne's Navy in the West Indies* (New Haven, 1939), p. 207): for the extremely complex liquidation of this cruise and the malversations which attended it, see M. Giraud, *Histoire de la Louisiane française*, i (Paris, 1953), 104 *seq.*

[4] This figure does not distinguish cases in which a ship but not the cargo (or part of the cargo) was condemned, or *vice versa*.

15

and Portuguese coin). By definition, the sums in question were usually small; they were smaller for Calais than for Dunkirk, but the average even for Dunkirk was below 1500 florins and for British ransoms little more than £100 in most years. It does not follow, of course, that the cumulative material and moral damage to the sufferers was comparably slight. Although the British and French governments in May 1708 arranged a truce to attacks on home fisheries, which was renewed in September 1710, the Dutch herring fishery endured this form of taxation to the bitter end, in addition to its total losses; there was some decline, though less than might have been expected, in the numbers of busses employed in it during most of the war years.[1] In Newfoundland waters, both English and French cod-fisheries suffered likewise from wasting raids at higher levels of ransom. On the other hand, it is likely enough that some ransom bills were simply the price paid for smuggled goods exchanged at sea. In all, the ransoms paid at sea, if reduced to sterling, may be estimated provisionally at £380,000.[2]

Measured by the crude numbers of prizes brought into port (less recaptures and releases), the Dunkirk admiralty easily led the field with 959, followed by Brest (506), Calais (461), Saint-Malo (374), Toulon (208), Morlaix (183), Marseilles (136), Le Havre (111), Vannes (110), La Rochelle (90), Bayonne (84), Dieppe (74), Nantes (67), Cherbourg (60), La Ciotat (47), Antibes (40), Quimper (32), Boulogne (26), and Collioure

[1] H. A. H. Kranenburg, *De Zeevisscherij van Holland in den Tijd der Republiek* (Amsterdam, 1946), pp. 219-20. Sailings to the Greenland whale fishery also fell off, but not to the same extent as in 1690-97: see Gerret van Sante (ed.), *Alphabetische Naam-Lyst van alle de Groenlandsche en Straat-Davische Commandeurs die zedert het jaar 1700 Groenland en zedert het jaar 1719 op de Straat-Davis, voor Holland en andere Provincien, hebben gevaaren* (Haarlem, 1770), pp. xxvi-xxvii.

[2] The variability of exchange rates makes any exact calculation mis-leading. I have used contemporary quotations for the Dutch florin at 2s. English; the standard piece of eight at 4s. 6d.; the silver ducat at 3s. 6d.; the *cruzado* at 4s.; and the *livre tournois* at 18 = £1. This last equation may silghtly undervalue the *livre*: according to information from Dr. John Sperling, the £ sterling averaged 17·2 *livres* from 1702 to 1707 and 18·3 *livres* from 1708 to 1714, if differences arising from price fluctuations and accounting procedures are ignored.

(21). Other French ports account for a further seventy-six prizes, the performance of Bordeaux (11) providing striking

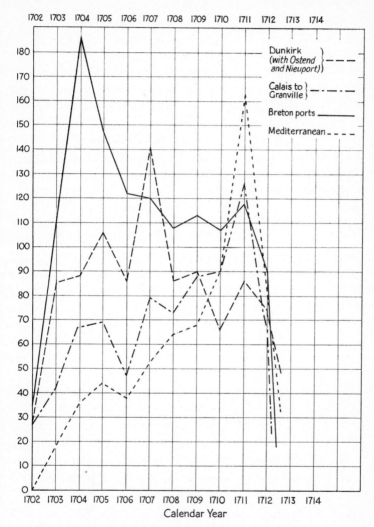

NUMBERS OF PRIZES (excluding ransoms, recaptures, and releases) adjudged by *Conseil des Prises,* October 1702–June 1713.

confirmation of the absence of a strong shipowning interest there in this period. In addition, thirty-four recorded French prizes were proceeded against at Ostend and Nieuport; twenty-six at San Sebastián, Bilbao, Corunna, and Vigo; five at Lisbon (in 1703); 180 at Cadiz; nineteen in the Canaries; eighty-eight at Málaga, Cartagena, Alicante, Almería, and Altea (in that order); sixty-five at Messina; sixteen at Malta; sixty-five at Leghorn; and eight at Smyrna, Syrian Tripoli, Tunis, and Algiers. The total for all Mediterranean (including French) ports is only 692, compared with a figure of 3618 for the eastern Atlantic (of which the Channel and North Sea ports from Brest to Ostend account for no less than 2852 or over three-quarters). Something may be learnt about the relative fertility of the European cruising-grounds if the figures are tabulated regionally, if somewhat arbitrarily, as follows:

Dunkirk, with Ostend and Nieuport	993
Calais to Granville	785
Saint-Malo to Nantes	1282
Sables d'Olonne to Bordeaux	107
Bayonne to Vigo	110
Lisbon, Cadiz, Canaries	204
Western Mediterranean	684
Eastern Mediterranean	8
	4173

A reference to the graph on page 215 will provide a rough comparison from year to year of the performance of the four leading groups above. The balance is made up of 370 prizes brought into the French colonies in America,[1] *viz.* 260 to Martinique, four to Guadeloupe, twelve to Cayenne, eighteen to Acadia, sixty-three to Placentia, seven to Quebec, and four simply described as in '*Amérique*'; the only reference to Saint-Domingue is a single ransom confirmed at Cap François. Even if this colonial total were doubled, however, it would not bear a significantly greater proportion to the whole than the Mediterranean quota. In fact, the captures reported by English and French colonial governors, when collated with the condemna-

---

[1] Four prizes were also sold at Pondicherry—two English and two Dutch: *Procès-verbaux des délibérations du Conseil Souverain de la Compagnie des Indes* (Pondichéry, n.d.), i, 15, 19-20, 70, 101-3, 106.

tions registered in Valincour's *dépouillement*, make a minimum of 700 French colonial prizes perfectly credible, and there were perhaps at least as many ransoms.

No reliable estimate of the total sales value of prize ships and goods is yet practicable, but Faulconnier, the historian of Dunkirk, is so nearly accurate about the numbers of prizes condemned there that it is tempting to accept his figure of 30 m. *livres*—say £1,666,000—for their gross sales value.[1] It is not absolutely clear whether he means gross or net product of sale, but other evidence strongly suggests that it is the former and throws serious doubt on Henri Malo's figure of 82 m. gross.[2] For an account also survives of the prize tenths remitted to Paris by the admiral's receiver at Saint-Malo throughout the war and these aggregate 1,316,071 *livres*.[3] Now, as the tenth was levied after deductions for certain expenses,[4] the Malouin sales must have amounted to more than 13,160,710 *livres* gross —that is, to perhaps as much as half Faulconnier's figure for Dunkirk. That this is probably a realistic relationship as between Saint-Malo and Dunkirk, in terms of gross sales, is confirmed by a statement of the admiralty tenths for *all* ports (including Spanish and colonial) for the single calendar year 1706,[5] when to a total of 1,356,595 *livres* Dunkirk contributed 293,634 and Saint-Malo 134,323 *livres*—rather less than half the Dunkirk value. A figure of 82 m. gross for Dunkirk would require us to believe that its sales fetched over six times those of Saint-Malo over the war as a whole. This is most unlikely. It

[1] *Description historique de Dunkerque*, 2 vols. (Bruges, 1730), ii, 166.

[2] Relying on H. Malo, *La Grande Guerre des corsaires*, p. 126 (where no explicit source is given for a gross value exceeding 82 m. *livres*), Sir George Clark considers that the Dunkirk figure 'far exceeded six millions sterling' ('War Trade and Trade War, 1701–1713', *Econ. Hist. Rev.*, 1st ser., i (1927), 263). In converting into sterling here, Sir George Clark seems to have used the higher rate for the *livre* which prevailed in the Nine Years War.

[3] A.N., G5 28[1]. See the graph below, p. 218.

[4] These were minor expenses as a rule; the *dixième* was levied *before* deducting the *frais de justice*, the Invalides tax of 3 *deniers* on every *livre* of the gross product of sale, and the cost of subsisting prisoners.

[5] A.N., G5 28[1]. This is an account from 15 December 1705 to 31 December 1706.

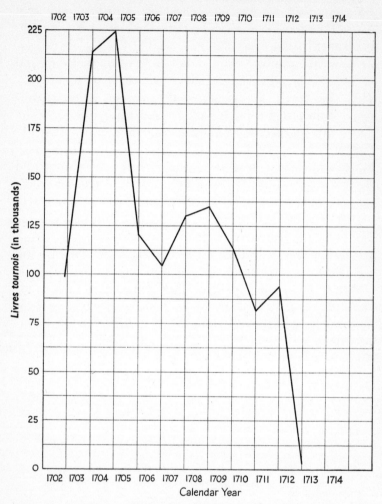

SAINT-MALO. Prize tenths (in *livres tournois*, in thousands) remitted by Admiralty Receiver in respect of ransoms and sales, 12 November 1702– end of 1713.

may be noted that, together with Ostend (38,921 *livres*), Dunkirk accounts for about 25 per cent of the whole yield in 1706, and Saint-Malo for only 10 per cent; but the Breton ports as a whole, into which many Malouin prizes were taken, then aggregated rather more than Dunkirk with Ostend—398,200 against 331,748 *livres*.[1] It is still more interesting that the Flemish and Breton groups together account for well over half the grand total of prize tenths in 1706. The next largest figures for that year are for Toulon (199,572 *livres*, compared with 162,694 for Brest), Cadiz (79,829), and Martinique (65,551). Calais, on the other hand, in spite of the great number of prizes for which its *barques longues* were responsible, paid only 43,313 *livres* in 1706.

If the assumption were made that Dunkirk's proportion of the total value of prize sales throughout the war amounted to about a quarter, we might tentatively compute that grand total at four times Faulconnier's figure, at about 120 m. *livres*. This is almost certainly too low. If Saint-Malo's 10 per cent share of the 1706 values is at all representative of its share of the war total, we should obtain a value for this last rather more than 10×10 times the tenth which Saint-Malo paid from beginning to end of the war—that is, $10 \times 10 \times 1,316,071 = 131,607,100$ *livres*. If, again, the year 1706 could be regarded as an average year for the yield of prizes as a whole—it was rather below average in terms of crude numbers,[2]—we should obtain a value, for nearly

[1] Such a comparison may give a more just impression of the rewards to Malouin capital, which had a considerable share in armaments at Morlaix, Brest, and Nantes. Moreover, Malouin corsairs not infrequently carried their prizes into other Breton ports (as well as into Cadiz). On the other hand, *armateurs* and government alike preferred prizes to be prosecuted and sold in the port of armament, near which also the majority of the crew had its home. The chief countervailing factors were the weather and the distance from home. Though captains were usually at liberty to cruise where they thought fit, they were also instructed to send prizes to a port where the principal *armateurs* had a correspondent, failing their own base, where the *directeur* or *procureur* could keep an eye on the proceedings. The Marseilles *escrittes d'armement* are particularly instructive on this score. Every privateer had to return to base for the disarmament and pay-off: in most cases they brought their prizes with them or came in empty-handed.

[2] The totals of prizes and ransoms condemned for each year of the war (excluding recaptures and releases) was as follows:

1702 (May–Dec.):	162	1706: 537	1710:		623
1703:	454	1707: 738	1711:		831
1704:	571	1708: 607	1712:		575
1705:	587	1709: 755	1713 (Jan.–April):		223

Total: 6663.   *Average for 1703–12*: 627·8.

[Footnote continued overleaf.]

eleven years of privateering, somewhat exceeding $11 \times 10 \times 1,356,595 = 149,225,450$ *livres*. Clearly, no great credence can be lent to these calculations at present; but they are perhaps sufficiently consonant to suggest a gross sales value, including ransoms, at least of the order of 140 m. *livres*, equivalent to roughly £8 m. sterling—a figure by no means out of line with the estimated value of £1 m. in London's losses alone down to 1708,[1] but scarcely compatible with a figure of £6 m. for Dunkirk gains alone.

The net product, available for distribution to the share-holder, would have been considerably less. It is probable that only some of the captains and principal *armateurs*—and the bankers behind them—made much by the *course*. Few share-holders (*intéressés*) seem to have held large fractions in a privateer, or to have subscribed large sums to the cost of armament when naval ships were chartered. The articles of agreement committed the subscribers as a rule to a single cam-paign only, this limitation being subject to review in the light of results, for corsairs might well come home without having recovered the cost of their outfitting and of advances in wages to often unreliable crews. That the game went on in spite of many discouragements, however, is a sure indication that gains exceeded losses, even if it is also a sign of the decline of normal trade outlets—the profitable Malouin sailings to Newfoundland fell significantly from eighty in 1702 to nineteen in 1703 (and

These figures provide only a rough indication of the number of captures *per annum*. Condemnation normally occurred within three months of capture in European waters, but there might be an interval of anything up to a year for overseas cases and longer than three months in any event if a case went on appeal. Delays in the *amirauté* proceedings were greatest precisely in the most successful ports and occasioned bitter complaints. The *Conseil des Prises* acted with dispatch but was often held up by the excessive sophistication of the *avocats* of the parties, according to the critical 'Mémoire sur la course par M. Valincour' of 1711 (A.N., Marine G 144).

[1] H[istorical] M[anuscripts] C[ommission], *House of Lords MSS.*, new ser., vii, 183. It is not to be assumed, of course, that the value of cargoes as prize was necessarily as high as if they had reached their intended market, though they might be higher on occasion.

never exceeded thirty till 1713), for example,[1]—and a symptom
of that speculative rage which was to culminate in the Rue
Quincampoix. There were certainly times when there were too
many *armateurs* chasing too few seamen.[2] These, rather than a
shortage of working capital, were normally the chief limitation
on the scale of French privateering, which would certainly not
have attained the dimensions it did had the navy more continuously employed its registered seamen. One reason for the
pre-eminence of Dunkirk, in any case a kind of maritime
Alsatia with a large floating population, was doubtless that
Flemish seamen were exempt from naval conscription;[3] but in
the later years of the war the machinery of the *inscription
maritime* did much to facilitate the close partnership between
the arsenal at Toulon and the Marseilles capital market
(with Lyons in the background), while the armaments of
Duguay at Brest were always manned by the *commissaires des
classes*.

Although the French Mediterranean *course* was largely conducted in the king's ships and galleys, 'accorded' to officers who
were fertile in projects, the sources reveal beyond doubt that it
was the mass of wholly private and usually small armaments

[1] A.D., Ille-et-Vilaine, Amirauté 9 B 402-408. In the Nine Years War,
the tonnage employed in the Saint-Malo codfishery fell to less than a quarter
of its peace-time level (J. Delumeau, 'Le Commerce malouin à la fin du
XVIIe siècle', *Annales de Bretagne*, lxvi (1959), 284-5). The codfishers
carried abnormally large crews: from this point of view, the decline in
sailings to the Antilles could hardly have released similar resources at Nantes
or La Rochelle. Moreover, the codfishing vessels were sometimes converted
into privateers (Morel, *op. cit.*, p. 40). The diminution of Malouin privateering from 1706, conversely, may have owed something to increased
involvement in South Sea trading: see *House of Commons Journals*, xv, 404-5.
For the impact of the Nine Years War on Malouin commerce, see J.
Delumeau, *Le Mouvement du port de Saint-Malo à la fin du XVIIe siècle, 1681–
1700* (Rennes, 1962).

[2] In August 1702, for example, it was stated that many Malouin corsairs
were held up for want of a full complement, and Pontchartrain's earlier
proposal that manpower be concentrated on half a dozen of the strongest
privateers seems not to have been followed (A.N., Marine G 144 and B³
120, fos. 475ᵛ-6). For a similar situation at Dunkirk and Calais in August
1711, cf. P.R.O., State Papers Dom. 34/16, fo. 54.

[3] Malo, *La Grande Guerre des corsaires*, p. 141.

which did most to distress the seagoing trade of the Allies in the Atlantic. It was their frigates and *barques longues*, of some twenty-six down to six guns or less,[1] capable of close inshore sailing and nimble enough to 'wrong' a man-of-war upon a wind, which kept up a more or less unremitting pressure on enemy coasts and sea-lanes and captured most of the prizes, with or without the countenance of small naval squadrons. They could, and often did, increase their fire-power by sailing in company, under a formal agreement either to share their winnings for the duration of a cruise—even in the event of separation for emergency repairs or for the safe-conduct of a prize—or else for a few days. They could keep the sea for two months or longer. Some of them returned to it several times a year, and year after year, without being caught. In the whole war the English captured less than 300 privateers of all strengths.[2] Losses, however, were not difficult to replace by capture or building: a new frigate could be constructed in three months—Saint-Malo alone built twenty-nine frigates in 1703–04.[3] These facilities, more than losses, explain the rapid turnover in privateering *vessels*. Losses were most serious if there were delays in the exchange of prisoners, especially of experienced captains. To have stopped the prisoner-of-war cartels altogether would have been the most certain means of destroying the routine privateers; but so totalitarian a measure seems only to have occurred to Governor Lowther of Barbados, and the most that was done was sometimes to dispatch captured French privateersmen from the Caribbean to Europe[4]

---

[1] In the early years of the war, the average Dunkirk *capre* carried 10 guns and 60-70 men—a few were armed only with hand weapons—but after 1705 these averages rose to about 15 and 100 respectively, according to the information assembled in the index to Malo, *op. cit*. The Calais privateers seldom carried more than half a dozen guns. Few of the Bretons carried as many as 26 guns and 170-200 men, which may be taken as the minimum strength of a big privateer.

[2] P.R.O., H.C.A. 32/47-86, 90, 92: prize papers.

[3] Morel, *op. cit*., p. 42.

[4] C[alendar of] S[tate] P[apers], Col[onial Series, America and West Indies], 1711–12, no. 77: Lowther to Council of Trade and Plantations, Barbados, 20 August 1711 (O.S.); A.N., Colonies C 8 A 15: Machault to Pontchartrain, Martinique, 18 August 1703 and 15 December 1704.

—prisoners being expensive to feed, while West India merchantmen usually went short-handed for the voyage home.

Once the 'partisan' or guerrilla character of most privateering is understood, it is not surprising that the cruising-grounds were normally within a few days' reach of the bases. As the sailors sang to the Spanish ladies, 'From Ushant to Scilly is thirty-five leagues'. The Bretons had only to steer a rhumbline across the Chops of the Channel to catch the plane-chart shipmasters from America and the Mediterranean making for the Blaskets or the Scillies.[1] A 'nor-'nor-easterly would carry the corsair even more easily to Cape Finisterre; indeed captains sometimes cruised off Cape St. Vincent and Cape Clear in a single campaign.[2] Brest, as Vauban saw, enjoyed an exceptionally advantageous situation with reference to all these stations and that may be why its share of the Breton prizes considerably exceeded that of Saint-Malo, and why the Malouins sometimes armed a few of their privateers there, as they did occasionally at Port-Louis and Lorient. Calais had a similar freedom of choice, as between the Channel and the North Sea; in the North Sea it was the only important competitor of the Dunkirkers. The Dunkirk squadron indeed sometimes marauded as high as Bergen and the Orkneys, and as far south as the Gibraltar Straits; but the Thames or Maas could be reached from Dunkirk in a single tide and most of its *capres* did well enough in the North Sea itself. When English cruisers took better care of the Soundings, after 1708, privateering became more active near the Portuguese coast, although it was exceptional for an Atlantic privateer to enter the Straits. Geographical factors thus invited what state direction could never have accomplished with such instruments—a convergence of numerous private interests against the trunk routes and junctions of Allied shipping in the eastern Atlantic, each main group having a limited radius of attack but composing in all a comprehensive

[1] Admiralty Library, Misc. Papers on Naval Matters, p. 49: Halley to Pepys, 17 February 1696 (O.S.), 'touching the yet imperfect measure of knowledge in our ordinary navigation'.

[2] A.D., Loire-Maritime, B 4572–4576: enregistrement des rapports des capitaines au long cours, 1705–13.

strategy based on inner lines which were lengthened by Bourbon Spain.

Here diplomacy underwrote geography, notably in negotiating the Spanish decrees of 13 April 1704 which absolved the French from payment of duties on prize goods and allowed them to examine foreign shipping in Spanish harbours. Nowhere, however, was French diplomatic pressure of more importance to the privateering war than in the western Mediterranean, where the chief cruising-grounds lay immediately within the Straits, in the Malta channel, and in the Sea of Tuscany (especially the Piombino channel, which separates Elba from the mainland). In 1706, the grand master was embarrassed at being asked to provide facilities for the sale of prizes and for the provisioning and cleaning of corsair frigates in Malta, but by 1711 this seems to have become a familiar practice.[1] The English accused both the Knights and the Italian states of failure to enforce respect for their neutrality—exhibiting, for instance, a pious horror of the arrest of the pope's alum[2]—and believed that French influence with them grew as a result of privateering successes in 1711, when, for the first time, the Mediterranean accounted for over a fifth of French prizes. Consul Molesworth wrote from Tuscany in May that year that the Italians themselves were saying that 'notwithstanding our powerfull fleets in the Mediterranean, we sometimes receive worse usage from Neutral Powers than they dare give the French . . .'. In July, Admiral Jennings was constrained to observe to the secretary of state that 'there is not one port in Italy, but countenances the Enemies ships, and setts lightly by any damages sustain'd on our parts', and the Admiralty ordered him not to confine himself 'to bare reprizals' if he

[1] A.N., Marine B³ 139, fos. 552-4; Royal Malta Library, MS. Arch. 1561, Perellos to Pontchartrain, 22 January 1711. I owe this last reference to Mr. Roderic E. Cavaliero, who kindly sent me a transcript. With some justification, the British came to regard Malta as a kind of French naval base: see Mr. Cavaliero's *The Last of the Crusaders: the Knights of St. John and Malta in the Eighteenth Century* (1960), p. 48. Cf. P.R.O., S.P. 99/58: Cole to Dartmouth, Venice, 8 August 1710.

[2] P.R.O., S.P. 79/6: Henshaw to Dartmouth, Genoa, 24 May 1711.

failed to obtain damages in such cases.[1] On the other hand, it is difficult to miss the point of French seizures of so many food cargoes—corn, cheese, rice, salted meat, and horse fodder— consigned to Barcelona and Lisbon, mainly in Catalan and Neapolitan vessels furnished with Austrian passports, but sufficiently often in Genoese bottoms to draw repeated diplomatic protests from the Genoese Senate:[2] in 1709 Genoese corn merchants had indeed contracted to supply the Allied armies in Catalonia,[3] but many of these arrests were wrongful and it says much for the *Conseil des Prises*, and for the development of prize law, that so many Genoese carriers were released. In bulk, these seizures probably had some influence on the later stages of the war in Spain, especially as they coincided with the intensification of attacks on provision-ships from the British Isles and Holland.

In American waters, the worst blows were to fall in 1711–13, from Duguay and Cassard, at Portuguese and Dutch expense. Measured by the number of prizes recorded in the prize judgments at Paris, routine privateering attained its maximum a little earlier, before the loss of its northern base at Acadian Port Royal in October 1710. This was the only 'nest of spoilers' against which action was taken before the demolition of Dunkirk: Sir Stephen Evans, governor of the Hudson's Bay Company, colourfully described it as the Dunkirk of North America.[4] Like Dunkirk, it damaged coastal trade and fisheries. But even Boston shipping seems to have had more to endure from Martinique. Certainly the 'Martinicos' have left an uglier mark on English colonial dispatches and the French admiralty

[1] Molesworth to Dartmouth, Florence, 19 May 1711, P.R.O., S.P. 98/23; Sir J. Jennings to same, Barcelona, 4 July 1711, S.P. 42/68; Lords of the Admiralty to same, 3 August 1711, S.P. 42/10, fo. 140.

[2] P. Bonnassieux and E. Lelong, *Inventaire analytique des procès-verbaux du Conseil de Commerce, 1700–1791* (Paris, 1900), pp. 59-60, 5 and 26 June 1711.

[3] B.M., Add. MS. 28153, fo. 34: George Carpenter to Sir J. Norris, Barcelona, 8 January 1710.

[4] J. P. Baxter (ed.), *Documentary History of the State of Maine*, ix, 212. Cf. G. M. Waller, *Samuel Vetch, Colonial Enterpriser* (Chapel Hill, 1960), esp. p. 171.

judgments bear witness to the number of New England and
New York prizes which they took. This was no accident, for
there were times when the French Antilles were desperately
short of food.[1] Their privateers seem chiefly to have cruised
to windward of Barbados and the Leewards, which were more
closely invested than was Jamaica (by the 'picaroons' of Léogane
and Petit Goave), although the Spanish trade of Jamaica was
certainly complicated by raids from Martinique in the vital
zone between Rio de la Hacha and the Rio Chagre.[2] The interest
shown by Martinique corsairs in slaveships was illustrated as
far afield as the Gambia, where they twice ransomed James
Fort.[3] Reinforced by refugees from St. Christopher and by
some of their English prisoners,[4] small enough to evade naval
guardships in shoal water, some of them ranged up the North
American coasts as high as Acadia.[5] Between these poles of
iniquity none of the mainland colonies could feel secure, least
of all the Virginians whose estates lay along open rivers: the
president of the Council of Virginia felt himself justified in
fitting out a ten-gun coastguard even if it did no more than
quiet the apprehensions of planters and induce them to prepare
crops: 'It is easy', he told the Board of Trade, 'for a Privateer

[1] On 28 February 1705, the governor-general of the French West Indies,
Machault, wrote to Pontchartrain that the dearth had worsened since no
prizes had been taken for some time (A.N., Colonies C 8 A 15); the loss of
manpower by capture would be a good reason for forbidding the *course*,
but 'elle fournit les Isles de vivres' (*ibid.*, 15 December 1704).

[2] P.R.O., Adm. 1/4089 A, fo. 625: Handasyd to Hedges, Jamaica, 17
September 1704 (O.S.); Adm. 1/4090, fo. 438: Heathcote to Hedges, 11
December 1705 (O.S.); S.P.Dom. 34/7, fo. 51: Dummer to Hedges, 10
January 1706 (O.S.); Adm. 1/4091, fo. 221: Sunderland to Lords of Ad-
miralty, 24 February 1707 (O.S.). Cf. H.M.C., *House of Lords MSS.*, n.s.,
vii, no. 2402.

[3] J. M. Gray, *A History of Gambia* (1940), pp. 142-3, 147-8.

[4] *Cal.S.P.Col., 1702*, no. 1137: Roberts to Nottingham, Barbados,
10 November 1702 (O.S.); P.R.O., S.P. 42/119, fo. 106.

[5] J. B. Bartlett (ed.), *Colonial Records of Rhode Island*, iii, 560-1: Governor
and Council to Board of Trade, Newport, 14 September 1706 (O.S.);
E. B. O'Callaghan (ed.), *Documents Relative to the Colonial History of the
State of New York*, v, 20: Cornbury to Board of Trade, 20 July 1707 (O.S.),
Minutes of the Provincial Council of Pennsylvania (Philadelphia, 1852), ii,
411-2: S. Finney and others to Cornbury, 3 July 1708 (O.S.).

to Land at any of those Places in the night, and surprize People in their Beds.' He also deplored what he called 'the drawing off of people to defend the coast' and the need to remove negroes lest they run to the enemy each time the alarm was raised.[1] When it is appreciated that a parliamentary indemnity of £100,000 did not suffice to compensate the inhabitants of Nevis and St. Christopher for what they had suffered from d'Iberville's raids,[2] the fears of planters on the Chesapeake seem well enough founded: like Indian war parties, the privateers could damage nerves as well as purses. But for this very reason colonial correspondence can be misleading as to the scale of shipping losses in American waters. The French evidence leaves little doubt that even the Anglo-American trades suffered most heavily at the European approaches, when the final returns came home from the whole complex of Atlantic trading.

The familiarity with which French privateers treated English coasts gave an edge to the storm in the City of London in the winter of 1707–08, beginning with the setting up of a select committee of the Lords to inquire into 'the State of the Nation in relation to the Fleet and Trade'.[3] This was, or became, a real merchants' revolt, not merely an opposition party stunt, though the Junto hoped to get rid of George Churchill, the dominant figure on the admiralty board, and secured a debate in the Lords before the Address of Thanks.[4] Prominent in the attack were the Leghorn merchants, angered as much by their ships 'being taken entring the Doors of our own home' as by the scale of their losses, which in January 1708 they estimated at £250,000 in the previous two months—£50,000 more, that is, than the Levant Company claimed to have lost in the whole of 1705. Others, notably the Jamaica and Virginia traders, soon echoed Edward Gould's reflection: 'The Book of Seldens

---

[1] P.R.O., Adm. 1/3815: Popple to Burchett, 27 October 1707, 29 June 1709, and 12 August 1712 (O.S.).

[2] R. Pares, *A West India Fortune* (1950), p. 49.

[3] The Committee was agreed to on 12 November 1707 (O.S.): *Journals of the House of Lords*, xviii, 338.

[4] R. R. Walcott, *English Politics in the Early Eighteenth Century* (1956), pp. 132–4.

called Mare Clausum hath been verifyed of late in a contrary sence'.[1] The last thing some Mediterranean merchants wanted was convoys, but 1707 was the year of Forbin's stroke at the Russia fleet, the rout of the autumn fleets to Virginia and Lisbon—with 1000 troop horses for the allegedly demoralized Portuguese—the detention of the out-going East Indiamen for seven months at Cork, and of unseasonable sailings to the West Indies. There were therefore demands for more efficient convoys and, above all, for more cruisers in the Channel Soundings and off the Straits of Gibraltar.

Was the English admiralty rightly held to blame? What had occurred was in part the price of the Mediterranean offensive—1707 was also the year of the Allied expedition to Toulon —and in part the consequence of convoying an overseas commerce which had grown not only in size but in complexity. The admiralty had foreseen this at least as early as December 1702, when it protested against ministers' demands for the Virginia and St. Helena convoys: 'It is much to be doubted that if the service should require the Body of the Fleete abroad the next yeare, as it did the last, and that all these ships be allowed as Convoys and Cruizers to protect the severall Trades, the Channell and Coasts of this Kingdome will be greatly exposed to the Insults of the Enemy . . .'.[2] In 1707 it could fairly claim that it was unable to spare ships to deal with the Martinique privateers 'in regard there was no small want of proper ships at home to guard the coast', even though it had added to the fourth- and fifth-rates at its disposal for trade defence.[3] Nor can anyone go through the secretary's Letter-Books[4] and fail to respect the tireless and ingenious manipulation of marginal resources there revealed: Josiah Burchett per-

---

[1] P.R.O., Adm. 1/3863: depositions of Edward Gould, 2 November and 8 December 1707 (O.S.); *House of Lords MSS.*, n.s., vii, 181 *seq.*: petition of Edward Gould and others, 29 January 1708 (O.S.). For the complaints of the colonial merchants, *ibid.*, p. 226 *seq.*

[2] P.R.O., S.P. 42/6, fo. 148 B: 'Statement of Convoys and Cruizers proposed for next year', 3 December 1702 (O.S.).

[3] H.M.C., *House of Lords MSS.*, n.s., vii, 315.

[4] P.R.O., Adm. 2/403–442.

haps had the kind of mind that used to refresh itself in Bradshaw. Yet the French evidence makes it clear at last that the
merchants did not grossly exaggerate the size of British shipping losses. Their total of 3600 ships may have been guesswork,
though perhaps not the figure of 1146 London ships—valued
with their cargoes at over £1 m.—included in it.[1] The *Conseil
des Prises* had in fact condemned 1969 ships and ratified the
ransom of 1020 others before 1707 was out—a round total of
3000, to which must be added at least 250 captures in the West
Indies recorded elsewhere. And at least three-quarters of these
prizes were ships of British register, to say nothing of cargo
carried on British account by the captured vessels of allies and
neutrals, or of unrecorded captures.

The proportion of British losses, though not so high, remained well above half that of the Allies as a whole during the
remainder of hostilities, when a failing and desperate enemy
took some 2600 prizes in addition to 1100 ransoms: hardly
more than 200 fell to him after the Anglo-French Cessation of
Arms had taken effect in the autumn of 1712. This argues only
a very limited success for the new emphasis on trade defence
in British naval policy which followed the Cruisers and Convoys Act[2] of March 1708. More sixth-rates were built and
rather more French privateers were captured—169, compared
with 125 before 1708—but many of them still, significantly,
near the North Foreland, the Isle of Wight, and the Lizard.[3]
The Dunkirkers did not quite recover the brilliance of 1707
and it is notable that many of the Malouins were failing to take
any prizes at all; but these were the best years for other ports,
including Calais. We no longer hear of the French killing
bullocks in Lundy Island and snatching sheep from County
Kerry, and it looks as if the Ordnance Office was better able
to assist local initiative in strengthening coastal fortifications;

[1] H.M.C., *House of Lords MSS.*, n.s., vii, 183. Cf. the figure of 1000
ships and £2 m. given by Warre to Burchett, 9 September 1704 (O.S.):
P.R.O., Adm. 1/4089, fo. 615.

[2] 6 Anne c. 65, summarised in Owen, *op. cit.*, pp. 284–5.

[3] Charles Derrick, *Memoirs of the Rise and Progress of the Royal Navy*
(1806), pp. 118–20; P.R.O., H.C.A. 32/47–86, 90, 92: prize papers.

16

yet the Lord Advocate of Scotland complained on 12 March
1709 'how much Our Forth and all our Coast northward
beyond Aberdeen is infested with small contemptible French
Privateers that take up our ships in our very view and how
little the Cruizers hitherto sent have assisted in this matter'.[1]
If London's coal stocks were never again reduced to one week's
supply, as happened in 1703,[2] that was not because interference
with Lowestoft and Yarmouth shipping was discontinued.
The privateers no longer 'laid a boom across British seas', as
they had done in 1707, and British cruisers more continuously
policed the Soundings gateway; but there was more French
activity near the Portuguese coast and within the Straits.
Insurance at Venice, in September 1710, was quoted at 20
guineas per cent 'owing to French privateers'—as high, that
is, as the rate for Straits-bound shipping in November 1707,
though six guineas below the rate for the homeward run in
that exceptionally perilous month.[3] Anglo-American trade,
too, now suffered less in the English 'Mare Clausum', but
homeward freights from Barbados did not fall below £6 per
ton of sugar (with one exception) until 1711: in 1710 they were
up to £8 or even £10—the rate ruling in 1708.[4] These rates
were two or three times pre-war and not, I think, entirely on
account of higher war-time wages (which might, however,
go far to explain why homeward freights from Jamaica were
double those from Barbados). It would be dangerous to read
too much into the general Balance of Trade figures, which in
1709-11 show a fall in British export values from the levels of
1707-8 and (more revealingly, perhaps) a drop in imports in
1711.[5] I cannot, however, follow Sir George Clark in denying

[1] P.R.O., Adm. 1/4092, fo. 228: Stewart to Queensberry, Edinburgh,
12 March 1709 (O.S.).
[2] T. S. Ashton and J. Sykes, *The Coal Industry of the Eighteenth Century*
(1929), p. 201.
[3] P.R.O., S.P. 99/58: Cole to Dartmouth, Venice, 19 September 1710.
Cf. H.M.C., *House of Lords MSS.*, n.s., vii, 182.
[4] This information was kindly communicated to me by Mr. K. G. Davies.
[5] Davenant's table in Sir G. N. Clark, *Guide to English Commercial
Statistics* (1938), p. 149. Import values throughout the war remained at
least one-quarter, and usually over one-third, below the levels of 1700 and

St. John's veracity when he claimed, in a letter to Drummond on 28 November 1710 (O.S.), that 'our trade sinks'.[1] Certainly no judgment on his peace policy or the Tory conduct of naval affairs should overlook the pressure of the French privateering war in those last strange years.

Further, when St. John wrote to Drummond that Dutch commerce 'flourishes to a great degree',[2] we may also believe him. From 1705 the Dutch had been trading at French ports in hundreds—they had taken off quantities of French prize goods, for one thing—and the ordinance revoking their passports had only just been published, on 19 November. This, according to Heinsius, was their most important trade.[3] The *Conseil du Roi* stopped it as the best way to dispose them to a peace, but also because the measure was expected to give the *course* a boost; the *armateurs* had continually complained of the abuse of French passes by Dutch ships bound to non-Dutch destinations.[4] In conjunction with the evidence of the prize *jugements*, this strongly suggests that during the greater part of this war Dutch commerce was not, after all, harder hit than British. The accepted view that it suffered more is only true, if at all, for the very last years. It is true, though not generally realised, that Dutch victims were more conspicuous at Dunkirk, trivial in value as were the numerous fishing doggers of Zierikzee and the Maas towns to be ransomed; but no other French bases, not even Calais, fattened primarily at Dutch expense. Almost certainly, the Dutch were far more deeply hurt by the loss of their French trade, following as it did, within less than a year, a renewal of naval hostilities in the Baltic. But in these new circumstances, clearly, they could the less afford an intensification of French privateering attacks.

1701. Cf. G. Chalmers, *Estimate of the Comparative Strength of Great Britain* (1794), p. 89. [1] *The Later Stuarts, 1660–1714* (1934), p. 225.
  [2] Quoted *ibid*.
  [3] The evidence for these statements is in my article, 'Le Commerce de la France de l'Ouest et la guerre maritime, 1702–1712', *Annales du Midi*, 65 (1953), 49–66.
  [4] A.N., F¹² 55, fos. 182–91: minutes of *Conseil de Commerce*, 11 and 18 July 1710.

X

THE RED PRIEST

H. K. Andrews

. . . the most popular composer for the violin, as well as player on that instrument, during these times, was DON ANTONIO VIVALDI, maestro di capella of the Conservatorio della Pietà, at Venice; who, besides sixteen operas which he set for the Venetian theatres, and several others for different parts of Italy, between the year 1714 and 1737, published eleven different works for instruments, of which a list is given in Walther, without including his pieces called *Stravaganze*, which among flashy players, whose chief merit was rapid execution, occupied the highest place of favour. His *Cuckoo Concerto*, during my youth, was a wonder and delight of all frequenters of country concerts; and *Woodcock*, one of the Hereford waits, was sent for far and near to perform it. If acute and rapid tones are evils, Vivaldi has much of the sin to answer for. His title of *Don* was derived from his clerical character. 'It is very usual,' says Mr. Wright in his Travels through Italy, from 1720 to 1722, 'to see priests play in the orchestra. The famous Vivaldi, whom they call the *Prete Rosso*, very well known among us for his concertos, was a topping man among them at Venice.'

Albinoni, Alberti, Tessarini, and Vivaldi are, however, classed among the light and irregular troops; the Roman school, formed by Corelli, having produced the greatest performers and composers for the violin which Italy could boast during the first fifty years of the present century.

CHARLES BURNEY, *General History of Music* (1789)

S o wrote Dr. Burney at a time when Vivaldi, his works, and his influence were almost totally forgotten in the world of music. It is evident that Burney himself knew little of Vivaldi's music, and it is probable that most of the details which the entry in his book contains were largely hearsay; nevertheless, there are some shrewd observations in the passage, and it shows how far from Venice Vivaldi's fame had spread in an age when the dissemination of music was a slow and uncertain matter.

The neglect of Vivaldi's music for more than a century and a half after his death and its subsequent reinstatement is one of those constantly recurring patterns which make the history of music so apparently illogical and at the same time so interesting. Many forces are at work in this: the natural 'swing of the pendulum'—the neglect and discrediting of men of strong artistic personality by the succeeding generation—the inevitable changes of fashion and the growing up of a 'new' musical style. These are the normal hazards of all creative work. A less obvious reason for the temporary or permanent eclipse of much music which had fame and popularity in its composer's lifetime is the purpose of the music itself. The bulk of the music written in the first half of the eighteenth century was produced for some specific occasion. Composers were crafts-men employed by masters—kings, princes, courts, ecclesiastical establishments, schools, or opera houses. The idea of a composer as an artist, working in splendid isolation for art's sake, did not arise until the Romantic age in the nineteenth century. The composer, moreover, was essentially a working practical musician, whose task was to produce and perform music to meet the needs of his employer, whether he played it himself or directed others in its performance. In many cases the demand for new music was so pressing that composers were forced to borrow from their own earlier works or from the works of other composers, with or without acknowledgment. Handel was a notorious example of this. It is not to be wondered at that a large amount of music written in such circumstances should be laid aside and forgotten as soon as it had served its immediate purpose, and in this process many fine works must have passed into oblivion.

These factors account, in part at least, for the neglect of Vivaldi after his death. The period of his eclipse, however, was unusually prolonged. It may be suggested that this was due to the nature of his music itself and the way in which the art developed in the centuries after his death. Vivaldi's music was direct in style, simple and concise in design, in no way deeply emotional, written for relatively small forces with no grandiose aspirations save the current requirement of giving the virtuoso soloist a chance of displaying his wares. In the age which followed, the chief emphasis lay in the perfection of musical structure, the nice balancing of formal design and musical content, and these factors, already present in some degree in the works of Vivaldi and his contemporaries, were raised to the highest limits by composers of supreme genius such as Haydn, Mozart, and Beethoven. The nineteenth century, the Romantic age, set a completely different target. The ideals of romanticism in music were poles apart from those of Vivaldi. Emotional fervour, highly coloured and grandiose forms of expression with rhapsodical structure, dramatic content and literary associations led the art far from its classical and pre-classical purpose. The composer was no longer a skilled crafts-man, but an interpreter of men's minds, emotions, and aspira-tions. It was not until musicians rebelled against the excessive romanticism of the end of the nineteenth century and the beginning of the twentieth, and turned again to the ideals of directness of approach and simplicity of expression that Vi-valdi's music could regain its place and once more be appreci-ated for what it was, music for its own sake.

Antonio Vivaldi was born about the year 1678 in Venice and died in Vienna in July 1741. His father, Giovanni Battista Vivaldi, was a violinist at St. Mark's, Venice. Little is known about his early musical training, but it is generally supposed that he received it from his father and Legrenzi, though Legrenzi's instruction must have been of short duration, since he died in 1690.

Antonio was 'tonsured' in 1693, received minor orders in 1696, became a sub-deacon in 1699 and was priested in 1703. His active career in the Church, however, was of short dura-tion. There was a story current in Venice at the time, which Roualle de Boisgelou recounts about 1800, that 'One day Vivaldi was saying mass when a fugue subject came into his mind. He at once left the altar where he was officiating and repaired to the sacristy to write out his theme; then he came back to finish the mass. He was reported to the Inquisition, which happily looked upon him as a musician. . . .' Vivaldi's own account in a letter to the Marchese Bentivoglio in 1737 gives a different view of the circumstance: 'After I was ordained priest I said mass for a little over a year, and then gave it up, as three times I had to leave the altar before the end on account of my illness.' He goes on to explain the nature of the illness, which appears to have been 'pain or constriction in my chest' brought on by exertion.

Vivaldi's career in the Church is of little importance, however, compared to his musical activities, save for the fact that it gave him his famous nick-name, 'the red priest'. (Apparently the whole Vivaldi tribe had red hair.)

From 1704 to 1740 Vivaldi was closely connected with the music at the Seminario Musicale dell' Ospedale della Pietà, and it is probable that he was in charge of the musical activities there for most of the period. The Pietà was one of the numerous charitable institutions in Italy which at this time became primarily famous for their schools of music. There were three other foundations of the kind in Venice, and others in Naples and Palermo. An excellent account of the musical accomplishment of these schools is given by Charles de Brosses, writing in 1739.

> The Ospedali have the best music here [Venice]. There are four of them, all for illegitimate or orphaned girls or [those] whose parents cannot support them. These are brought up at the State's expense and trained exclusively in music. Indeed they sing like angels, play the violin, flute, organ, cello, bassoon—in short, no instrument is large enough to frighten them. They are cloistered like nuns. . . .
> Where I go most often, and enjoy myself most is the Ospedale della Pietà. It ranks first for the perfection of its symphonies. What well-drilled execution! That is the only place to hear a first attack from the strings such as, quite undeservedly, the Paris opera is renowned for.

Vivaldi's duties at the Pietà gave ample opportunity and incentive for the use and development of his musical powers. He had to train his instrumentalists and singers from an early stage, and weld together the orchestra and choir into a highly skilled ensemble of professional standard. At the same time he was required to supply music in profusion and ensure its performance at the highest level. In these demands lay the ideal combination of the practical musician and the composer.

In addition to this formidable task, Vivaldi pursued his career as a virtuoso violinist, and opera composer and impresario. As his fame grew he began to travel widely with the encouragement and approval of the Pietà governors, who appear to have been eager that he should make the best of his talents beyond the confines of Venice as well as in their service. His travels took him not only to Rome, where he directed operas for three Carnival seasons, and the chief musical centres in Italy, but to many European capitals such as Amsterdam and Vienna where, eventually, he died. Yet his most important work was done in his native city, chiefly at the Pietà, which in itself provided him with enough scope for the full realisation of his talents—a first-rate group of instrumentalists and singers of his own making, and an appreciative and encouraging governing body.

Vivaldi has often been regarded only as a writer of instrumental music. Though in fact he achieved a very large output of dramatic works and music for the Church, it is probable that his best work and his most far-reaching influence lay in his instrumental compositions. Pincherle's list comprises 554 instrumental items; 454 concertos for varied combinations of instruments, seventy-five sonatas or trios, twenty-three *sinfonie* and two organ pieces. This was a very large output, even by eighteenth century standards, and, as might be expected at this period, only a small part of it was published in the composer's lifetime.

Nearly all the essential characteristics of Vivaldi's style and technique may be found in these instrumental works, especially in the concertos. He employed both the contrapuntal method of writing, in which the individual strands of melody and rhythm were woven together into a homogeneous texture, and the 'accompanied melody', where a single strand or instrument held the chief interest, the remaining forces accompanying it in a supporting role. The 'melody-with-accompaniment' style of writing had been a prominent feature of the early 'Baroque' revolt against the polyphony of the preceding era; it was, moreover, a medium in which the growing awareness of diatonic tonality could most easily develop. In the later part of the seventeenth century and the first half of the eighteenth the contrapuntal method had to some extent regained its place, combining readily with the now firmly established diatonic tonal system, and reaching a glorious climax in the tonal polyphony of John Sebastian Bach, only to be displaced once more by the so-called 'galant' melodic style of the classical era.

Vivaldi's great achievement lay in his ability to unite these seemingly diverse and even antagonistic elements within a single movement; this was made possible to a great extent by the rhythmic and harmonic nature of his themes. The harmonic basis of his subject-matter was nearly always clear-cut and economic. His habit of beginning a theme with a melodic statement of the tonic chord, and then progressing through a number of other clearly defined basic harmonies, each supporting the original key-chord and confirming it as the tonal centre, created a well-founded tonal orientation, whether the theme stood by itself as a melodic entity, or was supported by accompaniment. Against this harmonic framework of melody Vivaldi used rhythm equally clear-cut and pointed, though sometimes extremely subtle. His rhythmic subtlety may be seen in the irregular phrase-lengths of his melody, and in such favourite devices as six-pulse patterns used against a basic four-pulse measure.

Thematic material constructed on these lines is, at its best, equally suitable for treatment in a unison context with no accompaniment whatever, as melody with accompaniment, or in contrapuntal style using an imitative linear texture. It can be developed either by melodic extension of the phrases, or by splitting up the component parts of the rhythmic and melodic ideas and working them in combination in different strands. This type of material also lends itself readily to soloistic elaboration, and an almost endless supply of accompanimental figures may be drawn from it. The chief drawback lies in the fact that there is an inevitable similarity in the themes produced in this way. The number of different harmonic formulae within the diatonic key which may serve as a basis for melody of this kind is limited and the store of arresting and individual rhythmic patterns is not endless. The close kinship of much of Vivaldi's thematic material, especially in the first movements of concertos, is a matter which has given rise to a considerable amount of adverse criticism. The charge that 'Vivaldi did not write 454 concertos but one concerto 454 times' has just that trace of truth in it which would make it hard to refute completely were it not for its gross and facile exaggeration. It may be owned that Vivaldi does repeat himself from time to time both in the rhythmic pattern and harmonic basis of his themes, but over and over again he saves the situation by variety in design and lay-out, by subtlety in orchestration and ornamentation, or by sheer inventiveness which gives the music life and character of its own.

Orchestration—the combination and use of instruments—is a factor of paramount importance in Vivaldi's music. In Vivaldi's time the orchestra was by no means the stereotyped and stable instrument of the nineteenth and twentieth centuries. There is some truth in the statement that in the first half of the eighteenth century composers made use of whatever instruments they had at their disposal. It is, however, wrong to suppose that they were not very much aware of the tone colours and finer potentialities of those instruments.

Besides this instability and variation in its component parts, the eighteenth century orchestra differed from that of the nineteenth century in two other important respects. It was, in the first place, very much smaller; it might well be likened to the chamber orchestra of today. The number of players would probably not exceed a total of twenty-five, except in such untypical establishments as those at Mannheim and the Paris Concert Spirituel in the middle of the century. In the second place the presence of the continuo in the eighteenth century orchestra gave a completely different functional slant to its constitution. The continuo may be regarded as a characteristic and essential part of all 'Baroque' music, which lingered on into the classical period, and is still to be found, rather unexpectedly, as late as Beethoven's piano concerto in C major. It consisted of a bass line with 'figuring' indicating the harmony; this harmony was 'realised' by a keyboard instrument (harpsichord, organ or the like) which filled in the chords indicated by the figuring, and a bass stringed instrument which emphasised the bass line.

The 'filling in' function of the continuo was a means of binding together an often heterogeneous collection of instruments; it also gave the individual instruments freedom to develop their own melodic lines by absolving them from harmonic responsibilities. It did not, however, encourage the orchestra to develop into a standardised and self-contained unit such as it became in the later years of the century.

Vivaldi was a virtuoso violinist; it was on this asset of his musical personality rather than on his abilities as a composer, teacher or impresario that his international fame rested in his lifetime. He knew instinctively what string ensembles could accomplish most effectively, and used that knowledge to the full, sometimes exploring new technical devices, but more often drawing a wealth of richness and diversity of effect from normal technique by subtle use of groupings and placing of the timbres of the instruments.

Vivaldi occasionally wrote music for unusual stringed instruments such as the viola d' amore, English viols, lute, theorbo, and mandolin. The viola d' amore was generally used as a solo instrument; in this capacity Vivaldi wrote at least eight concertos for it, contrasting its unusual tone colour with the less individual ensemble of the other strings, and exploring its ability to cope with double and triple stops. The three 'viole d' Inglese' in the *Concerto funebre* are not easy to identify; Pincherle suggests that they were just an ensemble of ordinary viols which remained in favour in England as late as the beginning of the eighteenth century, despite the spread of the violin. The lute and the theorbo, both obsolescent at this time, are found very occasionally in Vivaldi's orchestra in a purely accompanimental capacity. The mandolin, however, attracted more attention from the composer, and he provided several concertos for the instrument which call for a considerable degree of virtuosity. He also made some use of it in accompaniment.

Brass instruments were no strangers to the Venetian musical tradition. From the time of Gabrieli they had found much favour. Unexpectedly Vivaldi rarely used trumpets and trombones. Only one concerto for two trumpets and one for two 'trombon da caccia' are known. Horns seem to have been more to his liking, and they occur in pairs in several of the *sinfonie* and concertos within the framework of the orchestral ensemble, sometimes brought into the foreground with elaborate solo passages.

It is generally thought that wood-wind instruments found little favour in Italy during the period, possibly because of defective construction. Vivaldi must be regarded as an exception to this generalisation; over ninety works in which these instruments play a prominent part are now known in his output. He seems to have had a special liking for the bassoon, and was probably the first composer to write virtuoso concertos for it, exploring its full range and technical possibilities. He combined it with violins, flutes, or oboes in concertino groups. His treatment of the flute was equally successful and enterprising; the six concertos for the instrument (Op. 10, c. 1730) were probably the first works of the kind to be published. In these he used the full range of flute technique, showing special interest in the higher ranges of the compass. He also seems to have realised the flutes' usefulness as accompanying instruments in the orchestra, and their role in wind ensembles. His interest in flute tone extended to the piccolo, for which he wrote three concertos.

Oboes at this time were mainly used doubling violins, or as substitutes for violins as solo instruments in cases where the solo parts were relatively simple and of suitable range. Vivaldi continued to employ them in this way, and also provided them with a number of concertos, either as soloists or in pairs or combined with other solo instruments.

The clarinet was almost a new instrument in Vivaldi's day. It is said to have been invented by J. C. Denner, a flute maker, at the beginning of the eighteenth century, though it probably developed out of the considerably older chalumeaux. With his usual enterprise, Vivaldi made use of them in at least three concertos. He also employed a 'salmò' (? chalumeau) in the *Concerto funebre* and in one of the concertos in the Dresden collection.

This brief summary of Vivaldi's instrumentation shows his enterprise and versatility in the use of almost all the resources available at the time, and also his capacity for incorporating unusual voices within the orchestral framework. Strings remained the backbone of his orchestra based on the firm foundation of the continuo, but it is possible to see the beginnings of other structures, such as the wind ensemble, taking shape. In concertino combinations he mixed his ingredients with daring and a great sense of effect. His orchestral accompaniments always show skilful calculation to give the soloists full scope; his tuttis display contrast and colour.

It is not always realised that at this period a considerable freedom was given to instrumentalists in the ornamentation and 'realisation' of their parts, especially in the solo combinations. They were expected to elaborate and interpret the written notes in improvisatory manner, and at times the written notes are not much more than a skeleton of the finished performance which skilled players would be able to produce. The more Vivaldi's work is studied the more does his skill and inventive capacity in handling the orchestra become apparent.

Possibly Vivaldi's greatest contribution to musical development in his age was in the matters of form and structure. His mastery of instrumental form, especially in the concerto, influenced many composers of the time including J. S. Bach, who is generally thought to have acquired his wonderful sense of design from the study and assiduous copying out of Vivaldi's music.

Vivaldi was not the inventor of the concerto or of any other instrumental form. His predecessors such as Corelli had gone far towards finding completely satisfactory structural basis for such works. His contribution lay rather in the work of consolidation and clarification. It is not necessary to attempt to trace the origin and growth of the concerto here. It was the natural outcome of the musical potentialities of contrasting one performer or group of performers with another, and probably received its initial impetus from the works for contrasted and separated bodies of singers which had been developed so successfully in Venice at the close of the sixteenth century by the Gabrielis. By the time of Vivaldi the concerto grosso and the solo concerto had settled down into a three-movement structure of two quick movements flanking a slow movement generally of lesser size and importance.

The general plan of the concerto first movement in Vivaldi's work may be outlined thus: (1) Ritornello for the orchestral tutti in the home key of the work, usually containing three or more motives of a clearly defined and striking nature; (2) a section by the 'concertino' group or soloist, either decorating some of the ritornello material or introducing new matter of a related kind; (3) a tutti section using part of the material from the ritornello, presented in a new key usually closely related to the home key of the movement; (4) another solo section; (5) a tutti using part of the ritornello material, and partly in another related key; (6) a third solo section; (7) a final recapitulation of the whole ritornello in the home key.

The chief thematic material was placed in the ritornello, and the key scheme of the tutti passages and the key balance of these created the real architecture of the movement. The solo sections provided contrast in texture; they usually consisted of decorative treatment of the ideas already put forward in the ritornello; yet their structural function was in no way confined to soloistic display, and at their best they could shed a new light on the material and develop it.

Within this general plan Vivaldi was able to find infinite variation both in key scheme, and in his method of treating the tutti and solo sections. Though the solo department was most often given over to pliable, decorative and rhapsodic figuration based on ritornello material as a contrast to the solid rhythmical statements of the 'tutti', it might also make use of individual subject-matter in strong contrast to the ritornello, producing an almost bithematic movement, as in Op. 3, no. 8. Nevertheless, whatever method was used for the solo sections, the basic principle of contrast of two forces remained constant and the true concerto idea was maintained.

Vivaldi's treatment of the middle (slow) movement of the concerto plan was probably his most important contribution to the development of the form. The middle movement had been, and indeed tended to remain to the end of the Baroque age, of considerably less importance than the outer movements. Sometimes it was little more than a brief connecting link between them; in extreme cases, such as Bach's third Brandenburg Concerto, it might be cut down to two chords, though probably in this and similar instances, improvisation by the soloist on a considerable scale was intended by the composer at this juncture.

Vivaldi made the middle movement the focal point of the concerto, with the solo instrument or group the centre of attention. Sometimes the orchestra was reduced to merely the continuo (harpsichord or organ, plus cello on the bass line) as an accompaniment to the solo; sometimes the strings of the orchestra were added as a discreet background.

Vivaldi gave his soloists extended outpourings of melody not encountered hitherto in concerto slow movements. The solo part, unhampered by a complex orchestral texture, was left free to embellish its melodic line at will and to express itself with complete freedom. The form of these slow movements varies from work to work; it may take the shape of a continuous melody with minimal accompaniment, a dialogue between solo and tutti, a solo melody framed by tutti passages, a Siciliano, a simple ternary movement, an ostinato bass with a lyrical melody written above it (a favourite and memorable device of Bach), or a dozen other variations of these. The influence of the expressive opera 'aria' may often be traced. There is no denying the beauty and originality of Vivaldi's slow movements at their best, or the influence that they had on his contemporaries and successors.

The final allegro movements of concertos were traditionally lighter in form and substance than the first movements. Vivaldi's 'finales' are no exception to this. They are usually rapid and light in texture and content, though they contain much variety of character and structure. In form they sometimes tend towards the rondo, the solo sections representing the episodes. Many other types occur; the dialogue, the fugal, and even straightforward dance movements, yet the essential concerto character, the interplay of solo and tutti, remains the foundation of the music.

The 'symphony' of the second half of the eighteenth century is generally considered to be a descendant of the opera overture, and its immediate genesis has often been attributed to Stamitz, Sammartini, or Mysliweček. Amongst the early precursors of the symphony proper, Vivaldi's *sinfonie* (about eighteen remain) and the works at Turin called *concerto a quattro* and *concerto ripieno* numbering some fifty compositions, have considerable significance. These works, though less highly developed than the true concertos and musically less interesting, show characteristics of thematic material, orchestration and structure which point the way to the classical symphony, and must be regarded as an important step in the evolution of the musical form which was to become the chief glory of the classical period.

What may be termed 'descriptive music' played an important part in Vivaldi's output. Two types of descriptive music must be kept in mind in considering this phenomenon: (1) the imitation of the sounds of nature or man in terms of music, and (2) the musical work which follows a programme or describes a situation or event in detail. These two types are often found in combination. Neither was new in Vivaldi's time; in fact both had long and fairly honourable histories. There was a marked increase in the popularity of both kinds of musical representation at the end of the seventeenth century and the early part of the eighteenth. Opera made copious use of both; the charming descriptive pieces of François Couperin and the Clavecinists, and the more complex programmatic works such as Kuhnau's *Bible Sonatas* and Biber's *Mystery Sonatas*, are good specimens in instrumental music. Vivaldi explores both types exhaustively. The *Cuckoo Concerto*, mentioned by Burney, is one of the more obvious and musically least satisfying examples of imitation of the sounds of nature. Far better is *Il cardellino* which is a charming essay in orchestration. Leaving the purely ornithological studies for representations of more man-made sounds, the *Concerto o sia il cornetto a posta* is a good example employing the traditional post-horn call. Coming nearer to real programme music are the two concertos (Op. 8, no. 5 and Op. 10, no. 1) called *La tempesta di mare*. The first of these is a very interesting work in which the descriptive elements are closely woven into the typical concerto pattern.

By far the most famous of Vivaldi's essays in programme music is the group of four concertos (Op. 8, 1-4) known as the Seasons. To each of the four is attached an explanatory sonnet, probably written and appended after the works were finished, giving a kind of running commentary on the events represented in the course of the unfolding of the concerto movements. Though not his highest achievements as music, these works are, nevertheless, fine examples of the concerto and at the same time of descriptive music of the period; their popularity was widespread and well deserved, and their influence on other composers very great.

Vivaldi's name has always been associated almost exclusively with instrumental music in general and the concerto in particular. His vocal works—opera, oratorio, and church music—have received little or no attention and have generally been regarded as of slight importance. Even at the height of his fame his contemporaries were reluctant to give him any credit for his works in these spheres. Charles de Brosses reports a saying of Tartini to the effect that 'Vivaldi tried to write both for his

17

instrument and for the theatre, and whereas he succeeded very well in the first, he always failed in the second'. His output of vocal music was large; about forty-six operas are listed among his works, and there are also oratorios, secular cantatas, and an abundance of church music written no doubt for his singers at the Pietà.

With regard to the operas, the number of commissioned works outside Venice and the widespread dissemination of copies of arias, etc., throughout the chief libraries of Europe suggest that there was a considerable demand for Vivaldi's operatic music during his lifetime. That his operas have not held a place in the repertory or been revived is probably due not so much to deficiency in the quality of the music as to the type of opera current in Italy at the time of their creation. D. J. Grout, an eminent expert on the history of opera, has summed up the situation thus:

> . . . opera is of all great musical forms the most sensitive to its environment. For this reason opera is one of the most perishable forms of music. Every educated musician knows something about Vivaldi's concertos and Handel's oratorios, but comparatively few know much about Vivaldi's or Handel's operas. It is not that the music of these operas is any less worthy of remembrance, but rather that it is so clearly bound by a hundred subtle ties to a certain way of life that has now disappeared—to bygone fashions in psychology, in poetry, in drama, in dress, manners, and customs—that we can hardly revive it with convincing effect without reviving the whole culture from which it was nourished.[1]

Vivaldi's operas were of their time. There is no doubt that when a careful study has been made of the Foà and Giordano collections which were given to the Turin Library 1927-30, much fine music will be discovered, but it seems very doubtful whether the works *qua* operas could ever regain their position in the repertory.

The sacred music is a more promising subject for revival. Most of it was probably written for the Pietà, and its practical aspect must have been carefully considered by the composer.

---

[1] *The Musical Quarterly*, October 1948.

Like the operas nothing of it was known till the Foà and Giordano collections came to light, and even now little is easily accessible for study. It seems to display a great variety of styles; the contrapuntal, the dramatic and the concerto-like instrumental. Sometimes the traditional Venetian lay-out for double choir and instruments is used in a way which is reminiscent of Gabrieli, as in *Laudate Pueri*, *Beatus Vir*, and *Lauda Jerusalem*. Even on scanty acquaintance there can be little doubt of the effectiveness of these works.

The history of music presents a picture not of a steady and inexorable progress towards a definite goal, but of a series of rises and falls—of peaks and valleys interspersed with smaller undulations. The polyphonic age moved through a long course of experiment and achievement to its eventual culmination in the sixteenth century in the works of Palestrina, Byrd, and Lassus. On the journey a number of other lesser heights had been scaled, for example in Machaut, Dunstable, and Josquin. The 'Baroque' period shows a like building up of achievement, punctuated by periods of mere experiment, till another great summit was attained in the music of Bach and Handel. It is a mistake to regard the summits as the only points of importance worthy of serious attention. On the way up to the summit and sometimes after it is passed many lesser peaks may be found. Works of lasting value, often little inferior to the highest achievements, are encountered, sometimes in unexpected places; the best works of lesser composers are frequently of as great intrinsic worth as the average work of the greatest.

Vivaldi has often been regarded merely as a composer who prepared the way for the great achievements of others. His work in the development of form and orchestration certainly influenced the course of music at one of its great moments, but it is in the intrinsic value of his best music itself that his true stature as a composer must be assessed. In his best work, such as some of the Dresden concertos, there is enough beauty and vitality to ensure for him a place of honour in music for all time.

XI

A NEW COLLEGE SCANDAL OF THE SEVENTEEN-TWENTIES

H. E. Bell

ROBERT LOWTH, the eighteenth century divine who wrote what is still the best Life of William of Wykeham, devoted the last chapter of his biography to an examination of such things as had been published to Wykeham's discredit. Almost half of this final section of Lowth's book consisted of a detailed refutation of the very adverse allegations about Wykeham that had been made by William Bohun—first in his *English Lawyer*,[1] and later in his edition of Nathaniel Bacon's *Historical and Political Discourse of the Laws and Government of England*.[2] According to Lowth, it was a personal grudge against New College that accounted for the virulence of the attack on the college's founder launched by Bohun—'who having without any just cause conceived a violent resentment against the Society of New College in Oxford, first endeavoured, in the impotence of his wrath, to revenge himself by a vexatious prosecution commenced against the person of their worthy Governor: but not satisfied with this, and thinking he could give them a blow which would affect them more sensibly by wounding the reputation of their Founder, set himself to collect everything he could meet with that was capable of being represented to his discredit, and to improve it with new and horrible calumnies of his own invention'.[3] In a footnote, Lowth explained some-

[1] *English Lawyer: showing the nature, Forms of Original Writs, Processes, and Mandates of the Courts at Westminster, also the Forms of Returns and Directions of Writs, Processes, etc. in English, with many curious observations on the whole,* 1732.   [2] 1739.
[3] *The Life of William of Wykeham* (1758), pp. 325-7.

248

thing of the circumstances that had created Bohun's bitterness, and the story that he outlined seems sufficiently interesting to justify its being told in greater detail than he gave. This fuller account of the quarrel between Bohun and New College is made possible by the survival, amongst the New College muniments, of a bunch of letters and legal memoranda relating to it.

Since the quarrel, as it developed, possessed elements of the fantastic, and even the ridiculous, it is not entirely inappropriate that the estate at issue and the names of the protagonists should be absurdly alliterative: the bone of contention was the leasehold estate of Birchanger, the rival claimants for its possession were Eustace Budgell and William Bohun, and the Warden of New College so embarrassingly involved in their disagreement was Henry Bigg. Birchanger, Budgell, Bohun, and Bigg—it will be well to say something of them all, both place and personalities, before attempting to describe the course of the dispute.

The manor of Birchanger lay in Essex, close to Bishop's Stortford and hard against the boundary of Hertfordshire, into which county, indeed, some of its lands extended. Part of the founder's endowment of New College, by the eighteenth century its lands had long been let as two leasehold estates—Birchanger Hall and Stansted Mill Farm—in this period normally let to the same lessee, but nevertheless the subject of separate leases: Birchanger Hall, the site of the manor as it was usually styled, carried with it 169 acres, Stansted Mill Farm 138. Of course New College continued to exercise and enjoy the rights of manorial lordship, and indeed the leases contained provisions for the holding of manor courts, and the entertainment of the warden when he came on progress, in Birchanger Hall itself. This fact has relevance to our story for, as will appear, it was in the Hall, and at the time of Warden Bigg's progress, that the quarrel reached its climax—a few moments of angry physical violence, preceded and succeeded by some years of tangled litigation. The house in which these serio-comic events took place is still standing, but so altered as to bear little similarity to its original state.

Of the personalities involved in the Birchanger dispute, the one with the most claim to be called a public figure was undoubtedly Eustace Budgell, and indeed he, alone of the three, made his mark on the general history of his time. On that history Budgell impinged at three points. In the first place, in that age of journalists he achieved some reputation as writer and editor. The first cousin once removed of Addison, he contributed to the *Tatler* and the *Spectator*, and even in the unhappy period towards the end of his life he wrote for the *Craftsman* and launched the *Bee* which, as has recently been pointed out, was one of the earliest digest magazines.[1] To Addison's influence, too, Budgell owed his start on an official career, for it was Addison who, in 1714, initially secured him the position of under-secretary to the Lord Lieutenant of Ireland. Still, Budgell pretty clearly possessed some administrative talent, and his Irish work as under-secretary, as chief secretary to the lords justices and, later (in 1717), as accountant-general, seems to have been effective enough. Finally, in the autumn of 1720, the South Sea Bubble gave him a moment of real fame, when, having, as he later claimed, lost £20,000 himself, he stood out at the General Court as the leader of the annuitants and subscribers at 1000.[2]

Yet Budgell's considerable abilities were unfortunately counterbalanced by grave defects. His vanity was infinite and his ambition inordinate. He was utterly extravagant in his mode of life, consistently living beyond his means: one of the New College leases describes him as being of Denton in Oxfordshire, but actually most of his letters are dated from his London house in Arundel Street where he maintained an expensive establishment. Above all, he was hopelessly and incorrigibly quarrelsome. His career in the Irish administration was terminated by conflict with Lord Bolton, who became lord-lieutenant in 1717, and thereafter, having set his heart on a political career at home in England, when he found his efforts

---

[1] Harold Herd, 'The Decline and Fall of Eustace Budgell', in *Seven Editors* (1955).

[2] John Carswell, *The South Sea Bubble* (1961), pp. 186-7.

frustrated, he became the victim of a positive persecution mania, seeing on every hand the malign influence of powerful enemies, of whom Sir Robert Walpole was the chief. The last fifteen years of his life, from 1722 on, were marked by prodigious litigation, increasingly egocentric pamphleteering, and finally, in the affair of Tindal's will, almost certain fraud. Utterly embittered, ruined in reputation and finance, in 1737 Budgell committed suicide. Even that last act had something of his usual flamboyance about it. Leaving a note on his desk—

> What Cato did and Addison approved
> Cannot be wrong,

he filled his pockets with stones, hired a Thames waterman, and plunged to his death in the river.

The interest of the Birchanger dispute, so far as Budgell is concerned, is that it occurred just at the time when his deterioration was beginning to set in. When he wrote on 8 October 1724 to inform New College that he had purchased the Birchanger leases, they must have thought him a sufficiently estimable tenant. 'I flatter myself', he said, 'I shall find the Colledge kind Landlords having had a brother who was a fellow, and having the happiness to know many of the present members'. Actually, William Budgell, the brother whom he mentioned, had died the year previous, and it is interesting that Eustace Budgell's earliest biographer, Theophilus Cibber, lays stress on William's death as the removal of a restraining influence—after William's death Eustace 'seemed to pay no regard to any person'.[1] Certainly the whole Birchanger episode is illustrative of all Budgell's mounting faults—his vanity, violent quarrelsomeness, and inability to keep his finances in order.[2]

In comparison with Budgell, his opponent William Bohun seems a far less picturesque character, and his own description of himself, written at the height of the Birchanger conflict, is

---

[1] *Lives of the Poets* (1753), v, 10.
[2] For general accounts of Eustace Budgell, see Cibber, *op. cit.*, and *D.N.B.*

perhaps in some ways fair enough—or at least was so until the quarrel roused his passions. He was, he wrote, 'an *Old Man*, a *Professor* of the *Law*, of a *Quiet Disposition* and peaceable behaviour'. Yet it would be a mistake to underrate Bohun. A Somerset man, he had been admitted to the Middle Temple as far back as 1701. In the course of his life he was the author of five substantial and reputable law books—the *Privilegia Londini*, the *Institutio Legalis*, the *Cursus Cancellariae*, the *Law of Tithes* and the *English Lawyer*—most of which were in use over a considerable period of years and ran into several editions, two of them—the *Institutio* and the *Law of Tithes*—commanding respectful treatment by Sir William Holdsworth.[1] Aside from these major works, he also published practical manuals and edited two works by other authors.[2] His was a solid and entirely respectable achievement.

Unhappily the Birchanger episode induced in Bohun a bitterness that made him almost as fanatically prejudiced as Budgell himself. Nor was his anger directed only at his rival for possession of the leaseholds but also most markedly against Henry Bigg, the Warden of New College. It is possible that Bohun was anti-clerical anyway—certainly the *Brief View of Ecclesiastical Jurisdiction as it is this day practised in England*, which he published in 1733, is markedly anti-clerical in tone; and of course Bigg was in holy orders. But neither this bias nor even his conviction, possibly genuine though it was, that he had suffered a grievous wrong over Birchanger justifies, or even explains, the violence of his attack on New College and its warden. In Bohun, scarcely less than in Budgell, there was an abnormal element, amounting in his case to near hysteria.

Entangled by circumstance with these two exceedingly difficult characters, the Warden of New College, the Rev.

---

[1] *History of English Law*, xii, 424, 621.
[2] Manuals: *Instructions for Clerks in the King's Bench and Common Pleas*, Part I (1732).
Practising Attorney: or, Lawyer's Office (1724).
Editions: Nicholas Covert, *The Scrivener's Guide*, 4th edition (1724).
Nathaniel Bacon, *Historical and Political Discourse of the Laws and Government of England*, edition of 1739.

Henry Bigg, was not among the most distinguished holders of that office. Matriculating in 1710 and graduating B.A. in 1714, Bigg became warden in 1724 at what, in modern eyes, appears the unduly early age of thirty-three. Even Hearne, a contemporary, thought it worthy of comment that Bigg was 'a Young Man'. Worse still from Hearne's point of view, he was 'a great Whig'. Not for the first or the last time the fellows were much blamed for the election they had made, in which, so Hearne asserted, there had been 'very foul dealing', Bradshaw, Bishop of Bristol, one of whose chaplains was a fellow of the college, having a great hand in the matter.[1] It no doubt gave Hearne a good deal of pleasure to hear, within the twelve-month, that Bigg was already weary of the wardenship and wished he had never taken it—an attitude that Hearne accounted for by Bigg being a rich man in his own right and by his having married an even richer wife.[2] If this report of Bigg's discontent was correct, within a further year the Birchanger affair was to give him another, and perhaps better, reason for regretting his election to the wardenship.

Of course Hearne's disapproval of Bigg proves very little—he was far too prejudiced a witness for his testimony by itself to be taken seriously. It does, however, receive some support from another quarter. When, after the pattern of the times, Bigg moved in 1729 from the wardenship of New College to that of Winchester, Burton, the headmaster, was later to make a comparison between him and his predecessor that was very much to Bigg's disadvantage. 'In Warden Dobson's time', Burton said, 'we were in the height of glory. In Bigg's time, a very different man, we just supported ourselves.'[3] Certainly Bigg has left behind no reputation as a scholar, nor did his headship of the Wykehamical foundations coincide with a period of distinction in either. On the other hand, in an age when such attitudes were rare, he did show as Warden of

---

[1] *Hearne's Collections*, viii, 314-16.   [2] *Ibid.*, ix, 67-8.
[3] A. K. Cook, *About Winchester College* (1917), p. 61. It is fair to say that Burton made a further comparison between Bigg and his successor, and that this was to Bigg's advantage.

Winchester some compunction about the uses to which the corporate revenue was put, in 1739 addressing a letter to the fellows in which he asserted that they and he were converting to their own use more of that income than they were entitled to enjoy in their personal capacities.[1] Moreover, if his handling of the Birchanger affair was not markedly adept, it does at least leave the impression of a fair-minded man, caught in a difficult situation that was not of his own making.

That situation—for it is time that we left personalities and turned to events—had its origins prior to Henry Bigg's wardenship. On 30 July 1718, apparently without the college's cognisance, the London milliner John Pheasant, who held both the Birchanger leaseholds, sold the unexpired portion of his interest in them to Daniel Combes for a sum of £1262. Although the surviving record is too incomplete to permit a satisfactory description of Combes's tenancy, three letters of his that do remain leave the impression that, at any rate from 1722, he was finding it difficult to pay the rent that he owed and that, in addition, he was burdened with certain legal charges. He later informed Hinde, the college steward, that he had suffered great losses in the year 1720—no doubt, like Budgell, in the South Sea Bubble. What really proved Combes's most serious embarrassment, however—and incidentally touched off the great Birchanger conflict—was that in November 1722, along with three of his relatives, he entered into bail for a certain John Talbot, arrested for non-payment of a debt on bond due to William Bohun, and he, failing to obtain satisfaction from Daniel Combes and the other sureties, instituted proceedings against them in the King's Bench. In Easter Term 1723 he obtained judgment in his favour in £800 from each of the defendants; but, doubtless as delaying tactics, the defendants brought writs of error in Exchequer Chamber, so that it was not until a whole year later that the judgment was affirmed, and a still further period of twelve months elapsed before Bohun obtained a *fieri facias* to levy £800 on Daniel Combes's goods and chattels.

[1] T. F. Kirby, *Annals of Winchester College* (1892), p. 400.

Now, of course, a leasehold interest is a chattel; and had Combes retained his Birchanger estate until such time as Bohun put his judgment into execution, the leasehold would have become vulnerable to Bohun's *fieri facias*. But on 15 May 1724, probably immediately after Bohun's favourable judgment, Combes assigned his leases to Eustace Budgell. Without question his motive for doing so was to prevent Bohun from levying his £800 on the Birchanger rents from the sub-tenants, and equally it is beyond doubt that Budgell, who appears to have been the nephew of Combes's wife, was assisting knowingly in Bohun's deprivation—indeed when, somewhat belatedly, he wrote on 8 October 1724 to inform New College that he had taken over the leases, he hinted as much. 'I shall not trouble you', he told them, 'with an account how I am in a Manner forced to be the Purchaser.'

To accept this diagnosis of motive, however, is very different from asserting that either Combes or Budgell was guilty of any illegality. There are two questions here—one of fact and one of law. As to the question of fact, Bohun was to allege later on that the witnesses to the assignment were men known to be adept in villainy and that the leases were procured long after his judgment and execution.[1] This allegation of fraudulent ante-dating of the instrument of transfer was quite clearly unjustified: Combes informed New College of his surrender to Budgell on 30 September 1724, and eight days later Budgell seems to have enclosed the relevant documents for the college's inspection—all of which preceded Bohun's *fieri facias* for execution by over six months. What advantage would there have been in ante-dating an assignment, made, say, in September to the May previous? Was it in order to make it appear to precede Bohun's judgment as distinct from his execution of judgment? This raises the second question—that of law. The Statute of Frauds and Perjuries, as counsel was subsequently to advise New College, expressly declares that the property of chattels is not bound by any judgment until the execution is delivered into the sheriff's hands. Until that happened, Combes

---

[1] *Letter to the Revd. Henry Bigg, D.D., Warden of New College* (1726).

was entirely free to assign his leasehold interests. He and Budgell
were technically in the right: between them they had out-
manoeuvred the learned professor of law. Perhaps it was really
because Bohun realised this that he took his defeat so hardly.

The Birchanger dispute, so far as we have described it, was
a conflict between Bohun, on the one hand, and Combes and
Budgell on the other. Initially New College as landlord was
not involved, and indeed it was not officially informed of
Bohun's claim until 16 April 1725. On that day, when the
college steward was holding the manor court in Birchanger
Hall, and Warden Bigg was himself present there on progress,
William Bohun appeared with his *fieri facias* to claim seizure of
the estates. As Bigg at a later date deposed, 'there came into the
said House a person who declar'd that he was Wiliam Bohun
Esqre., and pretended that he had a writ of *Fieri Facias* to
execute on the College Estate at Birchanger . . . but whether
he did or did not execute the same this Deponent knoweth not,
although the said Mr. Bohun did make a very great noise and
disturbance in the House, and did read some paper or other so
loud that this Deponent heard the same in the next Room, but
what were the partial Contents thereof this Deponent knoweth
not'. Certainly New College took no immediate notice of
Bohun's seizure of the leasehold, continuing to take rents from
Budgell and to regard him as the lawful tenant.

This no doubt very much annoyed Bohun, but what really
alarmed him was the possibility of the college renewing
Budgell's lease. About this, on 29 June 1725, he wrote a long
letter to a certain Adolphus Meetkirk who was acting for New
College in the Birchanger affair, setting out the details of his
case and urging Meetkirk to advise the college not to give
Budgell a new lease. Nine months later he maintained that
Meetkirk had been favourably disposed to his case, and, however that may be, it is true that the effect of Bohun's reiterated
claim was to make New College think twice before agreeing
to renew Budgell's tenancy. Indeed in the autumn they went
to the expense of securing counsel's opinion, putting the
specific question as to whether it was safe to renew with

Budgell. Armed with an affirmative answer, towards the end of the year they gave Budgell his renewal. This meant that, from Bohun's point of view, New College had lined up with the enemy: Combes, Budgell, Bigg were, in his eyes, confederates, and there was little to choose between them. His furious letter of 28 March 1726 to Bigg,[1] alleging a conspiracy between an under-sheriff and one of the college officers, shows how abnormal his state of mind had become. In view of the equal abnormality of his principal opponent, Eustace Budgell, a clash of the most melodramatic kind was possible.

The clash in fact came about on the last day of April, when once again the manor court was sitting in Birchanger Hall and when once again Warden Bigg was at Birchanger on his progress of the college estates. Aside from minor evidence in the depositions of John Coker, a fellow of New College who was accompanying Bigg on progress and no doubt acting as outrider, and of Thomas Pryor, the deputy steward, the story of the events of that 30 April 1726 has to be reconstructed from the information laid by Bohun and the deposition of Bigg. This is not an easy task since on several material points they are mutually contradictory.

Bohun apparently turned up at 10 a.m. and was kept cooling his heels until noon, when Bigg and Budgell, returning from viewing some trees to take their dinner in the Hall, were informed that he was about the place. And here is the first contradiction of the evidence. Bohun maintained—it was an important part of his attempt to prove conspiracy—that he was invited into the Hall both by a servant of Budgell's and a messenger sent by the warden, Bigg that he came into the parlour without being sent for at all.[2] However that may have been, there is no need to doubt Bigg's statement that he asked Bohun in a civil manner about his letter of a month previous and who was the college officer of whom he had complained, and Bohun's alleged reaction to this has an authentic ring—

---

[1] *Letter to the Revd. Henry Bigg, D.D., Warden of New College* (1726), to which it is printed as an appendix.

[2] Lowth says that Bigg sent for Bohun, *op. cit.*, p. 326, note.

'To which the said Mr. Bohun immediately reply'd in a very surly and insolent way, That he would give this Deponent an answer when he was call'd upon in a Legal manner, and when this Deponent was Archbishop of Canterbury, or such like words'. Bigg was fair-minded, or perhaps merely neutral, enough to state that what caused the first high words at this unhappy meeting was that Budgell charged Bohun with abusing him in a scurrilous pamphlet.[1] But—the second point at which the evidence is contradictory—while Bigg maintained, with the support of Coker and Pryor, that he thereupon left the room, Bohun asserted that the warden sat in such a position that he hemmed him in while Budgell furiously assaulted him 'with [an] Oaken Stick and with oathes'. Even by the details of Bohun's telling, this assault does not seem, in fact, to have amounted to much more than violent threats by Budgell, until Bohun sought to leave the room—'whereupon the said Mr. Budgell violently seized this Informant by the left Shoulder and turning this Informant about Gave him a blow with the said Oaken Stick on this Informant's right Shoulder and immediately afterwards two other violent blows with the same stick on this Informant's head which broke it in diverse places and Caused a Great Effusion of this Informant's blood and for some time Rendred this Informant altogether insensible'.

That there was a fight in the parlour of Birchanger Hall, and that Bohun got the worse of it, is certainly true. All the same, it is questionable how good a case he had. Coker deposed that it was Bohun, not Budgell, who struck the first blow and, as for Warden Bigg, he had withdrawn to his own chamber at the first sign that passions were running dangerously high and five minutes before actual violence began, preferring a discreet to a heroic role. Nevertheless Bohun exhibited articles of the peace in the court of King's Bench against both Budgell and Bigg. Budgell gave bail immediately, but the unfortunate warden, in ignorance of the whole affair, did nothing, and, as a result, was arrested. He had to find bail, first for his personal appearance in court and then to keep the peace for twelve

---

[1] This pamphlet has not been identified.

months. It seems to have been in connection with this case that William Bohun, in the autumn of 1726, wrote, and printed, his extraordinary *Letter to the Revd. Henry Bigg D.D., Warden of New College*, in which he contrived to quote the Book of Genesis, Proverbs, and the Gospel according to St. Luke, as well as to give some account of his ill-treatment at Birchanger and his grievance about the leasehold estate. As befitted an academic lawyer, he produced some splendidly medieval threats to the Warden and Scholars of New College—their lack of inquiries into his injuries might prove a forfeiture of their court leet; or again, under the Statute of Praemunire their lands and tenements, goods and chattels might well be forfeit to the king! Even more extraordinary, Bohun appears to have delivered copies of this letter to the judges concerned with the case, who, it was reported, very much resented his doing so. After all this, and in the upshot, he proceeded no further against Bigg, and the legal costs involved in the action were surprisingly modest—the college allowed the warden ten guineas, and of that sum two guineas was to meet the expense of his journeys to and from London.

Nevertheless, Lowth was wrong in implying that that was the end of the Birchanger affair: Bohun had still a number of shots in his locker. In Easter Term 1728 he sought relief in equity against New College in the Court of Exchequer. Amongst the college muniments there are copies of his bill and of the college's draft answer, which was drawn by the same counsel who had originally advised in favour of renewing Budgell's lease in 1725. Unfortunately the means of reference to legal records of the period are imperfect, and a search has failed to reveal the Exchequer decree or order in this case amongst the public records. However, the college accounts contain payments to the steward of £20:6:0 in 1730 for law charges against Bohun and of £4:6:10 in 1732 for receiving costs from him, while in the latter year there is noted the receipt of £15:0:0 costs from him. This would seem to suggest that the case terminated successfully for the college, but that the costs obtained did not balance the legal expenses involved.

Nor did this action exhaust William Bohun's persistence. Even while it was pending—and, indeed, perhaps since he realised that he was no more likely to obtain equitable, than legal, redress of his supposed grievance—he had lodged a formal complaint with the Bishop of Winchester, no doubt because the bishop was visitor of the college. The measure of how good a move this was, and how seriously Bigg took it, is the long and careful statement of the whole issue that he made in writing to the bishop on 3 April 1728. That account met with the bishop's approval, and yet another of Bohun's attacks upon the college had been parried. There only remained for him the literary revenge of seeking to damage the founder's reputation, with mention of which this paper started.

Yet for the long-suffering Warden Bigg and his college the Birchanger business was not yet over. It is the supreme irony of the whole episode that Eustace Budgell, whose acceptance as leasehold tenant, sound though it was in law, had led to so many embarrassments, should himself have proved utterly unsatisfactory in his relationship with the college. By 1728 Budgell's defects of character had become transparently obvious. It was, after all, his irascibility, and the too heavy hand with which he wielded his stick, which had led, two years previously, to Bigg's arrest. But there were also other matters that made him a tiresome tenant.

One of them, though it has no part in the main Birchanger dispute, concerned the watermill there. Although this had been leased to Pheasant, whether through oversight or from some other cause it had not been included in his assignment to Combes. Yet Budgell apparently persuaded New College to grant him a lease of it—certainly an irregular proceeding, as counsel subsequently pointed out. Moreover, he thereupon seems to have embarked on an ambitious plan of taking down the old mill and building a new one in its place, doing this without consulting the college about the scheme and using so much timber in the process that Bigg estimated its value at forty years' purchase of the rents. About all this very little can be said, for the sole source of information is a not very clear passage in a letter which Bigg wrote to Budgell in the summer of 1728. But items of expenditure in the college accounts, that year and the year previous, for special progresses to Birchanger show that something was going on there which was giving the college cause for concern. In any event, what little we do know about this matter of the mill seems sadly typical of Budgell in his later years, when he was so often both over-ambitious and disingenuous.

Most important of all, Budgell was unreliable in what especially concerns a landlord—the regular payment of rent. In the letter that he wrote on 8 October 1724 to inform the college that he had taken over Combes's lease, he told the steward, 'Since I am become a Tenant to the Colledge they may depend upon my being punctual in my payments to them'. This was, however, a promise that he most notably failed to keep. For the years 1728–29, four of his letters to Bigg survive, all of them making excuses for non-payment. The first excuse was that the principal sub-tenant, a man named Smith who occupied Birchanger Hall itself, was in financial difficulties and owed Budgell more than Budgell owed the college—'the poor fellow has two Executions served upon him . . . He has been up with me to beg for Godsake to forbear and assures me that with the assistance of his father and unkle he shall then get over everything.' This he followed up with descriptions of his own plight, either through sickness or the oppressions of great men. These are the oddest mixture of whining self-pity and quite unwarranted optimism that all will somehow come right. 'I have been so ill', he wrote on 26 April (1729?), 'that my Life was thought in the utmost danger but am now thanks be to God much better. . . . I have laboured under such Oppressions as all who know my Case are forced to allow are without a Precedent. I have had my goods seized by an Execution on an Action where I take Almighty God to witness I did not owe one single farthing. To say all in a Word my Oppressor is mighty yet I have some reason to hope that Providence will raise me up such friends as will deliver me out of his hands.' Something of his old flamboyant literary style

18

remained, but it is difficult to doubt that to Bigg, and to New College, the repeated excuses had come to wear thin.

The most notable example of Budgell's vanity, and of his impertinence, is found in a letter of 1 July 1728. There, after dismissing in the first half of the letter the reasons for his failure to pay his rent, he passed on in the second half to ask Warden Bigg to find him somebody in Oxford to translate into Latin verse his recently published poem on the king's journey to Cambridge.[1] 'I know', he added, 'I could have it translated by a gentleman of Cambridge, but I have so much affection for our own mother, that methinks I would have the Compliment compleated by none but an Oxford Man'. It is to Bigg's eternal credit that he gave very short shrift indeed to this irrelevance, refusing indeed to attend to it while so serious a business matter as Budgell's rent arrears was outstanding. Throughout the central part of the Birchanger dispute we are left with the impression that Bigg never grasped the nettle of the crisis; but by the summer of 1728 he had had enough, and the reply he sent to Budgell was admirable, firmly, though entirely courteously, describing the latter's faults. It is the very model of a letter to a defaulting debtor with whom the writer has previously enjoyed social relations, and Warden Bigg may be forgiven much for having written it.

Finally, in May 1729, New College served ejectment orders on Budgell's Birchanger tenants, though even then he seems to have found it difficult to believe that it was the college's intention to force him to confess a judgment in ejection: at any rate he tried one more appeal to Warden Bigg. When that failed, he mortgaged his estate in Birchanger to Benjamin Hoare, a London goldsmith, who in July paid the college rent arrears of £146:11:4. Three years later Hoare obtained a Chancery decree allowing him to foreclose, and he followed this up by seeking a new lease from New College in his own name. The attitude of the college in the negotiation leading to the lease was notably tough—perhaps not surprisingly, having regard to

---

[1] Eustace Budgell, *A Poem upon his Majesty's Late Journey to Cambridge and Newmarket*, 1728.

their recent experiences. In any event, that is another story, for by 1732 the protagonists of the Birchanger quarrel had gone their several ways—Budgell to continue his erratic career to its tragic end, Bohun to brood over the wrongs committed by William of Wykeham, and Bigg to find a peace in Winchester that he had not known in New College.

The Birchanger episode is perhaps not of great historical significance. Nevertheless, it does involve one interesting point of law—that the property of chattels is not bound by any judgment until the execution is delivered into the sheriff's hands. Again, it is illustrative of just how much litigation might arise from a comparatively small estate. It is indicative, too, of what sort of consequences stemmed from the South Sea Bubble. But, most of all, its interest lies in the interplay of vigorous and (perhaps fortunately) exceptional personalities.

A LIST OF THE BOOKS, ARTICLES, AND PRINCIPAL REVIEWS WRITTEN BY DAVID OGG

R. L. Rickard

1912

Cardinal de Retz 1613–1679. London. Methuen.

1918

Introduction. *Cardinal de Retz. Memoirs.* 2 vols. London. Everyman's Library.

1920

German Naval Propaganda. *Journal of the Royal United Services Institution,* lxv.

1921

Sully's Grand Design of Henry IV, from the Memoirs of Maximilien de Béthune duc de Sully (1559–1641). London. Grotius Society Publications, No. 2. Sweet and Maxwell.

1922

Review. *The Life of Sir John Leake,* by Stephen Martin-Leake, edited by Geoffrey Callender. *History,* vii, 144.

1924

Review. *Les Sources de l'histoire de France (1610–1715),* par E. Bourgeois et L. André. *History,* ix, 166-7.

1925

Ioannis Seldeni Ad Fletam Dissertatio. Cambridge. University Press.
Europe in the Seventeenth Century. London. A. & C. Black. Revised edtns. 1931, 1938, 1943, 1948, 1952, 1959, 1960. French edtn., see under 1932.

1929

Seventeenth century Dissent, Jansenism and Puritanism, in *History of Christianity in the Light of Modern Knowledge*, pp. 650-76. London. Blackie & Son.

1932

L'Europe du XVIIe siècle. Paris. Payot.

1933

Louis XIV. London. Home University Library. Thornton Butterworth.

1934

England in the Reign of Charles II. 2 vols. (2nd edtn., 1955.) Oxford. Clarendon Press.

John Selden (1584–1654), in *Encyclopaedia of the Social Sciences*, xiii, pp. 648-9. New York. Macmillan.

Renaissance and Reformation, in *Great Events in History*, edited by G. R. Stirling Taylor, pp. 275-342. London. Cassell.

1937

New England and New College, Oxford, a Link in Anglo-American Relations. Oxford. Clarendon Press.

1938

Review. *The Writings and Speeches of Oliver Cromwell, vol. I, 1599–1649*, edited by Wilbur Cortez Abbott. *E.H.R.* liii, 309-11.

1947

Herbert Fisher 1865–1940. London. Edward Arnold.

1948

Review. *John Aubrey and His Friends*, by Anthony Powell. *The Listener*, xl, 893.

1950

Chambers's Encyclopaedia, new edition, the following articles Queen Anne, 1st Earl of Arlington, Sir Richard Baker, Gilbert Burnet, Cavaliers and Roundheads, Charles I, Charles II, 1st Earl of

Clarendon, Oliver Cromwell, Richard Cromwell, Sir Kenelm Digby, Sir John Eliot, Thomas Fairfax, Guy Fawkes, Sir John Fenwick, William Goffe, John Hampden, Denzil Holles, Henry Ireton, James I, James II, William Laud, Long Parliament, Edmund Ludlow, Sarah Jennings (Marlborough), 1st Duke of Newcastle, Sir Thomas Overbury, William Penn, 3rd Earl of Peterborough, William Prynne, John Pym, Restoration, 1st Earl of Shaftesbury, Algernon Sidney, 1st Earl of Strafford, Sir Henry Vane, 1st Duke of Wharton, Whig Party, Bulstrode Whitelocke, William III.
London. George Newnes.

1951

Review. *The Age of Charles I*, by David Mathew. *The Listener*, xlv, 675.

1954

Review. *William III and the Respectable Revolution*, by Lucile Pinkham. *The Listener*, lii, 978-81.
'*Liberty above all Things.*' David Ogg gives the second of two talks on John Selden. *The Listener*, lii, 1062-3.

1955

England in the Reigns of James II and William III. Revised reprint 1957. Oxford. Clarendon Press.

1956

William III. London. Collins.

1961

Britain after the Restoration, in *New Cambridge Modern History*. V, ch. xiii. Cambridge. University Press.
The Achievements of France in Art, Thought and Literature, in *New Cambridge Modern History*. V, ch. xi. Cambridge. University Press.

INDEX